Racing Cars

Racing Cars

BY
PIERO CASUCCI

FULL-COLOR ILLUSTRATIONS
Maurizio Riccioni

RAND McNALLY & COMPANY
CHICAGO
NEW YORK
SAN FRANCISCO

Contents

Introduction

For as long as the car exists, and it is now approaching its first cente-
nary, the old, recurring question of whether or not technical progress is
helped by racing will remain without a definitive answer.

It is probably true to say that there could be less racing, but that is not
the same as saying that racing is not useful. It was and still is valuable to
all those (the organizers, sponsors, constructors, and drivers) promoting
racing. One learns by experience, and something has been learned from
racing—though often in a brutal, painful, and tragic way—on both the
technical and the human levels. The great improvements made in
brakes, tires, and road holding are in a large measure due to racing.

In the past, accidents caused by burst tires were commonplace, and
poor brake functioning or defective suspensions were frequent causes
of cars leaving the road. While today accidents are more varied, in the
vast majority of cases they are due to human error. Over-excitement
during the melée at the start of a Grand Prix can wreak havoc. The
heartbeat of some drivers rises to 200 beats a minute in the moments
before the starting flag is lowered.

Enzo Ferrari, who knows more about racing than anyone else, has
written, "The car has progressed with racing, and it continues its climb
towards perfection by learning from the fund of experience that racing
has to offer. It is only through the practical experience of racing that the
real worth, as opposed to what is claimed for it, of any new automotive
discovery or of any laboratory research or computation can be found.
During races drivers are forced to make maneuvers, to impose unpredictable strains and uses that are the result solely of the momentary
conditions in the race. Such unpredictable situations and circumstances
arise on normal roads and with everyday cars."

This collection of racing cars from their beginning up to the present is
intended to be a testimony to the technological progess made as a result
of racing. An idea of the great distance traveled can be gained even
through the schematism and synthesis imposed by the long period considered.

The material has been subdivided by periods, beginning, in a sense,
with the invention of the car. Though today the usefulness of racing is
debated, this was not the case at the beginning of the century. Races
were then a genuinely irreplaceable opportunity for experimentation. No
maker, large or small (and they were then, as a rule, very modest in
size), had the laboratories or equipment to evaluate in the factory the
success of an innovation or an improvement. Only the road could pro-

7

vide a suitable test. Car production, which was very low, benefitted immediately from the experience gained. The alterations could be made "overnight," possibly as soon as the day after the race. This phase might be termed the period of monsters, as it was characterized by very high engine capacities, necessary because of the modest specific and maximum power outputs. Cars such as these provided the starting point for true progress.

Next came the voiturettes, the exact opposites of the monsters. In a short time agile, light, small-capacity machines were being used in races. Motor racing was permanently enriched by this development since the voiturettes, and later Formula 2 and Formula 3 as well as the many other formulae—including the promotional ones—into which racing cars have been divided, have always clustered around the major competitions when, like Formula 2, they have not stood on their own.

With the Grand Prix, the principle of restrictions (weight, capacity, consumption) was reasserted as a means of restoring sense to the sport. The racing car became a practical object, much closer to mass-produced cars than it had been previously, and the age of monsters had passed forever. Because of this, modern motor races can be said to stem from the Grand Prix.

Since World War II the scene has been dominated by Formula 1 and Formula 2, which never cease to surprise and to astonish. In the last 30 years progress has been made through the shrewd mixing of sophisticated technical solutions (rear engines, disc brakes, fuel injection, broad section tires, ground effect cars). Weight has continued to be kept very low. As to the races of the future, there is the turbocharged engine.

Finally, sports cars, Indianapolis single-seaters, and record-breaking cars are also rich subjects for study, as are the epic feats performed by the people involved with them.

1

Beginnings

The early motor races, with their long distances, very uneven surfaces, lack of rescue services or assistance, and requiring hours behind the wheel where drivers were exposed to bad weather and dust, were major human undertakings. The 1903 Paris-Madrid was stopped at Bordeaux because, even before the halfway mark, so much damage had been suffered that to continue would have been madness.

Motoring, like aviation, quickly became synonymous with daring, with a contempt for danger and risk. It is estimated that between 1894 and 1905, when motor sport was in its infancy, as many as 35 important races were organized. Many historians of motoring hold that the first race was the "Concours des Voitures sans Chevaux" organized by the *Petit Journal* in 1894. However, Gerald Rose, one of the most authoritative historians—particularly in the field of sport—disputes this claim for the simple reason that the "Concours" was not a race. Bearing in mind the notions of speed and time, the first true race was organized by the *Velocipede* in 1887, though it is true that only one vehicle, Albert De Dion's four-wheeler, took part.

An essential precondition for entrance into the "Concours des Voitures sans Chevaux" of 1894 was to have put the vehicle through a preliminary trial, covering 50 km (31 miles) in three hours. The time was later raised to four hours since the required average speed of about 18 km per hour (11 mph) was believed to be dangerous to the competitors. The vehicles did not have to be professionally finished, but they had to be capable of moving under their own power. The race drew 102 cars. The prize of 5,000 francs was awarded jointly to Panhard & Levassor and Peugeot Frères of Valentigny, simply on the grounds that they were both powered by the engine invented by Daimler.

Less time meant greater speed. The makers were quickly forced to use higher and higher capacity engines to obtain the power outputs necessary for the desired performance. This need was the reason behind the 10,000 cc plus, 4-cylinder Snoeck Bolide and Mors of 1901, the 17,000 cc plus Napier of the same year, the 13,000 cc plus Panhard of 1902, culminating in the 26,000 cc of the Swiss Defaux engine, and the 28,353 cc of the S.76 Fiat of 1911, still with 4 cylinders. The capacity of the individual cylinders of this last engine was over 7,000 cc!

It was principally the Gordon Bennett Cup, in the period 1900–1905, that encouraged sensible progress in the technical field (increasing engine speed from 800 to 2,000 rpm, the spreading use of overhead inlet valves and side exhaust valves, overhead camshaft with pushrod and rocker, water cooling, honeycomb radiators, friction dampers, tubular chassis, and fuel mixtures based on benzene and alcohol).

This was a particularly fertile period for ideas, which flowed thick and fast; but perhaps the most original one was the De Dion rear axle, still in use today. Its uniqueness lies in offering the advantages of independent suspension with a rigid axle. The first car to be fitted with it was a De Dion of 1899, though the patent dates from 1893.

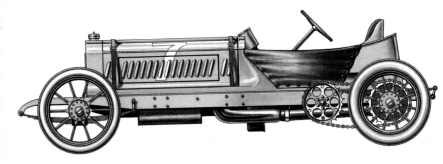

Richard-Brasier 1904: 4 cylinders, 9,896 cc, 80 bhp at 1,300 rpm

Locomobile 1905: 4 cylinders, 17,657 cc, 90 bhp at 1,050 rpm

The Mors was among the earliest cars to take part in racing (1897). Its creator, Emile Mors, was a convinced advocate of the sport because of both the publicity and technical advances derived from it. On the technical side, it is worth mentioning that one of the first Mors (1898) was powered by a water-cooled V-4. The 1901 Mors 60 HP is certainly one of the most famous machines built by Mors. In that year it gained two important successes (first place in the Paris-Bordeaux and in the Paris-Berlin), and on both occasions it was driven by Henri Fournier. Furthermore, because of the conditions of the roads at the time, the races were a great test of the mechanical aspects of cars. Despite the adverse conditions, Fournier averaged 85.460 km per hour (53.114 mph) in the Paris-Bordeaux and 70.970 km per hour (44.108 mph) in the Paris-Berlin.

The 60 HP of 1901 was powered by a 10,087 cc, 4-cylinder with low-tension magneto ignition and side valves. It had a four-speed transmission, a steel chassis,

Car: **Mors 60 HP**
Maker: **Mors**
Year: **1901**
Class: **Grand Prix**
Engine: **V-4**
Bore × Stroke: **130 × 190 mm**
Capacity: **10,087 cc**
Power: **60 bhp at 950 rpm**

chain drive, and brakes on the rear wheels only.

In the following year the capacity of the Mors was slightly reduced (9,236 cc). Though Mors did not achieve the same success as the year before, 1902 has a significant place in its history as the first year in which the French make fitted dampers to its cars. In 1908 Camille Jenatzy, who was much talked about as a world record holder, was one of Mor's drivers. Curiously, the French firm also had the services of another world record holder, Malcolm Campbell, though he acted merely as its representative in England.

Napier ceased business in 1925 with a luxury car, but it began by being involved mainly, if not solely, in racing. Its name is closely linked with one of the most famous drivers of the time, Selwyn Francis Edge, who was also a clever and effective promoter of cars in general and Napiers in particular.

The 30 HP was prepared for the Gordon Bennett Cup; unlike Napier's previous practice, it was powered by an engine with a relatively low capacity. Even so, it developed 45 bhp and not 30 as its designation suggested. Shaft drive was another novelty introduced by Napier on this car. With the retirement of René de Knyff, who was driving a Panhard, Edge won the 1902 Gordon Bennett, gaining a highly prestigious victory for his country and the Napier. The undertaking, including the construction of the car, cost Napier £1,418, a large sum at the time. But almost all of it, £1,200, was recouped by the sale of the car itself. For this race the maximum weight was 1,000 kg (2,204.6 lb). The result was the seemingly backward step of building cars with very light chassis. Napier was not thought to be capable of putting a maneuverable car in the field; but the astute Edge had not been wrong, and his victory enabled him to publicize the handling of his 30 HP and the fact that, according to him, it had the least powerful engine.

Car: **Napier 30 HP**
Maker: **Napier**
Year: **1902**
Class: **Grand Prix**
Engine: **4-cylinder in-line**
Bore × Stroke: **127 × 127 mm**
Capacity: **6,435 cc**
Power: **44.5 bhp at 950 rpm**

This car was designated the 96 because of the power that its 4-cylinder engine developed, but it was better known by the nickname "beetle" because of its hood and overall shape. The 96 had a transverse engine and was designed by Herbert Austin during the period between 1895 and 1905, when he worked for Wolseley. In 1906 he left to set up on his own, establishing a marque that bore his name.

Like other engineers throughout Europe, Austin believed racing to be useful and encouraged participation in it. It was he who persuaded Wolseley to enter the Paris-Madrid race and the Gordon Bennett Cup.

The 96 was the largest capacity machine to be built by this English make. In the fifth Gordon Bennett (1904) a 72 driven by Girling came in ninth and a 96 (Jarrott) came in twelfth. In the sixth Gordon Bennett a 96 came in eighth (Rolls) and another came in fourteenth (Bianchi). In 1905, both Rolls and Bianchi drove 96s in races on the Isle of Man.

Car: **Wolseley 96**
Maker: **Wolseley**
Year: **1904**
Class: **Grand Prix**
Engine: **4-cylinder in-line**
Bore × Stroke: **152.4 × 165.1 mm**
Capacity: **11,896 cc**
Power: **96 bhp at 1,300 rpm**

The departure of Austin from Wolseley led to a marked decline in the British firm's racing activities. Although races were an excellent means of publicity, they were also a heavy drain on the finances of the car firms that took part in them. In 1908 Wolseleys, or more precisely Wolseley-Siddeleys built under license in Italy by Legnano, took part in the Targa Florio and other Italian races.

The company became involved in racing again in 1921 with appreciably smaller capacity machines. Attention was also focused on individual teams taking part in long-distance events, such as the 1939 London-Capetown race, in which the distance was covered in 31 days and 22 hours.

Grand Prix – Voiturettes – Other

Voiturettes, or cyclecars, began to appear with the first road races at the very beginning of sport racing. As is well known, the earliest such activities were endurance races between one European capital and another, the starting point invariably being Paris. The French capital was also involved in transcontinental races such as the Peking-Paris and the New York-Paris.

A subdivision, initially by category and later by classes, was made almost immediately in order to establish a ranking that reflected merit. As early as 1903 Renault had demonstrated the effectiveness of its small cars in both the Paris-Madrid (which was stopped at Bordeaux) and in the Paris-Vienna races.

The term "voiturette" appears to have been first used in 1895 by Léon Bollée, one of the founding fathers of French motoring, who had built, among other things, a three-wheeled car. The new definition took account of the vehicle's small size. The term caught on and was used by other makers as well as by the press and eventually passed into common usage.

The Paris-Amsterdam race of 1898 was the first race in which voiturettes were classified separately. They were defined as cars that weighed less than 400 kg (881.8 lb). Subsequently the bore was also restricted but the stroke was not. This limitation was a highly questionable criterion for defining a class as it led to conceptually absurd engines. A good example is the 1910 Peugeot, a twin cylinder with a bore of 80 mm and a stroke of 280 mm. Given the strange shape of the engine (predominantly vertical), it is not surprising that the driver had to lean his head either to the left or to the right to see the road.

The voiturette formula—"formula" was already the accepted term—later had a stan-

Formulae – From 1907 to 1939

dard minimum weight of 700 kg (1,543 lb) set, which was reduced to 670 kg (1,477 lb) for single cylinders and raised to 850 kg (1,874 lb) for multi-cylinders. From 1911 onward a maximum capacity was fixed, initially 3,000 cc. It was later reduced to 1,500 cc and again to 1,100 cc. By then voiturettes had become an integral part of motor sport, though the limits were not always homogeneous and uniform.

With the demise of the Gordon Bennett Cup and the holding of the first French Grand Prix (Le Mans, 1906) motor sport underwent a profound change that was to influence all future racing technology. It is important to make clear at the outset the difference between then and now in the organizer's concept of a race. The first French Grand Prix took place on a circuit with a lap distance of 103 km (64 miles). It spanned two days, six laps being covered on the first day (over 619 km/385 miles) and six on the following, making a total of 1,250 km (777 miles).

This grueling race ended with the victory of François Szisz at the wheel of a Renault with a capacity of approximately 13,000 cc (Szisz was the French marque's chief test driver). His success hinged on the use of removeable wheel rims, enabling Szisz and his teammate to change tires quickly whenever they had a puncture.

The formula applying to Grand Prix cars set a maximum weight of 1,000 kg (2,204.6 lb) with a further 7 kg (15.4 lb) for the ignition magneto. A whole range of devices and fittings (horns, a variety of safety devices, upholstery and, when not used as a seat, the toolbox) was included in the weight of the chassis. It was also stipulated that the exhaust pipes must be horizontal with the ends turned upward to avoid raising clouds of dust when the cars were in motion.

In 1907 a restriction on fuel consumption (a maximum of 30 liters per 100 km/9.47

mpg) was introduced and all weight and capacity limits were abolished. In 1908 a minimum weight was brought back (1,150 kg/2,535.3 lb not including the fuel, cooling water, tools, safety devices, or spare wheels). A partial restriction was also placed on the capacity, a maximum bore of 155 mm being laid down for 4 cylinders and 127 mm for 6 cylinders, but no limit was placed on the stroke. Eight cylinders were not eligible for the French Grand Prix. From 1909 until 1911 there were no restrictions. In 1912 the maximum breadth of the body was limited to 175 cm (5 ft 8.9 in). In 1913 limits on weight (minimum 800 kg/1,763.7 lb, maximum 1,100 kg/2,425 lb) and consumption (20 liters per 100 km/14.13 mpg) were resumed. In 1914 an upper limit for capacity (4,500 cc) was established for the first time. The minimum weight was 1,100 kg (2,425 lb).

The outbreak of World War I marked a complete halt in sport racing. At its resumption, a new set of regulations came into operation, initially in the United States (1920), imposing a maximum capacity of 3,000 cc. This limit was ratified in 1921, and in the same year the minimum weight was fixed at 800 kg (1,763.7 lb).

In 1922 one of the more interesting formulae was launched, and it remained in force until 1923. It specified a maximum capacity of 2,000 cc with a minimum weight of 650 kg (1,433 lb). In addition it stipulated that the rear end of the car must not project more than 150 cm (4 ft 11.1 in) beyond the axis of the rear axle. A crew of two, with a minimum aggregate weight of 120 kg (264.6 lb), was also required.

In technical terms this was one of the most fertile and innovative periods, marked above all by the first racing car with a supercharged engine, the Fiat 805. Virtually the same formula was retained in 1925, but some extra rules were incorporated. The minimum breadth for the body was 80 cm (2 ft 7.5 in); and while two seats were retained, there was just the driver. The reasoning behind this change was to avoid exposing a second person, the mechanic, to unnecessary risks. By then the principal races took place at circuits, and the presence of a mechanic was almost superfluous. This arrangement was briefly abandoned in 1931 but was then permanently readopted.

True single-seaters did not appear until 1927. The minimum breadth of 80 cm (2 ft 7.5 in) was retained, and the new vehicles coexisted with two-seaters. In 1926 the maximum capacity was reduced to 1,500 cc and remained there in 1927, but the minimum weight rose to 700 kg (1,543 lb) from the 600 kg (1,323 lb) of 1926.

The subsequent formulae were based on weight, the distances or durations of the races and, once again, fuel consumption. In 1934 a completely new approach was devised. This was the so-called maximum weight formula, which stipulated that Grand Prix cars could not weigh more than 700 kg (1,543 lb). Its stated purpose was to place a curb on capacity without resorting to any specific restriction. Technology, however, shook off this fetter in no uncertain terms.

In 1938 three capacity limits were fixed: a minimum of 769 cc, a maximum of 3,000 cc for supercharged engines, and a maximum of 4,500 cc for normally aspirated engines. The minimum weight varied in proportion to the capacity from 400 kg (882 lb) to 800 kg (1,763.7 lb).

It was with this formula that racing activity was resumed immediately after the end of World War II, becoming the first Formula 1 of the new era.

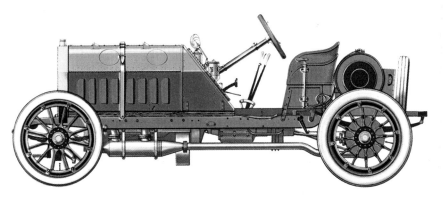

Itala 120 HP 1907: 4 cylinders, 14,442 cc, 120 bhp at 1,500 rpm

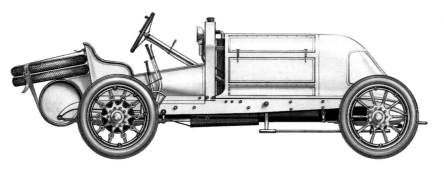

Panhard & Levassor 1907: 4 cylinders, 15,435 cc, 100 bhp at 1,200 rpm

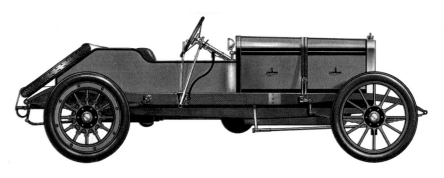

Austin 1908: 6 cylinders, 9,635 cc, 95 bhp at 1,350 rpm

Lancia-Alpha 1908: 4 cylinders, 2,453 cc, 53 bhp at 1,800 rpm

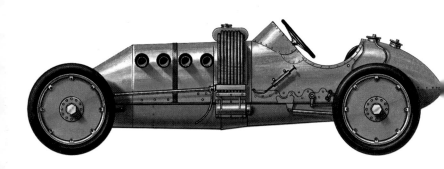

Marquette-Buick 1910: 4 cylinders, 5,750 cc, 130 bhp at 2,400 rpm

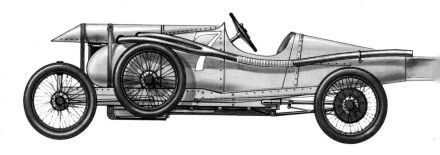

Sizaire-Naudin 1912: 4 cylinders, 2,982 cc, 95 bhp at 2,100 rpm

Peugeot 1912: 4 cylinders, 7,603 cc, 130 bhp at 2,200 rpm

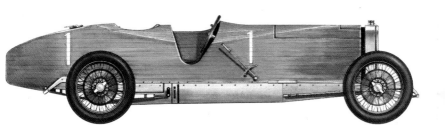

Hispano-Suiza 1919: 6 cylinders, 7,983 cc, 165 bhp at 4,100 rpm

Peugeot 1920: 4 cylinders, 2,996 cc, 105 bhp at 3,800 rpm

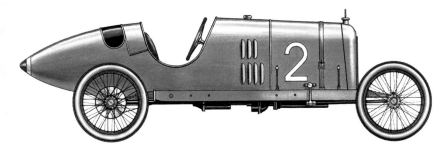

Salmson 1921: 4 cylinders, 1,097 cc, 38 bhp at 3,400 rpm

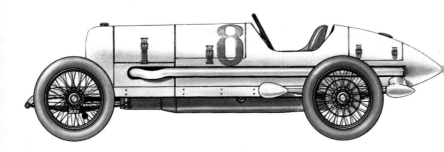

Austro Daimler 1921: 6 cylinders, 2,992 cc, 109 bhp at 4,500 rpm

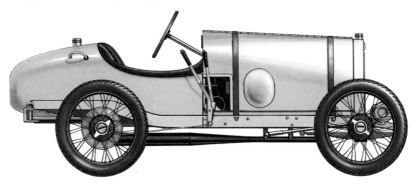

Bugatti Type 22 Brescia 1921: 4 cylinders, 1,453 cc, 30 bhp at 3,350 rpm

Bugatti 2000 1923: 8 cylinders, 1,991 cc, 90 bhp at 6,000 rpm

Benz Tropfen 1923: 6 cylinders, 1,995 cc, 95 bhp at 5,000 rpm

Rolland Pilain 1923: 8 cylinders, 1,968 cc, 135 bhp at 5,300 rpm

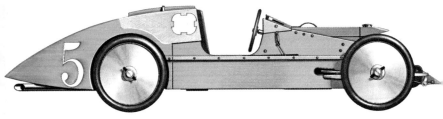

Voisin 1923: 6 cylinders, 1,978 cc, 90 bhp at 4,400 rpm

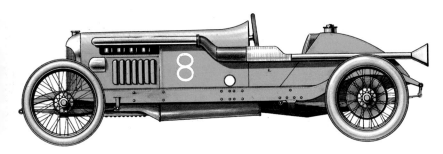

Bentley 3000 1924: 4 cylinders, 2,994 cc, 90 bhp at 3,900 rpm

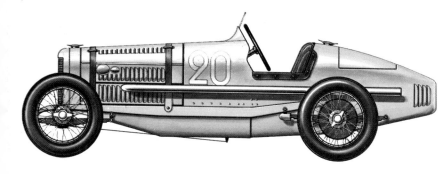

Talbot 1500 1924: 4 cylinders, 1,481 cc 100 bhp at 5,300 rpm

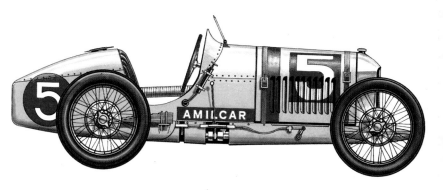

Amilcar 1925: 6 cylinders, 1,097 cc, 70 bhp at 5,500 rpm

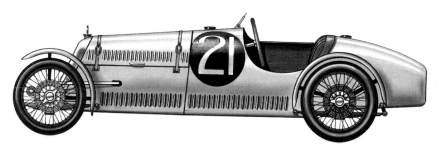

BNC 1927: 4 cylinders, 1098 cc, 61 bhp at 4,900 rpm

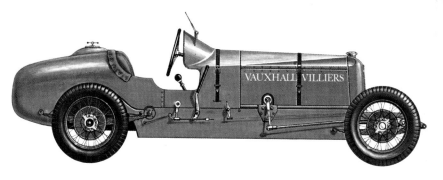

Vauxhall Villiers 1928: 4 cylinders, 4,224 cc, 250 bhp at 5,500 rpm

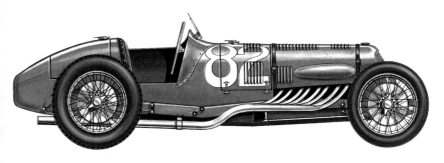

Maserati 4 CM 1933: 4 cylinders in line, 2,482.8 cc, 195 bhp at 5,300 rpm

Maserati 8 CM 1933: 8 cylinders, 2,991 cc, 220 bhp at 5,500 rpm

MG Magnette 1934: 6 cylinders, 1,087 cc, 120 bhp at 6,500 rpm

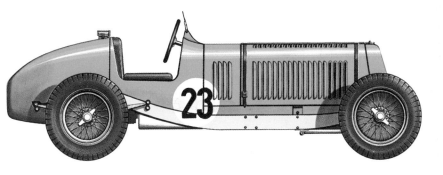

ERA 1500 1935: 6 cylinders, 1,488 cc, 150 bhp at 6,500 rpm

Riley 2000 1936: 6 cylinders, 1,950 cc, 250 bhp at 6,500 rpm

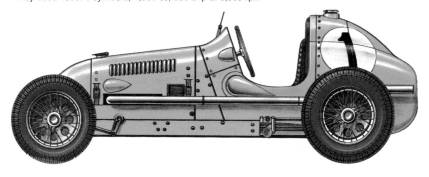

Austin 750 1936: 4 cylinders, 744 cc, 116 bhp at 7,600 rpm

Mercedes W 125/DAB 1937: 8 cylinders, 5,600 cc, 645 bhp at 5,800 rpm

Delahaye 1938: 12 cylinders, 4,490 cc, 245 bhp at 5,000 rpm

ERA 1939: 6 cylinders, 1,487 cc, 270 bhp at 7,500 rpm

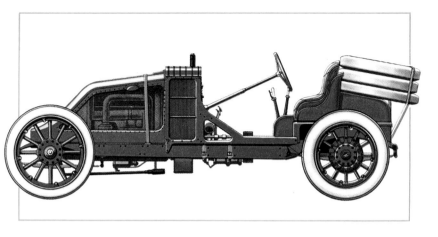

The 1906 Renault gained an important place in car racing history by winning the first French Grand Prix. The race was held at Le Mans and lasted two days (at the end of the first day the cars were parked in a restricted area). It was 1,250 km (777 miles) long, and Szisz covered it at the remarkable average of 102.772 km per hour (63.873 mph). The Renault was a thoroughly conventional machine, being powered by a 4-cylinder engine of about 13,000 cc that developed 90 bhp at 1,200 rpm. Technically it was much less interesting than the Fiats (Felice Nazzaro driving a Fiat came in second). The engine had side valves, a single carburetor, a three-speed transmission, shaft drive, and semi-elliptical leaf spring suspension front and rear. It also had hydraulic dampers, made by Renault itself and used for the first time on a racing car. Instead of being held in a container crudely mounted behind the driver and mechanic, the fuel was contained in a shaped tank, which also acted as the back of the car and to which the three

Car: **Renault**
Maker: **Renault**
Year: **1906**
Class: **Grand Prix**
Engine: **4-cylinder in-line**
Bore × Stroke: **166 × 150 mm**
Capacity: **12,986 cc**
Power: **90 bhp at 1,200 rpm**

spare wheels were fixed.

The secret of the Renault's success lay, to a great extent, in the adoption of rear wheels with removable rims, a decision taken on the eve of the race. The new rims enabled two people to change both rear wheels in less than 4 minutes as opposed to the 16 minutes required by fixed rims. Szisz, who was Renault's chief test driver, was stopped a total of nine times by punctures, and on the last lap he broke an upper leaf spring. However, he managed the 46-minute lead that he had over Nazzaro with such skill that he finished 32 minutes ahead of him.

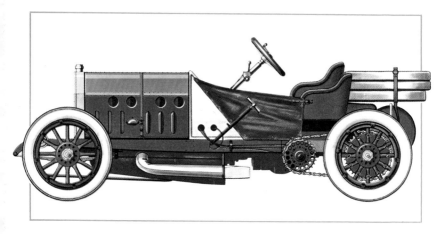

Up until 1906 Fiat had been intensely involved in racing. But the results, though good, remained unsatisfying. The main intention of the Turin firm was to end French supremacy.

For the 1907 season a new formula was introduced based on fuel consumption (a maximum of 30 liters per 100 km/9.42 mpg) without any weight or capacity limits. A 4-cylinder with a capacity of more than 16,000 cc was prepared following a design of Giovanni Enrico with the collaboration of Guido Fornaca and Carlo Cavalli. The oversquare engine (the bore was appreciably larger than the stroke) would today be thought of as modern. Further features of the 130 HP were overhead valves and hemispherical combustion chambers with centrally placed spark plugs. It had a Simms-Bosch magneto ignition and a single carburetor. It weighed more than 1,000 kg (2,204.6 lb) and each piston weighed 4.5 kg (9.9 lb).

The 130 HP performed superbly in the first race of the season, the Targa Florio,

Car: **Fiat 130 HP**
Maker: **Fiat**
Year: **1907**
Class: **Grand Prix**
Engine: **4-cylinder in-line twin block**
Bore × Stroke: **180 × 160 mm**
Capacity: **16,286 cc**
Power: **130 bhp at 1,600 rpm**

which was won by Felice Nazzaro followed by Vincenzo Lancia. Nazzaro also won the Coppa dell'Imperatore on the Taunus circuit. Fiat entered three cars in this race; Wagner came in fifth and Lancia sixth. The same team also entered the French Grand Prix at Dieppe, which ended with another victory for Felice Nazzaro, who also recorded the fastest lap. At one point in the race Fiat's total success seemed a possibility. Wagner led for three laps before being forced to drop out. First position then passed to Lancia, followed by Nazzaro; but in the end only Nazzaro escaped mechanical troubles—and justly so, as he never strained his vehicle.

Bearing in mind the date and the very high performance achieved by this car, it must be acknowledged that the sport of racing has driven car engineering forward by leaps and bounds. The S.B.-4 owes its fame to a challenge that Fiat received from one of the best known marques of the period, Napier of England. The meeting place was to be the renowned Brooklands circuit and the date July 8, 1908.

Car: **Fiat S.B.-4**
Maker: **Fiat**
Year: **1908**
Class: **Racer**
Engine: **4-cylinder in-line twin block**
Bore × Stroke: **190 × 160 mm**
Capacity: **18,146 cc**
Power: **175 bhp at 1,200 rpm**

The S.B.-4 was powered by a vertical twin block 4-cylinder with a bore and stroke of 190 × 160 mm, a total capacity of 18,146 cc developing 175 bhp at 1,200 rpm. It had chain drive.

During the trials Felice Nazzaro, the driver, had already reached 190 km per hour (119 mph) as opposed to the approximately 200 km per hour (125 mph) achieved by Newton, who was driving a 6-cylinder Napier that developed 200 bhp. For the challenge Newton replaced Napier's official test driver, Selwyn Francis Edge, who was one of the best known figures in international car racing. By shrewd driving Felice Nazzaro won the challenge (10 laps of the circuit, equal to 44.36 km/25.57 miles), covering the distance at an average of 152.155 km per hour (94.565 mph). In the final laps he exceeded 180 km per hour (112.5 mph).

The success of the Italian driver and Fiat made a great impression. The S.B.-4 was the second largest capacity machine built by the Turin firm for racing, the largest being the 1911 S.76, which had a 4-cylinder 28,353 cc engine developing 290 bhp at 1,900 rpm. It had a maximum speed of 220 km per hour (137.5 mph). The S.76 also had chain drive.

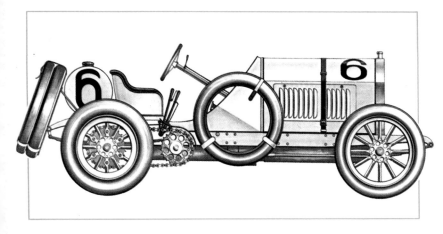

The Mercedes GP of 1908 was built in line with a new formula that specified a maximum weight of 1,100 kg (2,425 lb) and a maximum bore in 4-cyclinder engines of 155 mm; however, it did not restrict the piston stroke. Engines without 4 cylinders were to have the same total piston area as those that did. The Mercedes, designed by Paul Daimler, had a 4-cylinder engine with a capacity of about 13,000 cc and an appreciably higher stroke than bore. It had overhead inlet valves and side exhaust valves, a single carburetor, Bosch magneto ignition, a four-speed gearbox, chain drive, and semi-elliptical leaf spring suspension front and rear with Mercedes-built dampers. The wheel rims were removable (Michelin). Its top speed was a little over 160 km per hour (100 mph). This speed was actually achieved in the 1908 French Grand Prix at Dieppe, won by Christian Lautenschlager, the chief test driver of Mercedes Benz. Lautenschlager's victory was that much more important as it was won over a long distance (about 800

Car: **Mercedes GP**
Maker: **Mercedes**
Year: **1908**
Class: **Grand Prix**
Engine: **4-cylinder in-line**
Bore × Stroke: **154.7 × 170 mm**
Capacity: **12,781 cc**
Power: **135 bhp at 1,400 rpm**

km/500 miles) at an average speed of more than 101 km per hour (62.8 mph) and with a total field of 48 competitors.

The repercussions of this magnificent victory lasted only one season because in 1909 the formula was again altered. The 1908 Mercedes GP took part in hill races, however; the Italian-American Ralph De Palma drove it to victory in both the Vanderbilt Cup and the Elgin Trophy of 1912. The same machine, but with an engine of reduced capacity in accordance with the regulations, competed in the 1912 Indianapolis 500. It dropped out two laps from the finish.

The Sunbeam 3-liters of 1912 could be compared with the Formula 2 cars of to-day, so small were their engine capacities in relation to the larger class of the period. Sunbeam participated actively in racing; its chief designer, Louis Coatalen, was a highly admired though controversial engineer who was accused of copying other engineers' successful ideas rather too frequently

The 3-litre did very well in the 1912 Coupe de l'Auto, a race reserved for voiturettes. On that occasion the voiturettes raced alongside Grand Prix cars in the French Grand Prix at Dieppe. Out of the 47 starters, the Sunbeam was beaten only by Boillot's Peugeot, a 7,600 cc, and one of more than 14,000 cc. Driven by Victor Rigal, Dario Resta, and M. Médinger, Sunbeam 3-liters took first, second, and third places among the voiturettes and also won the team prize. The 3-liter was very similar to the English marque's production cars. In this class of racing the maximum engine speed allowed was 3,000 rpm. Rigal's and

Car: **Sunbeam 3-liter**
Maker: **Sunbeam**
Year: **1912**
Class: **Voiturette**
Engine: **4-cylinder in-line**
Bore × Stroke: **80 × 147.8 mm**
Capacity: **2,986 cc**
Power: **75 bhp at 2,800 rpm**

Resta's cars covered the distance in 14.5 hours, while Medinger's was delayed by a punctured fuel tank and took 16 hours. Their maximum speed on the fastest part of the Dieppe circuit was about 144 km per hour (90 mph). The 3-liter had a cone clutch, a four-speed gearbox, and semi-elliptical leaf spring suspension. It was fairly light, weighing less than a ton, and it had mechanical brakes that acted on the rear wheels only.

31

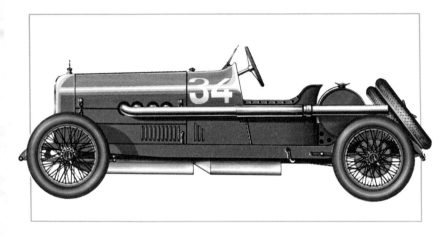

The first car to be entered in a race by A.L.F.A. was the 12 HP, which took part in the first Concorso di Regolarità at Modena in 1911. This race, however, was restricted to touring cars. The race covered 1,500 km (940 miles) in five stages; 19 cars took part, and the single A.L.F.A. was one of only six cars that were not penalized.

The 40/60, on the other hand, was conceived with the intention of producing a proper competition car as well. One of the two models selected, the Spyder, was described as a "two-seater racer." The fairly large capacity engine, 6,082 cc, had three different power ratings: 70 bhp at 2,200 rpm; 73 bhp at 2,000 rpm, and 82 bhp at 2,400 rpm. The last two versions were used, respectively, in the races of 1913–14 and 1920–22, their compression ratios being 5.5:1 and 4.35:1. Each cylinder had two overhead valves; the car had a light alloy crankcase, two crankcase-mounted camshafts with pushrods and rockers, two carburetors, high-tension magneto ignition,

Car: **A.L.F.A. 40/60**
Maker: **A.L.F.A.**
Year: **1913**
Class: **Racer**
Engine: **4-cylinder in-line twin block**
Bore × Stroke: **110 × 160 mm**
Capacity: **6,082 cc**
Power: **70 bhp at 2,200 rpm (1st series)**

shaft drive, and a transmission with four forward speeds.

The 40/60's first outing was in the Parma-Poggio di Berceto race of September 1913, where it took first and second places in its class. In the Targa Florio (May 1914) it came in third and fourth overall. The 40/60 was used again after the war, and in 1920 it won the Parma-Poggio di Berceto and a race at Mugello. The car displayed its potential for speed when one reached 147.605 km per hour (91.737 mph) in the Brescia flying kilometer. The 40/60's racing activity came to an end on October 22, 1922 at Monza. It was being driven by Giuseppe Campari who, though he did not finish, had the satisfaction of recording the fastest lap, at 141.605 km per hour.

At the beginning of the century, racing formulae were altered frequently even though there were few major events. The first formula was established in 1906, the second in 1907, the third in 1908, the fourth in 1909–11, the fifth in 1912, and the sixth in 1913.

The 1914 Mercedes GP was built in compliance with a formula that came into effect in that year and lasted only 12 months. It specified a minimum weight of 1,100 kg (2,425 lb) and a maximum capacity of 4,500 cc. After a careful study of the type of race for which the car would be used (the French Grand Prix at Lyons), and on the basis of experience gained from aircraft engines in the previous few years, the German factory chose a 4-cylinder with four overhead valves, aluminum monobloc engine with an overhead camshaft. There were three valves per cylinder angled at 60°, two Bosch magnetos, and one carburetor. The chassis had cruciform bracing, and the front and rear suspension was by semi-elliptical leaf springs. It had Rudge

Car: **Mercedes GP**
Maker: **Mercedes**
Year: **1914**
Class: **Grand Prix**
Engine: **4-cylinder in-line**
Bore × Stroke: **93 × 165 mm**
Capacity: **4,483 cc**
Power: **115 bhp at 3,200 rpm**

Whitworth spoked wheels, each of them balanced, which represented a completely new feature. The car's V radiator was another unique touch in its appearance.

Meticulous preparations for the French Grand Prix went on for months in advance. Mercedes drivers covered the course countless times in touring cars to learn all its secrets. Not surprisingly, this policy brought the company complete success. Victory went to Lautenschlager, followed by his teammates Wagner and Salzer. With the outbreak of the war, the 1914 GPs were scattered. Ralph De Palma managed to ship one to the United States and drove it to victory in the 1914 Elgin and the 1915 Indianapolis 500.

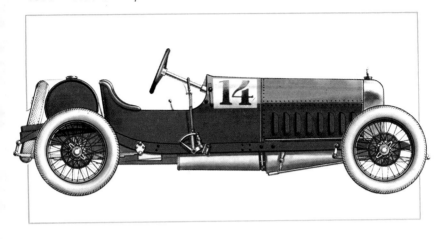

The S. 57/14 B and the S. 57 A/14 B, which appeared two years later, had much in common, with the exception of their capacity and shape. In the former the fuel tank was attached at the back and resembled a barrel, while in the A/14 B the tank was incorporated into the body, giving the car a far more compact and unified appearance.

Both the machines were designed during World War I, but they were not used until its end. The 14 B began to make a name for itself on August 24, 1919, when Nando Minoia won at the Fanöe Circuit in Denmark. Some months later Antonio Ascari came in first in a 14 B at the Parma-Poggio di Berceto race. Ascari, still in 1919, won another of the classics of the time, the Coppa della Consuma. Finally, on November 23, Giulio Masetti came in fourth overall in the Targa Florio, which in that year was won by Boillot in a Peugeot. In 1920 the 14 B scored just two successes: Giulio Masetti won the under 4,500 cc class in the Parma-Poggio di Berceto race, and a

Car: **Fiat S. 57/14 B**
Maker: **Fiat**
Year: **1914**
Class: **Grand Prix**
Engine: **4-cylinder in-line monobloc**
Bore × Stroke: **100 × 143 mm**
Capacity: **4,492 cc**
Power: **135 bhp at 3,000 rpm**

14 B driven by Niccolini came in first overall in the Coppa della Consuma, followed by Giulio Masetti in a second 14 B. However, although the A/14 B had already appeared, the earlier version's career had not completely ended. A 14 B took first place in the 1921 Targa Florio (Giulio Masetti) and first in the under 4,500 cc class (second overall) in the Susa-Moncenisio race of the same year.

Overall, this car had an excellent record. However, with its old-fashioned shape, reminiscent of the pioneering days of racing, it can be regarded as marking the end of motoring's heroic era.

The A/14 B was clearly derived from the 14 B. It was powered by an engine with the same characteristics (4-cylinder twin block) but with a slightly larger capacity (4,859 cc versus 4,492 cc). The increase was achieved by raising the bore from 100 mm to 104 mm. It developed 150 bhp as opposed to the earlier version's 135 bhp.

Although the two cars had the same general dimensions, the A/14 B could easily be distinguished from the 14 B because its fuel tank was incorporated in its body. This change made it the first modern Fiat racing car. The A/14 B's first racing season was 1921. On January 16 of that year, Masetti captured second place in an A/14 B in the over 4,500 cc class in the Vermicino-Rocca di Papa race. Niccolini took first place overall with the car in the Parma-Poggio di Berceto race on May 8. Niccolini then won the flying kilometer at the Settimana Automobilistica Toscana (Tuscan Motoring Week), reaching 151.901 km per hour (94.407 mph). The same driver won the

Car: **Fiat S. 57 A/14 B**
Maker: **Fiat**
Year: **1916**
Class: **Grand Prix**
Engine: **4-Cylinder in-line monobloc**
Bore × Stroke: **104 × 143 mm**
Capacity: **4,859 cc**
Power: **150 bhp at 3,500 rpm**

over 4,500 cc class in the Coppa della Consuma and the Brescia flying kilometer with the top speed of 177.399 km per hour (110.254 mph). Gaston Brilli Peri came in second in an identical car with a speed of 170.616 km per hour (106.039 mph).

Despite the appearance of more modern cars, the 803 for example, the A/14 B continued to be raced in 1922. Brilli Peri drove one to third place overall in the Parma-Poggio di Berceto race, and Niccolini and Brilli Peri came in second and fifth overall in the Coppa della Consuma. The A/14 B ended its racing career on a high note when Brilli Peri took first place overall in the 1923 Coppa della Consuma, and Niccolini, also in an A/14 B, came in second.

The specialist press frequently emphasizes the short time it takes to produce
modern racing cars. Such achievements,
however, are not restricted to our own
days. In fact they have been successfully
carried out right from the beginning of
motor racing. The 1919 Ballot, for example, was designed and built in 101 days.
It was intended for the 1919 Indianapolis
500, and the decision to produce it was
taken on Christmas Eve 1918. To be
ready, it had to be built, inspected, tried
out, and shipped by the following April
26, a period of 120 days. The renowned
Swiss Engineer Ernest Henri, who had
previously worked with great success for
Peugeot, was chosen to design it. The
straight-8 engine he chose had something in common with the Bugatti
straight-8 aircraft engine that Henri had
encountered during World War I and
which had a considerable influence on
motoring technology immediately after
the war.

The Ballot was the fastest in the time
trials, but it was discovered that the gear

Car: **Ballot**
Maker: **Ballot**
Year: **1919**
Class: **Racing**
Engine: **8-cylinder in-line**
Bore × Stroke: **74 × 140 mm**
Capacity: **4,820 cc**
Power: **140 bhp at 3,000 rpm**

ratios were too high. There was only time
to change the tires, an American make
being chosen. It was a disaster. Trouble
began before the first 100 miles had been
completed and continued throughout the
race. The victor was Wilcox in a Peugeot,
the second straight year the French
marque won this important race. A Ballot
8-cylinder, driven by René Thomas, took
part in another important race in 1919,
the Targa Florio; but the talented French
driver failed to achieve the hoped-for
success on the Madonia circuit.

The 1921 Ballot was a derivation of the 1919 car, with the substantial difference that the 4,900 cc straight-8 engine had been reduced to 3,000 cc. The change had been made in compliance with a new regulation in the United States restricting the capacity to three liters and the maximum weight to 800 kg (1,764 lb). Ernest Henri, who had previously designed the 4,900, reduced the bore and the stroke by 9 and 28 mm respectively.

Though the stablemate of the 4,900 did not have a brilliant career, the 3,000 did achieve considerable success. In the Indianapolis 500 of 1920, it held the lead for 465 miles before catching fire. Nevertheless, it managed to finish second. Ballot failed to win the 500 in 1921 as well, but De Palma and Goux did drive the French cars to second and third places at the French Grand Prix at Le Mans (won by Jimmy Murphy in a Duesenberg). In addition, Goux and Chassagne took first and second places in the first Italian Grand Prix at Brescia.

The short time Ernest Henri had to de-

Car: **Ballot**
Maker: **Ballot**
Year: **1921**
Class: **Grand Prix**
Engine: **8-cylinder in-line**
Bore × Stroke: **65 × 112 mm**
Power: **107 bhp at 3,800 rpm**

sign the 4,900 justifies, in a way, his basing it on both his own 1912 Peugeot and the 8-cylinder Bugatti engine. Quite a number of the Bugatti engines had been built for the Allied air forces during World War I, and one of the factories commissioned to produce them for the military was the French Bara factory in which Henri was employed during the war. The pistons were clearly derived from the 8-cylinder Bugatti while the lubrication system, the valves per cylinder, and the chain-driven overhead camshaft were reworkings of the 7,600 cc, 4-cylinder 1912 Peugeot.

The 20/30 ES was a direct descendant of the 24 HP with which A.L.F.A.'s racing activity began in the sixth Targa Florio of 1911. It was a historic car in the truest sense of the word, for it acted as the link between A.L.F.A. and Alfa Romeo. In 1915 about a hundred of the 24 HP's mechanical parts and units were stockpiled, and in 1920 these were used by Nicola Romeo's limited partnership. From then on the Milan factory was known as Alfa Romeo. In 1921 the 24 HP was improved and updated, reappearing as the 20/30 ES Sport. The factory produced 124 of these cars while, between 1910 and 1920, 680 of the 24 HPs were built.

The 20/20 ES Sport had a 4,250 cc, 4-cylinder engine that developed 67 bhp at 2,600 rpm, as opposed to the 4,084 cc and 42 bhp of the 24 HP's first version. The increase in capacity was achieved by raising the bore from 100 to 102 mm. Furthermore, the 20/30 ES had an electrical starting and lighting system as well as a wheelbase that had been

Car: **Alfa Romeo 20/30 ES**
Maker: **Alfa Romeo**
Year: **1921**
Class: **Racing**
Engine: **4-cylinder in-line, cast-iron monobloc**
Bore × Stroke: **102 × 130 mm**
Capacity: **4,250 cc**
Power: **67 bhp at 2,600 rpm**

reduced from 3.20 m (10 ft 6 in) to 2.90 m (9 ft 6 in). On request, it was fitted with spoked wheels that could be quickly removed. Another notable feature of this model was its top speed of 130 km per hour (81 mph), which was remarkable for the period. A two-seater version of the 20/30 ES criven by Sivocci and Marinoni took part in the thirteenth Targa Florio in 1921. The race was won that year and the next by Masetti driving a Mercedes. Alfa Romeo had its first success in the 1923 Sicilian race with an RL driven by Sivocci, but it was with the 20/30 ES that the company began to make a name for itself in the racing world.

Fiat 801 – 1921
Fiat 804 – 1922
Fiat 805 – 1923
Fiat 806 – 1927

The Fiat 801 was produced with two different engines; because of this it had two designations: the 801-401 and the 801-402. The first was powered by a 2,973 cc engine with four 85 × 131 mm vertical cylinders, developing 112 bhp at 4,000 rpm. The 801-402 had eight 65 × 112 mm cylinders in line and the same total capacity as the first version, developing 120 bhp at 4,400 rpm. The two cars also had the same wheelbase and track but differed in their overall length, the 801-401 being 3.73 m (12 ft 5 in) and the 801-402 being 4.65 (15 ft 3 in). They also differed in weight, the former weighing 810 kg (1,786 lb) and the latter 920 kg (2,028 lb).

The 801-402 performed superbly in the 1921 Italian Grand Prix at Brescia, in which there was a hard-fought duel between Pietro Bordino and the Frenchman Jules Goux in a Ballot. On the thirteenth lap Bordino had a puncture and lost the lead. He recovered brilliantly only to suffer a broken oil pump, which dashed his chances. The Italian driver did, however, record the fastest lap, with an average of over 150 km per hour (93 mph). Weber drove an 801-401 to victory in its class in the 1921 Coppa della Consuma, and an 801-402 driven by Wagner came in third in the Italian Grand Prix of the same year.

In that era racing formulae often lasted only a year. As a result, it is not surprising that Fiat produced the 803 (1,500 cc, 4-cylinder) and the 804 (2,000 cc, 6-cylinder twin block) in 1922; the 805 (2,000 cc, 8 cylinder in line) in 1923; and

the 806 (1,500 cc, 12-cylinder with two groups of 6) in 1927.

The 804 was a response to the new formula that came into effect in 1922 and limited engine capacity to 2,000 cc with a minimum weight of 650 kg (1,433 lb). It also specified that the rear of the car must not project more than 150 cm (4 ft 11 in) beyond the axis of the rear axle. A crew of two was required, with a total weight of not less than 120 kg (265 lb).

The 804 was powered by a 6-cylinder engine (designed by Giulio Cesare Cappa) with two blocks of 3 cylinders. It had an engine speed of 5,000 rpm, exceptionally high for the period; nickel-chrome connecting rods; two valves per cylinder; a four-speed transmission forming one unit with the engine; semi-elliptical leaf spring suspension; and a tubular front axle, which was first used in the 1914 Vauxhall.

The 804 had a brilliant debut in the French Grand Prix at Strasbourg, which was won by Felice Nazzaro at an average of 127.202 km per hour (79.06 mph). However, the success of this car, which could have been outstanding, was in the end tempered by the retirement of two out of the three Fiats at the moment when both were excellently placed. In one case a flange on the rear axle broke; the car lost a wheel and went out of control, killing Biagio Nazzaro, Felice's nephew. Bordino, who was driving the third Fiat, was accused of straining his car in an attempt to close the gap between him
(continued on page 42)

Car: **Fiat 801**
Maker: **Fiat**
Year: **1921**
Class: **Grand Prix**

Engine: **8-cylinder in-line monobloc**
Bore × Stroke: **65 × 112 mm**
Capacity: **2,973 cc**
Power: **120 bhp at 4,400 rpm**

1922 - Fiat 804

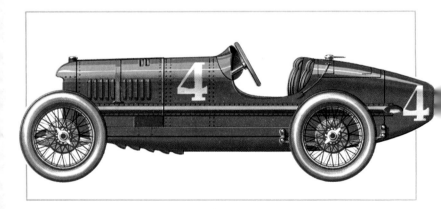

Car: **Fiat 804**
Maker: **Fiat**
Year: **1922**
Class: **Grand Prix**

Engine: **6-cylinder in-line, in two blocks**
Bore × Stroke: **65 × 100 mm**
Capacity: **1,991 cc**
Power: **112 bhp at 5,000 rpm**

Fiat 805 - 1923

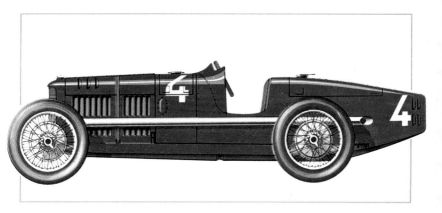

Car: **Fiat 805**
Maker: **Fiat**
Year: **1923**
Class: **Grand Prix**

Engine: **Supercharged 8-cylinder in-line**
Bore × Stroke: **60 × 87.5 mm**
Capacity: **1,979 cc**
Power: **130 bhp at 5,500 rpm**

Fiat 806 - 1927

Car: **Fiat 806**
Maker: **Fiat**
Year: **1927**
Class: **Grand Prix**

Engine: **Supercharged 12-cylinder in-line, in
two groups of 6**
Bore × Stroke: **50 × 63 mm**
Capacity: **1,484 cc**
Power: **177 bhp at 8,500 rpm**

(continued from page 39)

and Nazzaro. However, Bordino went on to win the Italian Grand Prix, the inaugural race at the new Autodromo di Monza (Monza motor racing circuit), followed by Felice Nazzaro in second place. Bordino recorded the fastest lap, at an average of 150.362 km per hour (93.45 mph). Fiat dominated the season with these two victories and wiped out their defeat the previous year at the hands of Goux in a Ballot in the first Italian Grand Prix.

The Fiat 805 was the first racing car in the world to be fitted with a supercharger. Initially, a Whitting centrifugal supercharger was used, later replaced by a Roots rotary pump. Both were positioned above the carburetor.

The 805's straight-eight 405 engine had a capacity of 1,979 cc and developed 130 bhp at 5,500 rpm with the Whitting supercharger and, subsequently, 150 bhp with the Roots. With the earlier supercharger the car's maximum speed was about 200 km per hour (124 mph), and it reached 219 km per hour (136 mph) with the later one.

The 805's first appearance was at the 1923 French Grand Prix at Tours. However, the circuit did not allow the car to develop its full power; and it was, after all, the machine's first run. The 805 appeared again at Monza in the Italian Grand Prix (which was also the European Grand Prix of that year), driven by Carlo Salamano. It had a clear victory. Though the 805 was little used, it established a technical concept that was to be extensively developed in the years immediately following.

Fiat's involvement in racing did not continue much longer. The 806 marked the end of Fiat's 30 years in racing.

Whatever the true reason for this withdrawal—a sad event for maker, drivers, and the public alike—it was in some way connected to the departure of Vincenzo Bertarione and Walter Becchia for Sunbeam of England and Vittoria Jano for Alfa Romeo. In both cases the designers took with them a wealth of experience (it is said that they even carried off projects and designs). The Turin factory, stating that it had to concentrate entirely on mass production, terminated its involvement with racing.

The 806 was powered by a 12-cylinder engine that had two rows of 6 cylinders and a Roots supercharger; it developed 177 bhp. The car raced only once, in the 1927 Italian Grand Prix at Monza. The race was won by Pietro Bordino at an average speed of about 151 km per hour (94 mph) and a top speed of 240 km per hour (149 mph). Bordino had a rather slow start and at the end of the first lap he was lying third, but by the following lap he had taken the lead, and he kept it until the finish. A technical novelty of the 806 was its three camshafts, the central one controlling the inlet valves of the two rows of 6 cylinders. The coupling of the cylinders, 2 to 2, enabled the number of main bearings to be reduced to four, and roller bearings were replaced by plain ones. The engine weighed 173 kg (381 lb).

The departures of Jano, Becchia, and Bertarione and the suspicion that they had taken the details of important projects and technical innovations to their new employers angered Giovanni Agnelli. He put an end, forever, to a glorious tradition. Fiat was ahead of its time in this decision as well, since it anticipated, though by many years, similar actions by Mercedes and Alfa Romeo.

The Sunbeam 2-liter Grand Prix was a much talked about machine, not so much for its results, though these were outstanding, but because it was regarded as too close a copy of the 1922 Fiat 804. The Sunbeam's designer was Louis Coatalen, the marque's English technical manager, who had the reputation of basing his products too closely on those of his rivals. In the case of the Sunbeam 2-liter the similarity to the Fiat 804 was the result of an astute move by Coatalen. He employed the Italians Vincenzo Bertarione and Walter Becchia who had worked in close contact with the Fiat engineers (Fornaca, Cappa, and Cavalli) in the Turin marque's racing department.

The 2-liter used the same chassis as the 16-valve, 4-cylinder car of 1922, but it was fitted with a 6-cylinder, 12-valve engine. It had a bore of 67 mm and a stroke of 94 mm as opposed to the Fiat's 65 × 100 mm. The engine was fed by a Solex carburetor and had a Bosch magneto. Sunbeam beat Fiat in the French Grand Prix at Tours, Segrave taking first place

Car: **Sunbeam 2-liter**
Maker: **Sunbeam**
Year: **1923**
Class: **Grand Prix**
Engine: **6-cylinder in-line**
Bore × Stroke: **67 × 94 mm**
Capacity: **1,988 cc**
Power: **108 bhp at 5,000 rpm**

overall; but it did not enter the Italian Grand Prix. In the Spanish Grand Prix it had a lucky win after Zborowski, who was leading in an 8-cylinder Miller, was delayed two laps from the finish by a burst tire.

In 1924 the Sunbeams were supercharged, raising the power output from 108 bhp to 138 bhp at 5,500 rpm. However, the chassis had to be modified substantially (lengthened and widened) in order to take the supercharger. The three-speed transmission of the 1923 machine was replaced by a four-speed one. These modifications increased the weight by more than 130 kg (287 lb).

Alfa Romeo P2 - 1924
Alfa Romeo P3 - 1932

Enzo Ferrari did not find it easy to tear Vittorio Jano away from Fiat, but once he had succeeded the results were very profitable for Alfa Romeo. Vittorio Jano was reared in the Fiat school. He attended races on behalf of the Turin firm and gained very useful experience from them. The P2 was the first car that he designed for Alfa Romeo, and his work for the Milan firm could not have had a better start. This twin-seater was unbeaten throughout its racing career. Jano arrived in Milan in September 1923; and the P2 appeared on June 9, 1924 in the 200 Miglia of the second Circuito di Cremona, where it quickly aroused great interest. It won at an average of more than 158 km per hour (98 mph) and reached 195 km per hour (121 mph) over the flying ten kilometers. In the space of just nine months, therefore, this car had been designed, built, and raced. Among other victories, a P2 driven by Gastone Brilli Peri won the first World Championship (the World Championship was only resumed in 1950).

The initial version of the straight-8 engine P2 developed 140 bhp at 5,500 rpm; this was later raised to 175 bhp at the same engine speed and with the same compression ratio of 6:1. In 1930 the three remaining cars out of the total of six that had been built were modified. They took part successfully in a number of races, including the Targo Florio, the Trieste-Opicina, the Cuneo-Colle della Maddalena, and the Vittorio-Cansiglio. The most original feature of the 1930 version's appearance was the housing of the spare wheel in a longitudinal slot in the tail of the car. However, this feature reduced the capacity of the fuel tank.

The P3, also known as the Type B, was another of Vittorio Jano's masterpieces. It was prepared for the open formula of 1932 and, like the P2, won its first race. This car's important technical peculiarities were the unusual position of the differential (at the output of the gearbox) and its two propeller shafts arranged in a V, each driving one rear wheel. The driver's seat was in the center.

The P3 competed in the 1932 and the 1933 racing seasons, the period provided for by the open formula, and in the 1934 races as well, with the single modification of increasing the engine capacity from 2,654 cc to 2,905 cc. The 1934 season was very demanding for Alfa Romeo, as it had to face Mercedes and Auto Union. The job of defending the Milan factory's name was taken on by Enzo Ferrari. Ferrari's Scuderia (racing organization) competed in the major races of the period; in 1933 management of the six P3s that had been built was handed over to the Scuderia, with excellent results. The formula in effect in 1934 specified a maximum weight (750 kg/1,623 lb) rather than a minimum, as had always been the case up until then. Ferrari had to work feverishly in order to be able to face the Germans. Alfa Romeo notched up a good number of wins with the 1934 Type B, which developed 255 bhp at 5,400 rpm. It was designed by Pallavicino, who was an engineer with Breda and therefore had aeronautical experience. His knowledge showed in the Type B's aerodynamic body and a top speed 20 km per hour (12.5 mph) more than the version with a normal body.

Alfa Romeo P2 - 1924

Car: **Alfa Romeo P2**
Maker: **Alfa Romeo**
Year: **1924**
Class: **Grand Prix**

Engine: **8-cylinder in-line**
Bore × Stroke: **61 × 85 mm**
Capacity: **1,987 cc**
Power: **140 bhp at 5,500 rpm**

Alfa Romeo P3 - 1932

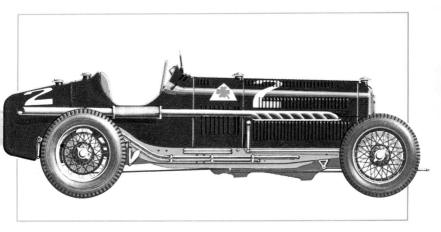

Car: **Alfa Romeo P3**
Maker: **Alfa Romeo**
Year: **1932**
Class: **Grand Prix**

Engine: **8-cylinder in-line**
Bore × Stroke: **65 × 100 mm**
Power: **215 bhp at 5,600 rpm**

Bugatti 35 – 1930
Bugatti Type 59 – 1933

The 35 constitutes a milestone in the history of this Italian-French marque for two principal reasons. First, it was one of the cars with the greatest number of victories; second, it was the first car that Ettore Bugatti sold to private competitors. In a period dominated by the Alfa Romeo P2 and the Delage V-12, the 35 did not, at the beginning of its career, have a chance to shine; but it subsequently achieved a record number of wins. According to the factory's official records, it scored 577 wins in 1926 and 806 in 1927. These figures admittedly include wins in relatively unimportant races; but in the course of its career the 35 did win 68 major races, including five Targa Florios, four French Grand Prix, three European Grand Prix, three San Sebastiano Grand Prix, two Monaco Grand Prix, and one Italian and one German Grand Prix. Masetti drove a 35 to its first important success, in the Rome Grand Prix.

The 35 won its outstanding reputation more for the way in which it was built and for its excellent road holding than for the power of its engine. Commercially the 35 was very important to Bugatti, as confirmed by the fact that about 400 were produced (of which about 40 had twin camshaft engines). The principal historians of the marque have been able to establish that between 1927 and 1929 the 35 cost a maximum of 120,000 francs, the 35 T cost 135,000 francs, and the 35 C cost 150,000 francs. It is unusual to obtain precise figures on most racing cars.

The necessity of replacing the Type 35, which had by then reached the limits of its potential, led Ettore Bugatti to build a new racing car—the Type 51, which was the last Bugatti racing car sold to the public. The Type 51 had a straight-8 engine with twin overhead camshafts. However, the car had only a brief career, though Chiron-Varzi drove one to victory in the 1931 French Grand Prix at Montlhery, and Varzi won the 1933 Monaco Grand Prix in it. The Type 51 was quickly superseded by the Type 53, which had four-wheel drive but was never actually used, and the Type 54, which did not achieve the results that had been hoped for. Ettore Bugatti spent the whole of 1933 designing and building the Type 59, which is considered to be the last of the classic Grand Prix cars. It complied with the new 1934 formula specifying maximum weight, even though its first appearance was at the San Sebastiano Grand Prix of 1933. The chassis was derived from the Type 54's and had inverted semi-elliptical leaf spring rear suspension, a tubular front axle, and Ram dampers. The clutch had a hydraulic control mechanism. The straight-8 engine initially had a capacity of below 3,000 cc, but it was increased to 3,257 cc. It had pinion-driven twin overhead camshafts. The pinions were housed at the rear of the engine and drove the water pump and supercharger as well.

The wheels were entirely original. The spokes were merely load bearing, while an aluminium disc, fixed to the drum of the brake and to the hub, engaged the rim by means of its many small teeth and transmitted the drive and braking forces.

Bugatti 35 - 1930

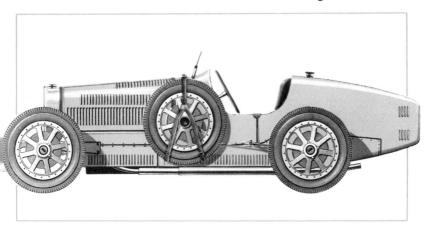

Car: **Bugatti 35**
Maker: **Bugatti**
Year: **1930**
Class: **Grand Prix**

Engine: **8-cylinder in-line**
Bore × Stroke: **60 × 88 mm**
Capacity: **1,955 cc**
Power: **135 bhp at 5,300 rpm**

Bugatti Type 59 - 1933

Car: **Bugatti Type 59**
Maker: **Bugatti**
Year: **1933**
Class: **Grand Prix**

Engine: **Supercharged 8-cylinder in-line**
Bore × Stroke: **72 × 100 mm**
Capacity: **3,257 cc**
Power: **240 bhp at 5,400 rpm**

Cyril Posthumus relates in his *Classic Racing Cars* that the Führer decided to grant a subsidy totaling 450,000 marks to Mercedes and Auto Union to help them prepare two Grand Prix cars worthy of the German tradition. According to Posthumus, the decision stemmed from the crushing defeat the Germans suffered in Hitler's presence at the 1933 Avus Grand Prix, when the Bugatti 4,900 cc took first and second places followed by three Alfa Romeos.

Mercedes prepared the W 25 for the 1934 weight formula. It was powered by a 3,360 cc straight-8 engine, enlarged in 1935 to 3,900 cc (W 25 B). Driven by von Brauchitsch and Luigi Fagioli, it made its debut in May 1934 at Eifelrenen, where there were also two Alfa Romeos and two Auto Unions competing. Von Brauchitsch was the winner, followed by an Auto Union and an Alfa Romeo. During the race Alfred Neubauer ordered Luigi Fagioli to yield first place to his teammate, and the Italian driver reacted by abandoning his car on the circuit.

Car: **Mercedes W 25**
Maker: **Mercedes**
Year: **1934**
Class: **Grand Prix**
Engine: **8-cylinder in-line**
Bore × Stroke: **78 × 80 mm**
Capacity: **3,360 cc**
Power: **354 bhp at 5,800 rpm**

Alfa Romeo recovered to take the French Grand Prix at Montlhery, Chiron driving; but this was the only success that the Italian marque achieved that year. Mercedes took four of the remaining seven major races in 1934, and Auto Union took the other three.

The 450,000 marks that had been granted to the two German marques did not even cover the design costs of the 8-cylinder Mercedes and the 16-cylinder Auto Union, but the money did provide a considerable boost. It has been justly observed that Hitler's action marked the first time a politician understood the importance of racing in supporting national prestige.

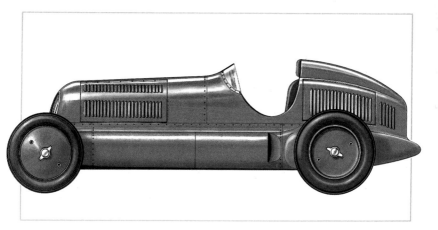

The formula with a maximum weight of 750 kg (1,653.4 lb), which was in force from 1934 until 1937, had an effect opposite to the International Automobile Federation's intention of reducing power. By using light metals, both Mercedes and Auto Union managed to achieve very high power ratings without exceeding the weight limit; and Alfa Romeo felt forced to respond quickly. The decision to build the Bimotore was a consequence of this technological race, and the car was prepared in less than four months.

The brilliance of Alfa Romeo's solution lay in the positioning of the two engines, one at the front, one at the rear, with the gearbox, clutch, and driver's seat in between. This enabled the same frontal section to be retained. The two engines that were chosen were taken from the 1934 Type B, though their capacity was increased by raising the bore from 68 mm to 71 mm. Each engine had a capacity of 3,165 cc, making a total of 6,330 cc and a power rating of 540 bhp at 5,400 rpm. According to Enzo Ferrari, the impetus

Car: **Alfa Romeo Bimotore**
Make: **Scuderia Ferrari**
Year: **1935**
Class: **Grand Prix**
Engine: **16-cylinder, consisting of two 8-cylinder, 3,165 cc engines**
Bore × Stroke: **71 × 100 mm**
Total capacity: **6,330 cc**
Power: **540 bhp at 5,400 rpm**

for a car of this kind came from Luigi Bazzi. The Bimotore made its first appearance at the ninth Tripoli Grand Prix, on May 12, 1936.

The Bimotore was actually built at the Scuderia Ferrari in Modena. Other distinctive features of this single-seater were: the gearbox with three forward speeds; the transmission with two shafts diverging from the differential (as in the Type B); the central steering wheel; the independent Dubonnet front suspension; and two lateral fuel tanks. The placement of the fuel tanks, which with the advent of rear engines has become universal, was also used on the 1938 Auto Union and therefore boasts an excellent pedigree.

Auto Union Type C – 1936
Auto Union Type C – 1937

Designed by Ferdinand Porsche, this car took the name of the new car group Auto Union, which was formed in 1933 by the merger of Horch, Audi, DKW, and Wanderer. Ferdinand Porsche was Wanderer's technical consultant; however, the single-seater racing car project intended for the maximum weight formula that came into force in 1934 was a personal venture undertaken with his business partner, Adolf Rosenberger. It was via Wanderer that the Porsche project subsequently reached Auto Union and acquired its name. An important feature of this single-seater was its V-16 engine, positioned at the back of the driver's seat, behind the fuel tank and in front of the rear axle. The gearbox was driven by a gearwheel mounted behind the rear axle. It had a tubular chassis, part of which was used to pipe cooling water between the radiator, at the front of the car, and the engine. There was independent suspension on all wheels, the front having Porsche half-axles and torsion bars, the rear having wishbones and a transverse leaf spring.

Initially the engine had a capacity of 4,360 cc and developed 295 bhp at 4,500 rpm. It made its first appearance on March 6, 1934 at the Avus circuit in Berlin, where Hans Stuck broke three world speed records. In the same year he won the German, Swiss, and Czechoslovakian Grand Prix. In 1935 the capacity was increased to 4,950 (Type B) and the power to 375 bhp at 4,700 rpm. For the Type C the capacity was increased yet again, to 6,006 cc, and it developed 520 bhp at 5,000 rpm. In 1935 Auto Union

and the Type B won only one important race, the Italian Grand Prix, while in 1936 the Type C took the German and Italian Grand Prix and in 1937 the Belgian Grand Prix.

With the advent of the new 1938-40 formula, Auto Union abandoned the 16-cylinder, like Mercedes selecting the 12-cylinder instead. Two events led to a decisive change at this point in its history. The first was the departure of Ferdinand Porsche, who wished to devote himself entirely to the design of the Volkswagen Beetle. The other was the death of Bernard Rosemeyer in a record attempt. Rosemeyer was not only a highly talented driver but also Auto Union's key figure in the complicated task of tuning a car which, as it was rear-engined, posed many problems for the drivers of the time. The place of Ferdinand Porsche was taken by another highly regarded technician, Eberan von Eberhorst, while Rosemeyer's was taken by Tazio Nuvolari.

The new 12-cylinder had three camshafts, the central one controlling the inlet valves and the two lateral ones controlling the exhaust valves. It had a Roots supercharger, and initially it developed 420 bhp at 7,000 rpm. This increased to 485 bhp at the same engine speed in 1939 with a two-stage supercharger. One of the major innovations von Eberhorst made with respect to the V-16 of 1937 was the replacement of the single fuel tank between the engine and the driver's seat by two lateral ones. This solution greatly improved the weight distribution and the road holding.

Auto Union Type C - 1936

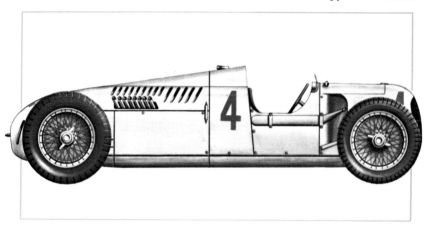

Car: **Auto Union Type C**
Maker: **Auto Union**
Year: **1936**
Class: **Grand Prix**

Engine: **45° V-16**
Bore × Stroke: **75 × 85 mm**
Capacity: **6,006 cc**
Power: **520 bhp at 5,000 rpm**

Auto Union Type C - 1937

Car: **Auto Union Type C**
Maker: **Auto Union**
Year: **1937**
Class: **Grand Prix**

Engine: **V-16**
Bore × Stroke: **75 × 85 mm**
Capacity: **6,006 cc**
Power: **520 bhp at 5,000 rpm**

The 1937 W 125 was a transitional single-seater hastily built by the German factory; despite this fact, the car was one of Mercedes's most interesting. The reason behind the car's makeshift nature was a change of mind by the highest motoring authority of the time, the Association Internationale des Automobile Clubs Reconnus (AIACR). Faced with the complete failure of its maximum weight formula, which was to remain in force throughout 1937, it decided on a new formula that specified a minimum weight, 850 kg (1,873.9 lb), and two maximum capacities, 3,460 cc for supercharged engines and 4,500 for engines without superchargers. However, this formula was never applied; in September 1936 the AIACR altered its decision again, retaining the upper limit for normally aspirated engines but fixing a new one (3,000 cc) for supercharged engines.

With only three months left in 1936, the AIACR retained the maximum weight formula for another year. The W 125 was therefore a development of the W 25 B of

Car: **Mercedes W 125**
Maker: **Mercedes**
Year: **1937**
Class: **Grand Prix**
Engine: **8-cylinder in-line**
Bore × Strike: **94 × 102 mm**
Capacity: **5,660 cc**
Power: **646 bhp at 5,800 rpm**

1935–36. Keeping within the 750 kg (1,653.4 lb) weight limit that was in force at the time, the W 125 was powered by a 5,660 cc straight-8 engine that developed 646 bhp at 5,800 rpm.

In 1937 a W 125 driven by Caracciola won the German Grand Prix; von Brauchitsch won the Monaco Grand Prix in one; and Caracciola won the Italian and then the Swiss Grand Prix. In the fastest stretches of the circuits where it was competing, the W 125 reached a top speed of 320 km per hour (198.9 mph). An interesting feature of this car is that in 1937 it was fueled by a mixture consisting of 86% methyl alcohol, 8.8% acetone, 4.4% nitrobenzene, and 0.8% sulphuric ether.

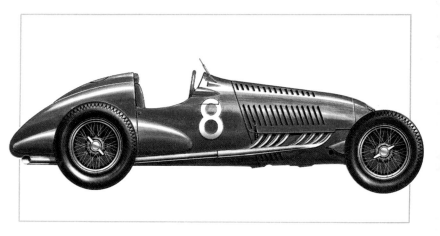

Although the 308 and the 158 were closely related, the latter was derived from the former. The 308 was built by Alfa Corse (Alfa Racing) at Milan while the 158 was built by Scuderia Ferrari at Modena.

The 308 was the first single-seater produced by Alfa Romeo for the new 3,000 cc formula, which came into force in 1938 and which would have remained in effect until 1940 had the outbreak of World War II not intervened. In addition to 3,000 cc engines, 4,500 cc engines were permitted without superchargers. The weight varied from a minimum of 400 kg (881.8 lb) to a maximum of 800 kg (1,763.7 lb) in proportion to the engine capacity. There were no restrictions on fuel. In practice, the capacity advantage of normally aspirated engines to supercharged ones was slight; as a result, 3,000 cc engines were highly favored.

The 308 had a straight-8 light alloy engine that developed 295 bhp at 6,000 rpm and was fed by two vertical two-lobed superchargers built by Alfa Romeo

Car: **Alfa Romeo 308**
Maker: **Alfa Romeo**
Year: **1938**
Class: **Grand Prix**
Engine: **8-cylinder in-line**
Bore × Stroke: **69 × 100 mm**
Capacity: **2,991 cc**
Power: **295 bhp at 6,000 rpm**

itself. It had a four-speed transmission, a transverse leaf spring rear suspension, and a central steering wheel.

The 308 was derived from the 8C 2900 B of 1937–39, which originated as a two-seater spyder and not as a racing car. The 308 differed not only in its chassis and in the driver's position but also in capacity (2,991 cc for the 308 versus 2,905 cc for the other model). The 8C 2900 B had 2 two-lobed superchargers and developed 180 bhp at 5,200 rpm.

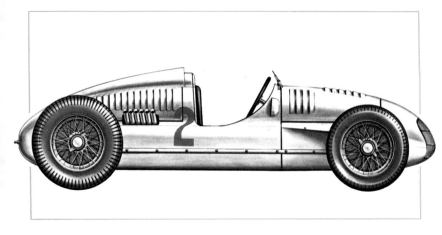

The Type D complied with the formula instituted in 1938. Like Mercedes, Auto Union chose a 12-cylinder engine after much hesitation about continuing in racing; moreover, it had lost the services of Ferdinand Porsche, who was by then taken up with the Volkswagen project. His successor was Eberan von Eberhorst, another talented engineer, who made a number of important modifications to the 1935–37 car besides reducing the number of cylinders. The new 3,000 cc, 12-cylinder had three camshafts; the central one controlled the 12 inlet valves and the other two (one for each bank of cylinders) controlled the exhaust valves. It had a vertical Roots supercharger, a five-speed ZF transmission, half-axle and torsion bar front suspension (as used on the 1935–37 single-seater), while De Dion rear suspension was adopted. The radiator remained at the front; but the fuel tank, instead of being placed behind the driver and in front of the engine, was split into two tanks located beside the driving seat.

Car: **Auto Union Type D**
Maker: **Auto Union**
Year: **1938**
Class: **Grand Prix**
Engine: **60° V-12**
Bore × Stroke: **65 × 75 mm**
Capacity: **2,990 cc**
Power: **420 bhp at 7,000 rpm**

This allowed the seat to be moved further back, giving better weight distribution. This substantial change altered the car's behavior from oversteering to understeering. Initially the engine developed 420 bhp at 7,000 rpm, but in 1939 this was increased to 485 bhp with the installation of a two-stage supercharger.

The car's preparation took more time than expected, and Auto Union was unable to take part in the first three races of 1938. The Type D then had a disastrous debut in the French Grand Prix. Only Tazio Nuvolari was able to stem the tide of defeat: the Italian driver won the Yugoslavian Grand Prix on the day that France and Britain declared war on Germany.

Mercedes W 154–163–1938–39
Mercedes W 165–1939

The W 154 and W 163 single-seaters were virtually the same thing, the second being a development of the first while the basic specifications remained unaltered. The W 154 was built in compliance with the 1938–40 formula, which specified a maximum capacity of 3,000 cc for super-charged engines and 4,500 cc for nor-mally aspirated ones. Rather than de-velop its 1934–37 formula straight-8, Mercedes, like Auto Union, built a 60° V-12. The W 154's powerful 12-cylinder engine had 48 valves (the exhaust valves being mercury cooled), and it was fed by two Roots superchargers and a Mer-cedes-built carburetor. Initially, it de-veloped 425 bhp at 8,000 rpm, but this was progressively increased to 466 bhp. The engine and the transmission were offset so as to give the driver more room. It had a five-speed, transaxle (i.e., rear-mounted) transmission; independent front suspension; and a De Dion rear axle. All these features made the W 154 a highly advanced machine. In addition, it excited great interest because of the then highly secret method for preparing its fuel mixtures. These mixtures contained a large amount of methyl alcohol, nitroben-zene, acetone, and sulphuric ether.

The car consumed about a liter of fuel for every kilometer (2.8 mpg) covered. The W 154 carried more than 400 liters (88 gal) of fuel in two tanks, one in the tail with a capacity of 227 liters (50 gal) and the other between the rear of the en-gine and the driver's seat, which held 181 liters (40 gal). Both were filled at the same time through a single filler placed at the top of the headrest.

In 1938 the W 154 won six out of eight races, demonstrating a clear superiority over the Auto Unions. However, its two defeats by Auto Union at the end of the season worried the Mercedes techni-cians, and during the winter of 1938–39 they strove to improve this already for-midable car. Its power output was in-creased by 60 bhp, the lubrication was improved, and the weight was reduced by more than 60 kg (132 lb). Mercedes also altered its appearance by giving it a new, more streamlined and aggressively shaped body. In 1939 the W 154 became the W 163.

In historical terms this latter designa-tion is incorrect since it refers simply to the engine, which was modified during the winter of 1938–39 and numbered the M 163. In the 1939 racing season, when this engine was installed in both the new body and, sometimes, the W 154's, it finished up with five additional victories. The W 154-163 continues to be regarded as one of the most successful racing cars ever built by Mercedes.

In 1951, when General Peron was an enthusiastic supporter of motor racing, the car was dusted off and raced in Argentina. However, the German car was soundly beaten by the supercharged Fer-rari 2000 of Gonzales. The W 163 was also entered in the 1947 and 1948 In-dianapolis 500s, but without success.

The decision to build the W 165, which was done in record time, was due to the rivalry that existed between the Germans and the Italians immediately before the war. Auto Union and Mercedes had swept the board in the major motor races and had made life extremely hard for Alfa Romeo and Maserati. The then FAI (Federazione Italiana dell'Automobile) devised a rather underhanded plan to put an end to this situation. It secretly decided to reserve the 1939 Italian races, beginning with the famous Tripoli Grand Prix, for voiturettes—single-seaters with engines below 1,500 cc—instead of the 3,000 to 4,500 cc engines specified by the formula then in force. This choice was motivated by the fact that the Germans did not have any cars with that engine capacity and probably would not have time to build them.

Neubauer learned of the Italian decision the day after the Italian Grand Prix of September 1938; the Tripoli Grand Prix was to take place in the spring of 1939. Neubauer reported the news to the Mercedes management as soon as he returned to Stuttgart, and an immediate decision was taken to build two 1,500 cc cars. These were ready by March 1939, their preparation having been speeded up by making use of many of the parts—including the suspension, brakes, and wheels—of the 3,000 cc W 154. The new car had a 90° V-8 engine, the first such to be produced by this German marque; it had Roots superchargers and initially was able to develop 256 bhp, which was progressively increased to 278 bhp at 8,250 rpm.

Drivers Lang and Caracciola were ready for Tripoli, and they took first and second place, respectively. The Mercedes engineers had thus achieved the miracle of building a virtually new car in less than six months.

1938 - Mercedes W 154

Car: **Mercedes W 154**
Maker: **Mercedes**
Year: **1938**
Class: **Racing**

Engine: **60° V-12**
Bore × Stroke: **67 × 70 mm**
Capacity: **2,962 cc**
Power: **425 bhp at 8,000 rpm**

Mercedes W 163 - 1939

Car: **Mercedes W 163**
Maker: **Mercedes**
Year: **1939**
Class: **Grand Prix**

Engine: **Supercharged 60° V-12**
Bore × Stroke: **67 × 70 mm**
Capacity: **2,962 cc**
Power: **425 bhp at 8,000 rpm**

Mercedes W 165 - 1939

Car: **Mercedes W 165**
Maker: **Mercedes**
Year: **1939**
Class: **Voiturette**

Engine: **90° V-8**
Bore × Stroke: **64 × 58 mm**
Capacity: **1,495 cc**
Power: **263–278 bhp at 8,250 rpm**

3

Formula 1 – Formula 2 From 1948 to the Present

The principal reason Formula 1, which came into effect in 1947, was divided into two very different capacity classes—1,500 cc for supercharged engines and 4,500 cc for normally aspirated ones—was the chance it offered to make use of racing material saved from the destruction and ravages of the war. There were no weight or fuel limitations.

The equivalence ratio of 3:1 took account of the difference in power obtainable from supercharged and normally aspirated engines. However, it was primarily the result of the extensive amount of material which had, miraculously, remained hidden during the conflict. The best way of resuming sport racing, and resuming it quickly, was to combine the 4,500 cc single-seaters of the old 1938–40 formula and the voiturettes (1,500 cc with supercharger). This fusion satisfied everybody: the Italians, British, French, and Germans, though the Germans were not immediately readmitted to the FIA, since they were held responsible for starting the war.

This mixture of machines turned out to be a good choice, one that produced excellent results. The best evidence for the soundness of the first Formula 1 was the decision not to alter it even when the World Championship was inaugurated in 1950. This formula was intended to remain in force up to and including 1953. However, it was abandoned at the end of 1951, through no fault of its own as will be seen.

In 1948 the Federation Internationale de l'Automobile, which had replaced the AIACR, decided to institute a Formula 2 for cars powered by 500 cc supercharged engines or 2,000 cc engines without a supercharger. Formula 2 cars were, in effect, the new voiturettes. They rose to prominence at the end of 1951 when the organizers of the Formula 1 Grand Prix were faced with the prospect of seeing their efforts frustrated by too few competitors. Crucial in this respect were the withdrawal of Alfa Romeo at the end of the 1951 season and the failures of BRM. The Formula 2 cars were promoted, taking the place of the Formula 1 cars in the Grand Prix. They fulfilled their task admirably, helped by the fact that the simple technology on which they were based

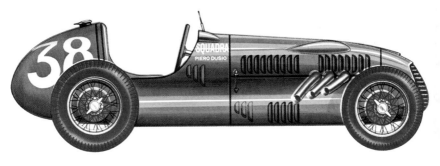

Cisitalia 1948: 4 cylinders in line (Fiat), 1,089 cc, 62 bhp at 5,500 rpm

excited considerable interest. That all the makers of Formula 2 cars used 2,000 cc engines exclusively had a marked impact on the public, since in the public's eye the Formula 2 cars had a great deal in common with normal production cars. Through 1952 and 1953, Grand Prix were the province of Formula 2 in 14 out of 15 races, the fifteenth won by the Ferrari 500.

From 1954 until 1960 it was the turn of the planned Formula 1 (2,500 cc engines without superchargers or 750 cc with, no fuel or weight limits; from 1958 onward it became obligatory to use commercial fuel, and no maker was allowed to resort to special mixtures). The advent of this formula marked the return of Mercedes to the major competitions after an absence of 16 years. Technical innovations made by Mer-

AFM 1950: 6 cylinders in line, 1,971 cc, 140 bhp at 5,800 rpm

cedes were the use of fuel injection and, on the faster circuits, a faired body. The latter was badly copied by other makers and was subsequently banned by the FIA, who stipulated that the front wheels had to be visible from the driver's seat. In the seven years in which this formula was in force, a total of 55 races were run, of which 13 were won by Ferrari, 13 by Cooper, 9 by Mercedes (in only two years of activity), 9 by Vanwall, 8 by Maserati, 2 by Lotus, and one by BRM. The total of 25 victories by British cars bears witness to the revolution that took place during this period. First Vanwall, then Cooper, and finally Lotus put an end to Italian supremacy. It was the beginning of the era of the assembler and the sponsor. The world of motor sport had been transformed.

Like Mercedes, Cooper introduced a profound innovation adopted by every Formula 1 maker. This was the moving of the engine to the rear of the car. The rear engine became universal on both sides of the Atlantic and in the smaller formulae as well as in Formula 1. In 1961 it was decided to lower the capacity further, to 1,500 cc (minimum 1,300 cc), and superchargers were not allowed under any circumstances. There was a minimum weight of 450 kg (992 lb) including water and oil but not fuel. It was forbidden to boost the weight with ballast. Commercial fuel had to be used. This formula was retained for five years with a total of 47 Grand Prix. Of these, 22 were won by Lotus, 11 by BRM, 9 by Ferrari, 2 by Brabham, and one each by Cooper, Porsche, and Honda. Porsche and Honda made only a fleeting appearance in Formula 1. Both considered the commitment required for participation in major races too heavy in terms of economics and human resources.

In 1966 a new Formula 1 came into force, and this is due to expire at the end of 1982. It makes allowance for two types of engines: 1,500 cc with a supercharger, 3,000 cc without. The minimum weight was initially fixed at 500 kg (1,102.3 lb) but this was raised to 530 kg (1,168.4 lb) in 1969 and to 575 kg (1,267.6 lb) in 1975 to accommodate various safety measures (roll bar, belts, fire extinguishers, and the like). In 1973 safety requirements dictated that each fuel tank could contain no more than 80 liters (17.6 gal) and that the car's total fuel capacity must not exceed 250 liters (55 gal).

The Ford-Cosworth V-8, which came to be used by all the British Formula 1 makers, appeared in 1967. It is this engine more than anything else that characterizes the period. Its dominance is shown by the fact that up until 1979 it had won 125 races (the 125th being won by Alan Jones driving a Williams in the 1979 Canadian Grand Prix) as opposed to the 40 victories over 14 years gained by the Ferrari 12-cylinders, both boxer and 60° V.

Another radical innovation, introduced in the last two years of the period in question, is the ground effect or wing car. Introduced by Lotus in 1978, the 79, which with Mario Andretti won the World Championship of that year, was quickly imitated by all Formula 1 makers. It is remarkable that the Ferrari T4, which reached the top with Jody Scheckter in 1979, was not a full-fledged ground effect car; the arrangement and the horizontal dimensions of its engine prevented it from fully exploiting the principles of underside aerodynamics that are a feature of such cars.

The advent of very broad section tires has revolutionized the behavior as well as the appearance of single-seater racing cars in recent years, but it has yet to be established

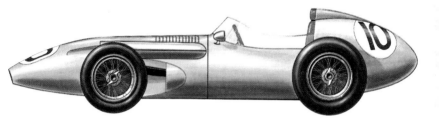

Aston Martin 1959: 6 cylinders in line, 2,492 cc, 280 bhp at 8,250 rpm

to what extent they are an advance. The failure of the six-wheeled Tyrrell confirms the difficulties of striking out along new paths without considerable financial resources.

Formula 2 has continued alongside the larger formula, providing an effective launching pad for young drivers. All the winners of the European Trophy (including Regazzoni, Jabouille, and Gacomelli) have successfully moved on to Formula 1. From the technical point of view, however, this formula has lost the stimulus it once provided to racing. The 2,000 cc engines of 1948 were replaced after ten years by 1,500 cc (again normally aspirated) ones and in 1964 by 1,000 cc engines with no more than 4 cylinders. In 1966 the capacity was raised to 1,600 cc with a maximum of 6 cylinders and a monobloc from a car sanctioned in the Grand Tourer class with a minimum production of 500 (the engine must have no more than five main bearings). This link led to an agreement between Fiat and Ferrari and later a permanent union between the two firms. The capacity has been 2,000 cc since 1972.

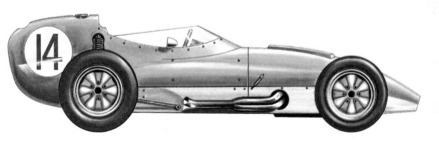

Lotus F 1 1958: 4 cylinders in line (Climax), 2,207 cc, 194 bhp at 6,250 rpm

Italian by birth, Amédée Gordini moved to France after visiting as a tourist. For many years active as a builder of racing cars, his fame is based on his ingenuity and on an agreement linking him for a while with Simca.

Simca had been founded in France by Fiat and at the time was run by Pigozzi, who was a native of Turin. The Simca-Gordinis were effective means of publicity for the young car firm. Amédée Gordini transformed the Fiat 1100 engine and used it in both sports cars and single-seaters. In addition, he encouraged the use of many young drivers— Maurice Trintignant, André Simon, and Robert Manzon in particular. One of Gordini's most successful single-seaters was the 1500 of 1948. Its engine was derived from the Fiat 1100, the capacity having been progressively increased to 1,220 cc in 1947 and 1,443 cc in 1948. The strong points of this car were its lightness and handling; but its power rating was rather low, particularly when compared with the supercharged Alfa 158s and 159s.

Car: **Simca-Gordini**
Maker: **Gordini**
Year: **1948**
Class: **Formula 1**
Engine: **4-cylinder in-line**
Bore × Stroke: **78 × 75 mm**
Capacity: **1,433 cc**
Power: **105 bhp**

The Gordini 1500 frequently upset the Italians, winning in 1948 the Perpignan, Angouleme, and Stockholm Grand Prix. The Drivers World Championship had yet to be started, but such successes encouraged Simca to continue its collaboration with Gordini. This relationship was broken when Gordini rejected the firm's suggestion that he become an employee and run its racing department.

The earliest Ferraris had 12-cylinder engines and were designated 125, after the capacity of the individual cylinders. They included a Grand Prix single-seater that was similar in all respects (bore 55 mm, stroke 52.5 mm, and total capacity 1,496.77 cc) to the GT and the S. This single-seater complied with the Formula 1 of the time (1,500 cc with supercharger, 4,500 cc for a normally aspirated engine). Ferrari and his designer, Gioacchino Colombo, chose a 1,500 cc engine above all others because of their experience with Alfa Romeo. Ironically, the most effective car of the period also came from the Scuderia Ferrari at Modena and was designed by Colombo himself. It was the Alfetta, another car with a supercharged engine.

The 125's monobloc 12-cylinder engine had a magnesium alloy crankcase and engine block. It had a single chain-driven overhead camshaft for each bank of cylinders; a single Weber 40 DC3C carburetor and a single-stage Roots supercharger; one spark plug per cylin-

Car: **Ferrari 125**
Maker: **Ferrari**
Year: **1949**
Class: **Formula 1**
Engine: **60 V-12**
Bore × Stroke: **55 × 52.5 mm**
Capacity: **1,496.77 cc**
Power: **Single-stage supercharger: 225 bhp at 7,000 rpm**
   Two-stage supercharger: 290 bhp at 7,500 rpm

der; and two magnetos. Its maximum declared power was 225 bhp at 7,000 rpm. It had a five-speed transmission and a tubular chassis with side members which were oval in section. The front suspension had triangular arms (wishbones), transverse leaf springs, and Houdaille hydraulic dampers. The overall weight was 700 kg (1,543 lb). While the basic features remained unchanged, in 1949 the 125 was fitted with two camshafts and a two-stage Roots supercharger; the power rating increased to 290 bhp at 7,500 rpm and the weight to 730 kg (1,609 lb). In 1950 the power rating was increased again, to 315 bhp at 7,500 rpm, and the De Dion rear axle was adopted.

The 4 CLT was derived from the highly popular 4 CL of 1946–51, which had sold well to private racing organizations. The first 4 CL appeared at Brooklands in 1939. Its most prominent feature was its square engine, both bore and stroke being 78 mm. It had a Roots supercharger and developed 210 bhp. The 4 CLT appeared in 1947; it differed from its stablemate by having a tubular chassis and a two-stage supercharger that increased the engine's power to about 225 bhp. The 48-valve 4 CLT made its debut by winning the 1949 San Remo Grand Prix. From then on, the car carried the city's name.

As it was the policy of the Orsi, the new owners of Maserati, numerous examples of the 4 CLT were built and sold to private individuals. For a number of years quite a few races were based on this car. Maserati's attempt to improve it, which was mainly concentrated on increasing its power, failed to give the hoped-for results. However, various private organizations such as "Milan" and the one behind

Car: **Maserati 4 CLT**
Maker: **Maserati**
Year: **1949**
Class: **Grand Prix**
Engine: **Supercharged 4-cylinder in-line**
Bore × Stroke: **78 × 78 mm**
Capacity: **1,498 cc**
Power: **240 bhp at 7,000 rpm**

the driver Enrico Patlé, both based in Milan, did succeed in increasing the power to 275 bhp (in one case the capacity was increased to 1,720 cc). However, the results were poor, and the engine suffered increased wear.

Along with the later 250 F, the 4 CL and the 4 CLT were among the most successful of Maserati's cars, and they have been the delight of many individual drivers. When racing was resumed in 1946–47, the 4 CL was one of the most familiar shapes.

Like the P2, the 158 was one of Alfa Romeo's most successful single-seaters, and it occupies a prominent place in the marque's history. It was designed by Gioacchino Colombo at the Scuderia Ferrari in Modena in 1937. The 158 followed the traditional Alfa Romeo scheme in its engine structure and in the arrangement of its mechanical parts, with the exception of transverse leaf springs. The 158 began well by taking first and second places overall in the 1938 Coppa Ciano in Leghorn. A second victory, at Monza, in the same year demonstrated its consistency. In 1939 and 1940 several major improvements were made, particularly to the engine. Initially it developed 195 bhp at 7,200 rpm, which was increased to 225 bhp at 7,500 rpm, while the compression ratio remained constant. It concluded the prewar period by winning the 1940 Tripoli Grand Prix.

Miraculously, the car escaped Allied bombing and looting by German troops, and it got a new lease on life when Alfa Romeo resumed racing in 1946. The en-

Car: **Alfa Romeo 158**
Maker: **Alfa Romeo**
Year: **1950**
Class: **Formula 1**
Engine: **Supercharged 8-cylinder in-line**
Bore × Stroke: **58 × 70 mm**
Capacity: **1,479 cc**
Power: **350 bhp at 8,500 rpm**

gine was fitted with a two-stage supercharger, and the power output increased considerably, to 350 bhp at 8,500 rpm. The 158, nicknamed the Alfetta, dominated the circuits in 1947 and 1948, but it wasn't raced in 1949. In 1950 it was ready for the first World Championship, which it won through the driving of Giuseppe (Nino) Farina assisted by Juan Manuel Fangio and Luigi Fagioli. Since the three drivers all had last names beginning with the letter F, the Milanese team came to be known as the "squadra dei tre F" (the team of the three Fs). The Alfetta won all six of the championship races in 1950, three going to Farina and three to Fangio.

In conjunction with Darracq the name of Talbot goes back to the beginning of the century, but the Talbot-Lago belongs only to the period after World War II. For quite a few years this machine, together with the Delahaye, effectively defended the French colors, even though Antonio Lago had emigrated to France from Brescia, as had most of his technicians.

The Talbot-Lago had a 4,500 cc 6-cylinder engine. Although not in the forefront technically, this engine had sound qualities such as its long working life and excellent fuel consumption. The specifications of the engine—the piston stroke was markedly greater than the bore—imply that it had a relatively low engine speed, which is associated with long life and economy. The leading car of the time was the Alfa Romeo 158; a comparison of the Talbot-Lago and this Italian car reveals the substantial difference in their fuel consumption. The 158 was unable to cover even a kilometer on one liter of fuel (2.83 mpg), while the Talbot-Lago could cover from 3.5 to 4.5

Car: **Talbot-Lago**
Maker: **Lago**
Year: **1950**
Class: **Formula 1**
Engine: **6-cylinder in-line**
Bore × Stroke: **93 × 110 mm**
Capacity: **4,485 cc**
Power: **275 bhp at 5,000 rpm**

kilometers (9.89–12.72 mpg). This meant that the Alfa was forced to refuel at least once, while the Talbot could easily avoid doing so. The Alfas, however, were fast enough to build up a sufficient lead to compensate for the time lost in the pits. On the other hand, the sustained performance of the Talbot-Lago frequently caused trouble for its rival single-seaters, in particular Maserati. In 1950 the Talbot underwent an important modification with the adoption of two spark plugs per cylinder and three horizontal carburetors instead of down-draft carburetors, and the power output increased to 275 bhp from 240 bhp. At the same time the mechanically controlled brakes were replaced by hydraulic brakes.

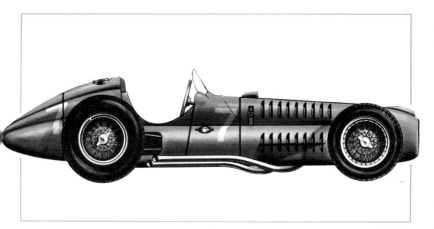

Never, from the sporting angle, has a racing car created such a stir as the BRM V-16 of 1950. Raymond Mays, an ex-driver, was the leading spirit of the project, as he was, in its time, of the ERA. His stated intention was to provide British motor racing with a car capable of competing with the Italians, Germans, and French. The design was entrusted to Peter Berthon, who also came from the ERA. He chose a V-16 that looked highly promising on paper. Although the car was built by BRM, it involved 150 British manufacturers both small and large, each one specializing in a particular branch of the motor industry. It was probably due to the extent and complexity of the undertaking that it failed completely. The car was ready in 1949, having been begun in 1946. It made its debut in the International Trophy at Silverstone, where it remained stranded on the starting line because of a broken drive shaft. The event was an omen. The V-16 never managed to show its true potential. Its best result in a championship race was in

Car: **BRM V-16**
Maker: **BRM**
Year: **1950**
Class: **Formula 1**
Engine: **Supercharged 135° V-16**
Bore × Stroke: **49.5 × 48.2 mm**
Capacity: **1,488 cc**
Power: **475 bhp at 11,500 rpm**

the British Grand Prix of 1951, when Parnell and Walker took fifth and seventh places. This was also the race in which Ferrari beat Alfa Romeo for the first time.

The V-16 ended its ignominious career by competing in some open formula races. The withdrawal of Alfa Romeo, which led to the premature end of the 1,500 to 4,500 cc formula, also involved BRM, whose costly efforts were bedeviled by a series of sensational failures.

Ferrari came to the 375 having found it impossible to compete with Alfa Romeo when using supercharged engines. Although the two companies were alike in using superchargers, they differed in engine layout, Ferrari using V-12s and the Milanese single-seaters straight-8s. Another reason leading Ferrari to abandon the supercharger was the search for lower fuel consumption, which would allow eliminating a refueling stop. Events proved Ferrari right. The 375 was the third stage in a project aimed at quickly increasing the engine capacity to the 4,500 cc upper limit allowed for normally aspirated engines. It was with a 375 driven by Froilan Gonzales that Ferrari first beat Alfa Romeo, in the 1951 British Grand Prix, and humbled the 159, then at the summit of its development. In the same year the 375, driven in both cases by Alberto Ascari, won the German and Italian Grand Prix.

The first step toward producing a single-seater with a normally aspirated engine capable of competing with the

Car: **Ferrari 375**
Maker: **Ferrari**
Year: **1951**
Class: **Formula 1**
Engine: **60° V-12**
Bore × Stroke: **80 × 74.5 mm**
Capacity: **4,493.73 cc**
Power: **380 bhp at 7,000 rpm**

Alfetta was the construction of the 275 (3,322 cc) in 1950. This engine developed 280 bhp at 7,000 rpm and had a compression ratio of 10:1. It was almost immediately succeeded by the 340, which differed from its stablemate only in having a capacity of 4,101 cc, developing 325 bhp at 7,000 rpm with a compression ratio of 11:1.

The 375 took shape over the winter of 1950–51. It differed substantially from the 275 and the 340 in its engine capacity, which was 4,493 cc. The 375 developed 350 bhp at 7,000 rpm and had a compression ratio of 11:1. In the course of 1951, it underwent important modifications (double ignition, power 380 bhp at 7,500 rpm, and a compression ratio of 12:1).

Although the Alfa Romeo 158 dominated the 1950 racing season, the advances made by Ferrari (who had abandoned their single-seaters with supercharged engines and successfully undertaken the construction of normally aspirated engines) were clearly apparent. Alfa Romeo was therefore compelled to improve its Alfetta as much as possible, and its power output was increased yet again to 425 bhp at 9,300 rpm, more than double its 1937 output. The adjustment of the components of the transmission, the more powerful brakes, and the adoption of the De Dion rear axle with double-jointed (universal) half-shafts transformed the car to such an extent as to justify a new designation, 159. Whereas 158 had referred to the specifications of the car, 1,500 cc and 8 cylinders, the new designation no longer did so, the higher number merely suggesting improvement.

The 1951 World Championship included seven races. Alfa Romeo got off to a flying start. Fangio won the Swiss Grand Prix, Farina the Belgian Grand

Car: **Alfa Romeo 159**
Maker: **Alfa Romeo**
Year: **1951**
Class: **Formula 1**
Engine: **Supercharged 8-cylinder in-line**
Bore × Stroke: **58 × 70 mm**
Capacity: **1,479 cc**
Power: **425 bhp at 9,300 rpm**

Prix, and Fangio the French. By then the season was almost halfway through. Then a Ferrari, driven by Gonzles, beat Alfa for the first time in Britain. This event made history, but it was no isolated incident. In the following Grand Prix, the German, Ascari beat Alfa Romeo, and he did so again in the Italian Grand Prix. This meant that Ferrari had managed to even the score with its great rival, who was by then in decline, in the space of three races. Only the Spanish Grand Prix remained. Ferrari was in an excellent position to win it but chose to use 16-inch rear wheels; this cost Ferrari the race and the championship.

Another marque that had its moment of glory was born through the enterprise of two English amateur drivers, John Heath and George Abecassis. The two owned Hersham and Walton Motors, a small factory in which the cars were built and which gave the marque its name. The marque made a significant contribution in developing the careers of such budding talents as Stirling Moss and Peter Collins. The first machine was ready in 1948 for Formula 2 races; it used a 4-cylinder Alta (named after another small English factory). The design made a promising start, and in 1950 Heath and Abecassis formed a proper team with three cars, on various occasions driving the cars themselves. Although it was built as a twin-seater, the HWM mainly took part in Formula 2 races. In 1951 a single-seater was produced, also powered by an Alta engine with twin overhead camshafts. It had a gearbox with a Wilson preselector, a De Dion rear axle with semi-elliptical leaf springs, and coil springs at the front. In 1952 and 1953 it was fitted with a tor-

Car: **HWM 2000**
Maker: **HWM**
Year: **1952**
Class: **Formula 2**
Engine: **4-cylinder in-line Alta**
Bore × Stroke: **83.5 × 90 mm**
Capacity: **1,960 cc**
Power: **150 bhp at 6,000 rpm**

sion bar rear suspension and inboard brakes, and the power output of the engine was raised from 125 bhp to 150 bhp. Its successes in 1952 included Lance Macklin's victory in the Daily Express Trophy at Silverstone and Paul Frère's in the Grand Prix des Frontières. Later on, HWM also built sports cars with Cadillac and Jaguar engines, creating in 1956 a sports car with a streamlined body and powered by the Jaguar D engine. However, the death of John Heath in that year's Mille Miglia put an end to the marque's activity, as George Abecassis did not feel he could continue alone.

Ferrari 500 – 1952
Ferrari 500 – 1953

The 500 occupies a unique position in the Ferrari family tree for a number of reasons. First, it won the greatest number of races in the two-year period during which it was used. Second, it stood out from the other Ferrari single-seaters in that its engine was designed in a single day (and that a Sunday) by Aurelio Lampredi, who was then in charge of the Modena factory's technical office. Third, apart from the 815, which used Fiat mechanical components, it was the first Ferrari-built racer to use a 4-cylinder engine.

The 500 originated as a Formula 2 car. It would have competed solely in such races but for the withdrawal of Alfa Romeo from racing at the end of 1951 and the lack of cars for the top formula. This threw the whole of Grand Prix racing into a crisis and forced the Fédération Internationale de l'Automobile to open the Drivers World Championship to the smaller Formula 2 cars, a formula in which even quite small makers were active.

The Ferrari 500 won all seven of the races that counted toward the world title in 1952, Alberto Ascari taking six of them and Piero Taruffi taking one. The main feature of the 500 was its outstanding reliability, which was mainly due to the simplicity of its design. The 4-cylinder was chosen primarily to reduce fuel consumption and to enable the car to cover the entire race without having to refuel.

The 500 excelled again in 1953, enabling Alberto Ascari to win his second world title. Its basic structure remained the same, but it was improved by the adoption of four Weber 45 DOE carburetors and an increase in its compression ratio to 12.8:1. Its power output reached approximately 190 bhp at the end of the season. Its weight rose to 580 kg (1,280 lb) and later to 615 kg (1.355 lb).

The 500 won seven of the eight championship races in 1953—Alberto Ascari taking five, Nino Farina one, and Mike Hawthorn one. Maserati put up a much more vigorous challenge, as in the French Grand Prix at Rheims on July 5. In this race Mike Hawthorn and Manuel Fangio engaged in one of the most thrilling duels in the history of motor racing, which ended with the Englishman crossing the finish line just ahead of his great rival. Fangio gained Maserati's only success of the season by winning the Italian Grand Prix, although he needed several lucky breaks to do so. Alberto Ascari, who went into the last bend in the lead, found his way blocked by the slower English driver Fairman, who had already been lapped. To avoid colliding with him, Ascari finished up off the track. For the same reason, Nino Farina was forced to take a longer line, ending up on the opposite side. This left the way clear for Fangio, lying third, to cross the finish line in the lead.

With the 500, Ferrari renounced the 12-cylinder, though only for a short time. The 625, built for the new Formula 1 (2,500 cc) that came into force in 1954, was also a 4-cylinder. It was an obvious derivative of the 500, but it achieved little.

Car: **Ferrari 500**
Maker: **Ferrari**
Years: **1952-53**
Class: **Formula 2**
Engine: **4-cylinder in-line**
Bore × Stroke: **98 × 76 mm (1952); 90 × 78 mm (1953)**
Capacity: **1,984.85 cc**
Power: **185 bhp at 7,500 rpm (1952; 190 bhp at 7,500 rpm (1953)**

1953 - Ferrari 500

In the wake of the success enjoyed by the 500, the 625 was also powered by a 4-cylinder in-line engine, derived from its smaller stablemate's. In the meantime, however, the formula had been changed, and the 625 found itself competing with the Mercedes W 196, the car with which the German marque made its re-entry into Grand Prix racing.

Initially the 4-cylinder 625 developed 210 bhp at 7,000 rpm; then, in 1954, 230 bhp at 7,800 rpm; and finally, in the course of the same season, 245 bhp at 7,500. The compression ratio, which rose to 12.8:1, was among the highest ever achieved in a Ferrari engine. The two victories gained by this car in 1954 and 1955 were mainly due to mishaps suffered by the Mercedes. The first victory was achieved by Froilan Gonzales in the 1954 British Grand Prix. In this race Mercedes entered a version of the W 196 with a faired body. As the fairing covered the front wheels, the drivers found it difficult to select the right line through bends, one moment mounting the curb

Car: **Ferrari 625**
Maker: **Ferrari**
Year: **1953**
Class: **Formula 1**
Engine: **4-cylinder in-line**
Bore × Stroke: **94 × 90 mm**
Capacity: **2,498.32 cc**
Power: **210 bhp at 7,000 rpm**

and another steering too wide. In short they lost precious fractions of seconds at every bend, often inadvertently providing a show by sending the rubber marker cones flying.

Maurice Trintignant gained the 625's second victory, in the Monaco Grand Prix of 1955; but of the three Mercedes in the race, two—Fangio and Simon—were forced to drop out and Moss came in ninth. All in all, the 625 was one of the least successful Ferrari single-seaters. Its poor reliability made the job of the Mercedes W 196 that much easier. The Mercedes, for its part, owed its reputation for invincibility more to the exploits of Fangio than any real, intrinsic superiority.

This was one of the few Ferrari single-seaters to have both a name and a number. Unlike the numbers used for all the other single-seaters, which indicated the number of cylinders and the capacity (e.g., 625 stood for six cylinders and 2,500 cc), its number, 555, meant nothing.

The Squalo (Shark) has a significant place in Ferrari's history in that it was an attempt, though unsuccessful, to distribute the weight of the fuel differently. Fuel storage has always created problems of trim; as the rear tank empties, the driver has to exercise great skill to hold his line through the turns. In the Squalo the fuel was kept in two central tanks to the side of the driver's seat.

The Squalo originated in 1953 as a Formula 2 machine and was designated the 553. By 1954 it had an engine that was similar to the 625's, though differing in bore and stroke, which developed 240 bhp at 7,500 rpm. In a later version, known as the Supersqualo, the power of the engine was increased to 270 bhp at

Car: **Ferrari Squalo**
Maker: **Ferrari**
Year: **1954**
Class: **Formula 1**
Engine: **4-cylinder in-line**
Bore × Stroke: **100 × 79.5 mm**
Capacity: **2,479.6 cc**
Power: **240 bhp at 7,500 rpm**

7,500 rpm and had a very high compression ratio of 14:1. It subsequently had a five-speed transmission and, finally, the engine from the Lancia D 50.

The Squalo was not liked by the drivers, who regarded it as unstable; and it gained only one victory, when driven by Mike Hawthorn in the 1954 Spanish Grand Prix. The Mercedes of Fangio and Kling came in third and fifth, respectively, and Herrmann was forced to retire. The 625 and the Squalo were the last Ferrari single-seaters to have 4-cylinder engines.

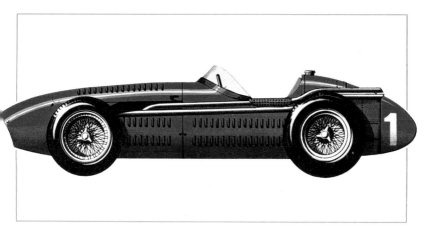

Gioacchino Colombo, regarded as one of the most ingenious and versatile minds involved in racing car design, was associated with this Formula 1 single-seater, which was one of Maserati's most successful cars. In addition to Colombo, Vittorio Bellentani and Giulio Alfieri were also connected with this car; the latter was to become Maserati's technical manager until Alessandro De Tommaso took charge of the Modena firm. It was Colombo, however, who improved the Maserati F 2 from which the 250 F was derived. The F 2 was born in 1952–53. Colombo fitted it with double ignition, increased its power from 175 to 190 bhp, and modified the suspension and brakes. It was rechristened the A6SSG and proved a worthy opponent to the powerful Ferrari 500 of 1953. The preparation of the 250 F for the new Formula 1 of 1954 relied on the experience of Colombo, particularly in regard to the double camshaft engine with two valves per cylinder, which was fed by three Weber down-draft carburetors and two Marelli magnetos.

Car: **Maserati 250 F**
Maker: **Maserati**
Year: **1954**
Class: **Formula 1**
Engine: **6-cylinder in-line**
Bore × Stroke: **84 × 75 mm**
Capacity: **2,493 cc**
Power: **270 bhp at 8,000 rpm**

It developed 270 bhp at 8,000 rpm and had a four-speed transmission and a tubular chassis. The car had wishbones and coil springs in the front suspension and De Dion rear suspension with transverse leaf springs and Houdaille hydraulic dampers.

The 250 F achieved the rare feat of winning on its first outing, being driven to victory by Juan Manuel Fangio in the 1954 Argentine Grand Prix, as well as in the following race, the Belgian Grand Prix. After the French Grand Prix, the Argentine driver moved to Mercedes, taking with him a good tally of points which, together with those he won at the wheel of the German cars, gave him his second world title.

Mercedes W 196 – 1954–55

The W 196 was another of the historic Mercedes single-seaters, both for its technical conception and because it signaled the German marque's return to racing after a 20-year absence. For reasons of weight a V-8 was rejected, and instead a straight-eight 2,496 cc engine was chosen with a central power take-off, double overhead camshafts, desmodromic valves, and Bosch direct injection. It developed 257 bhp at 8,200 rpm, later increased to 290 bhp at 8,500 rpm. It had a five-speed transmission, a tubular chassis, torsion bar and deformable wishbone front suspension, and torsion bar and hydraulic damper rear suspension. In the two years that Mercedes was active on the circuits, three versions of the W 196 were built: one had a faired body which even enclosed the front and rear wheels, one had a long wheelbase, and one had a short wheelbase. A further important modification was the use—from the 1955 Monaco Grand Prix onward—of outboard front brakes.

The faired version of the W 196 made its debut in the French Grand Prix at Rheims in 1954 where, driven by Juan Manuel Fangio, Karl Kling, and Hans Herrmann, it excited great interest. Fangio won with relative ease and Kling came in second, but Herrmann was forced to retire with a broken piston. The streamlined body that had played such a key role in the French Grand Prix proved to be completely unsuitable for the next race, the British Grand Prix at Silverstone. The tire fairings prevented the drivers from taking the correct line through the curves. Gonzales won at Silverstone in a Ferrari, followed by his teammates Hawthorn and Marimon in a Maserati, while Fangio had to struggle to take fourth place. This unexpected debacle forced Mercedes to advance the planned use of a single-seater with uncovered wheels. Fangio drove it to victory in the following race, the German Grand Prix. The Argentine also won the Swiss and Italian Grand Prix, but in Spain he was beaten by Hawthorn and also by Musso in a Maserati. Fangio, who had competed in the first two races of the season (the Argentine and Belgian Grand Prix) in a Maserati, took his second world title that year. He won his third in 1955 by capturing the Argentine, Belgian, Dutch, and Italian Grand Prix. The British Grand Prix was won by Stirling Moss, who had also moved to Mercedes. Of the 12 World Championship races in which the Mercedes took part in 1954–55, they lost only three: the British and Spanish Grand Prix in 1954 and the Monaco Grand Prix in 1955. The streamlined body was used in only four races —the French, British, and Italian Grand Prix of 1954 and the Italian Grand Prix of 1955.

Car: **Mercedes W 196**
Maker: **Mercedes**
Year: **1954–55**
Class: **Formula 1**
Engine: **8-cylinder in-line**
Bore × Stroke: **76 × 68.8 mm**
Capacity: **2,496 cc**
Power: **257 bhp at 8,200 rpm in 1954; 290 bhp at 8,500 rpm in 1955**

Mercedes W 196 - 1954-55

faired body - 1954

short wheelbase - 1955

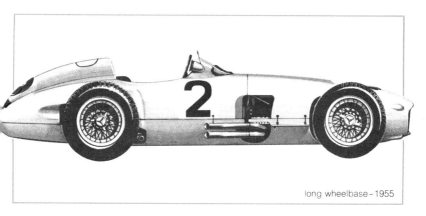

long wheelbase - 1955

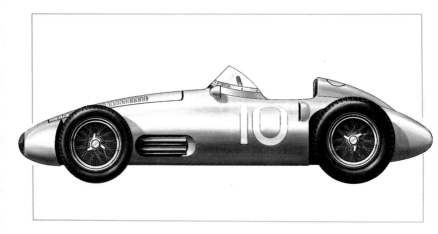

The straight-8 was one of the few engines that Amédée Gordini designed and built from start to finish. He did so during the period when, having parted company with Simca, he was struggling on his own and had not yet found in Renault a partner to shield him from difficulties.

Like all Gordini's cars the 8-cylinder was very simple in conception. The engine had two overhead camshafts, two valves per cylinder, four Weber twin choke carburetors, and two spark plugs per cylinder. It had independent suspension, using compound torsion bars which functioned in respect to one another to eliminate the gyroscopic effect and to make sure that the wheels adhered to the surface in all conditions. With this car Gordini was among the first, if not the first, to use disc brakes (Messier). It had a five-speed synchromesh transmission and a tubular chassis. Gordini's modest resources prevented him from competing regularly in the Championship. He missed the Belgian Grand Prix, and could only achieve poor placings: two seventh

Car: **Gordini F 1**
Maker: **Gordini**
Year: **1955**
Class: **Formula 1**
Engine: **8-cylinder in-line**
Bore × Stroke: **75 × 70 mm**
Capacity: **2,498 cc**
Power: **245 bhp at 7,000 rpm**

positions (Pollet at Monaco and Sparker in Great Britain) and one eighth place (Da Silva-Ramos in Holland).

The Italian-French maker also failed to achieve any great success with the same car in 1956, but its chief driver was able to steal the limelight on more than one occasion. He was Robert Manzon, who had had his moment of glory in 1954 as an official Ferrari driver, though it was Gordini who had given him his start.

The British Connaught is a typical example of the involvement of small makers, particularly the English ones, in the field of motor racing and of their misfortunes. Connaught began to build racing cars in 1949, using a 1,767 cc Lea-Francis engine. In 1950 it concentrated mainly on Formula 2 with the A-Type. This had a Wilson preselector, and in the following year it was fitted with a De Dion rear axle. When, at the beginning of 1952, the Formula 2s became Grand Prix cars, Connaught was extremely active. Among other things, it was one of the first, if not the first, to try fuel injection, in 1953. In 1954 it began a Formula 1 car with a 4-cylinder Alta engine; initially this was fed by SU injection and later by Weber carburetors, developing 240 bhp at 6,400 rpm. During the period when it was being tested and improved, disc brakes and magnesium wheels were added. It had a rather disappointing season on the English circuits; however, it was rebuilt for the Syracuse Grand Prix, which it won, driven by Tony Brooks. In memory of its

Car: **Connaught**
Maker: **Connaught**
Year: **1955**
Class: **Formula 1**
Engine: **4-cylinder in-line Alta**
Bore × Stroke: **93.5 × 90 mm**
Capacity: **2,470 cc**
Power: **250 bhp at 6,700 rpm**

greatest success, the car was renamed after the Sicilian city.

This small firm, which was frequently running at a loss, stumbled on until 1959, when it was forced to go out of business. The 1957 Formula 1 is remembered for its strange body, which ended in a conspicuous fin. This feature earned it the nickname of the "toothpaste tube." An overhauled and improved version of it appeared in the 1962 Indianapolis 500, though without success. Today the Connaught is often entered in races for cars of that period.

79

World War II put an end to any sport racing by Bugatti, though in this they were by no means alone. Instead Bugatti concentrated on designing aircraft engines for the Allies. The end of the conflict marked the almost complete disappearance of this famous marque with the death during that period of its leading spirit, Ettore Bugatti.

The entire racing world was surprised when in 1956 the firm made a comeback by commissioning a single-seater racing car for the existing Formula 1 from the Italian engineer Gioacchino Colombo. His enormous experience in the field of racing cars seemed a guarantee of success.

Colombo devised a highly advanced concept for the single-seater. Its main innovation was the transverse mounting of the engine just behind the driver. The straight-8 engine had two chain-driven overhead camshafts and was fed by four Weber horizontal carburetors. A peculiarity of the engine was the central power take-off on the crankshaft. It had a five-

Car: **Bugatti 251**
Maker: **Bugatti**
Year: **1956**
Class: **Formula 1**
Engine: **8-cylinder in-line**
Bore × Stroke: **75 × 68.8 mm**
Capacity: **2,430 cc**
Power: **245 bhp at 8,000 rpm**

speed transmission, and the differential was mounted in a single unit with the crankcase. It had De Dion front and rear suspension with coil springs.

Driven by Maurice Trintignant, the car made its debut at the French Grand Prix of 1956. A minor accident, the sticking of the accelerator pedal, forced it to drop out on the eighteenth lap. However, the 8-cylinders' lack of power, believed to be the chief reason that Trintignant was relegated to the next to last row on the starting grid, was sufficient cause for this very interesting machine never to compete again.

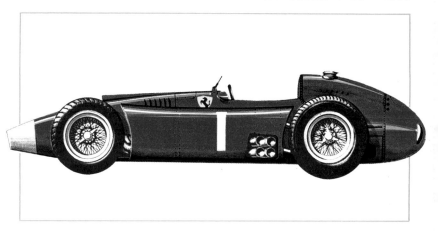

Lateral fuel tanks were also a feature of the Lancia D 50, Vittorio Jano's last design, which was powered by a 90° V-8, developing 250 bhp at 8,100 rpm. Though an excellent design, the D 50 was unable to display its qualities to the full as Lancia's involvement in Formula 1 racing lasted barely two years. This was too short a period to build up a good team and the fund of experience that only regular participation in racing can bring. The D 50 was not ready for the track until the Spanish Grand Prix at the end of the 1954 season. For the ten laps in which he was in the race, Alberto Ascari, the head of the Turin firm's team, held the lead; but clutch trouble forced him to retire. In 1955 the D 50 officially took part in only two races, the Argentine and Monaco Grand Prix. With Ascari's death at Monza while testing a Ferrari, Lancia withdrew from racing and gave all its Formula 1 equipment to Ferrari. In 1956 the engine's power was increased to 260 bhp at 8,000 rpm; and, though the lateral fuel tanks were retained, part of the fuel was trans-

Car: **Ferrari-Lancia D 50**
Maker: **Ferrari**
Year: **1956**
Class: **Formula 1**
Engine: **90° V-8**
Bore × Stroke: **73.6 × 73.1 mm**
Capacity: **2,488 cc**
Power: **260 bhp at 8,000 rpm**

ferred to the rear. With a new 8-cylinder engine, it reached 265 bhp and then 275 bhp. The structure of the car, designated the 801 F 1, altered substantially when the lateral fuel tanks were completely abandoned.

Through a continuous and feverish process of renewal, the ex-Lancia D 50 enabled Juan Manuel Fangio to earn his fourth World Championship. In the single year in which Ferrari used the car, 1956, it won a total of five Grand Prix.

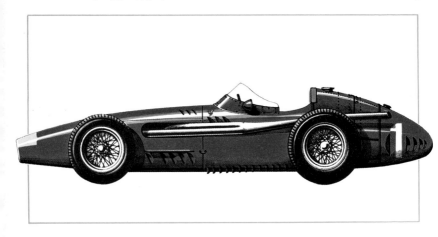

The 250 F, one of the most admired front-engined single-seaters in the history of racing, ended its career in 1957, the year in which it took Juan Manuel Fangio to his fifth World Championship. Foremost among those who acclaimed the car were Fangio and Stirling Moss, both of whom had driven it with success on several occasions.

In its four years of competition it underwent a lightening of its chassis, increased ventilation of the brakes, the fitting of a five forward speed gearbox, and improvements to the streamlining. Fangio drove the 250 F in his last race, the French Grand Prix at Rheims, coming in fourth. It was said that the death in that race of Luigi Musso persuaded the Argentinian to retire from racing. In actual fact Fangio, though he was very close to the Italian driver, had by then realized that his powers were declining. His decision was final.

The 250 F's career came to an end at the same time with 40 victories to its credit, not counting minor races. It

Car: **Maserati 250 F**
Maker: **Maserati**
Year: **1957**
Class: **Formula 1**
Engine: **6-cylinder in-line**
Bore × Stroke: **84 × 75 mm**
Capacity: **2,493 cc**
Power: **270 bhp at 8,000 rpm**

won six major races in 1954, five in 1955, four in 1956, and seven in 1957. Its outstanding year was 1957, when Manuel Fangio won the Argentine, Monaco, French, and German Grand Prix. The victory gained by Fangio in the last race is justly considered his greatest achievement, just as Tazio Nuvolari's in the 1935 German Grand Prix is regarded as his. On both occasions Fangio and Nuvolari had to face particularly strong opposition, and only through their personal mastery did they succeed in overcoming it.

The Vanwall was a patriotic venture by British industrialist and racing enthusiast Tony Vanderwell. He had followed the disappointing development of the 16-cylinder BRM, which had been started in 1946. Vanderwell began this new venture in racing cars with the Thin Wall Special. This car was initially a modified Ferrari 125 with a supercharger, then later a Ferrari 4500 without a supercharger. In 1952, however, Vanderwell decided to produce his own car. Being a director of Norton, he used four of its motorcycle engines. The car met the specifications of the Formula 2 then in force but wasn't ready for the track until two years later. By then it had become a Formula 1 car since a new Formula 1, open to 2,500 cc engines, had come into force in 1954. The British industrialist used a tubular Cooper chassis and a suspension inspired by those of Ferrari. Vanderwell was also among the first to use disc brakes (Goodyear) on a Formula 1 single-seater. Initially, it had a 1,998 cc engine that developed 235 bhp at 7,500

Car: **Vanwall**
Maker: **Vanwall**
Year: **1957**
Class: **Formula 1**
Engine: **4-cylinder in-line Norton**
Bore × Stroke: **96 × 86 mm**
Capacity: **2,490 cc**
Power: **285 bhp at 7,300 rpm**

rpm and was fed by four Amal motorcycle carburetors. In this form, the car made its debut in the 1954 International Trophy at Silverstone. With Alan Brown at the wheel, the Vanwall came in fifth—not a bad performance considering all its rivals had 2,500 cc engines. It was not until halfway through 1954 that the English single-seater, with its capacity raised to 2,300 cc, appeared in the World Championship. Peter Collins competed in two Grand Prix in it, retiring in the British and coming in seventh in the Italian. The engine was then enlarged to 2,500 cc and fitted with Bosch fuel injection. In 1957 the De Dion rear axle was abandoned and the engine's power was raised to 285 bhp at 7,300 rpm. In the same year Tony Vanderwell formed a true team of English drivers.

Like the BRM 16-cylinder of ten years previously, this car was designed by Peter Berthon. The 4-cylinder that powered it was unusually oversquare (bore 102.87 mm, stroke 74.93 mm). This exceptional feature gave the engine a total capacity of 2,491 cc, in line with the 2,500 cc maximum of the Formula 1 then in force. The 1957 BRM also had a single rear (disc) brake, mounted transversely behind the gearbox.

The car showed much more promise than its 16-cylinder stablemate and in several races demonstrated that it could hold its own against the competition. However, it was frequently eliminated by problems with its valves, which were made in three pieces. Replacing these with heavy, one-piece valves caused a drastic fall in engine speed (from 9,000 to 8,000 rpm).

Its poor road holding was markedly improved by Colin Chapman, whose assistance had been requested by Peter Berthon. Chapman suggested that the transverse leaf springs in both the front

Car: **BRM F 1**
Maker: **BRM**
Year: **1957**
Class: **Formula 1**
Engine: **4-cylinder in-line**
Bore × Stroke: **102.87 × 74.93 mm**
Capacity: **2,491 cc**
Power: **280 bhp at 8,000 rpm**

and rear suspensions be replaced by dampers with coil springs.

This car's best results were its victory at the Caen Circuit and its first, second, and third place sweep in the 1957 International Trophy at Silverstone. In 1959 the Swedish driver Jo Bonnier won the Dutch Grand Prix, achieving both his and the car's only success in the World Championship.

In 1962 BRM finally found its feet with the rear-engined, 90° V-8 P 56.

The 246, and its twin the 256, represented major innovations in Ferrari's engineering. They were powered by a V-6 called the Dino after Enzo Ferrari's only son Alfredino, who had died of an incurable disease while still very young.

Like the 500 and the Squalo, the 246 originated as a Formula 2 (1,500 cc) car with a gearbox mounted transversely at the rear—an arrangement adopted many years later for the 312 T. Another important feature of the Formula 2 was its De Dion rear axle. In 1957 the Dino Formula 2 was promoted to Formula 1, initially with an 1,860 cc engine (215 bhp at 8,500 rpm), then one of 2,417 cc (250 bhp at 8,500 rpm). In 1958 it was increased slightly to 2,474 cc (290 bhp at 7,500 rpm) and again in 1959, to 2,497 cc (the last two versions being designated as 256s). In 1960 the main features of the 2,497 cc remained unaltered, but the engine was positioned slightly across the car's axis. Later on in the season it was reworked, returning to a capacity of 2,417 cc with the same bore and stroke

Car: **Ferrari 246**
Maker: **Ferrari**
Year: **1958**
Class: **Formula 1**
Engine: **65° V-6**
Bore × Stroke: **85 × 71 mm**
Capacity: **2,417.3 cc**
Power: **270 bhp at 8,300 rpm (mid-season)**

as the second version of 1957 (85 × 71 mm), but this one developed 280 bhp at 8,500 rpm.

The 246 and 256 did not have outstanding careers; even so the 246-256 still took Mike Hawthorn to the 1958 World Championship. After achieving the title he decided to retire from racing, only to be killed in a road accident in England the following January. The 246-256 won two Grand Prix in 1958 (Hawthorn in France and Collins in Great Britain), two in 1959 (Brooks in France and Germany), and one in 1960 (Phil Hill in Italy).

Cooper-Climax – 1959
Cooper-Climax – 1960

Compared to the government-backed involvement of Mercedes and Auto Union in 1934 in Formula 1, the history of the Cooper Formula 1s is a lesson in spontaneity. Charles and John Cooper, father and son, owned a garage in Surbiton, Surrey. Their thoughts first turned to racing cars immediately after the war. To realize their ideas, they did not turn to famous designers or sophisticated solutions, relying instead on their own experience, built up through years of work. An example of their inventive genius is the fact that they were among the first to use independent suspension, but they did so in the cheapest way possible, salvaging Fiat Topolino rear suspensions from car wreckers. They used Japanese motorcycle engines and mounted them at the rear, as Ferdinand Porsche had done in 1934. Their first single-seater was extremely cheap, and one of its good points was that it was aimed at young motor racers with limited means, such as Stirling Moss. Helped by an understanding patron, Rob Walker, the Coopers gradually progressed toward Formula 1 while retaining their basic plan. The first Cooper-Coventry Climax made its debut driven by Jack Brabham in the 1957 Monaco Grand Prix. In the following year the car underwent important modifications with the replacement of the rear suspension's transverse leaf springs by coil springs, the fitting of disc brakes, a four-speed ZF transmission, and a self-locking differential. As it turned out, 1959 was a fortunate year for Jack Brabham, the English firm's chief driver. Although he managed to win only the Monaco and British Grand Prix, he took the World Championship. Moss and Bruce McLaren also drove Coopers, the former winning two races and the latter one.

In 1960 Cooper demonstrated emphatically that the successes achieved in 1959 were not due to luck. The improvements made to the preceding year's car were neither important nor fundamental and were mainly concerned with making the chassis more rigid and the body more pointed and streamlined. In 1960 Cooper also had a five-speed transmission, and the positions of the fuel tanks were altered. The overall result was a more compact and better balanced car.

The worth of John and Charles Cooper's underlying concept of the rear engine was proved by the almost instantaneous disappearance of the front-engined car. The revolution in single-seater racing cars and later in sports cars stemmed, in short, from this small English firm. This revolution was similar in extent and importance to the one sparked by the Mini in the field of small touring cars. Paradoxically, the Mini, with its transverse front engine, introduced a concept that was the direct opposite of the Coopers'.

Cooper began the 1960 season magnificently with Bruce McLaren's victory in Argentina. Jack Brabham then won five races in a row (the Dutch, Belgian, French, British, and Portuguese Grand Prix), which gave him his second world title, though there was some question about his superiority. Cooper won five of

the nine Championship races, and its two drivers came in first and second in the World Championship. After this achievement the English marque declined, but by then its message had been understood and carried forward.

Car: **Cooper-Climax**
Maker: **Cooper**
Years: **1959–60**
Class: **Formula 1**
Engine: **4-cylinder in-line Coventry-Climax**
Bore × Stroke: **94 × 89.9 mm**
Capacity: **2,495 cc**
Power: **240 bhp at 6,750 rpm**

Cooper-Climax - 1960

The 156 is a milestone in Ferrari's history, being its first rear-engined Formula 1 single-seater. Even when Charles and John Cooper had emphatically demonstrated the advantages of the rear engine, going back to an old idea of Ferdinand iPorsche's (Auto Union 1934–37), Enzo Ferrari had been reluctant to follow suit. However, once converted he had the shrewdness to obtain the services of a clever and original engineer, Carlo Chiti. Returning to an old tradition, the 156 began as a Formula 2 car (1,500 cc); however, the fact that the new Formula 1 (1961–65) specified engines of 1,500 cc as a maximum enabled the "small" single-seater to be rapidly adapted to play the role of the "large" one. The only difference was that the 65° V-6 was supplemented by a 120° V-6 engine, which was later used more extensively.

The 156 had a good opening season (1961), winning a total of five races (Von Trips won the Dutch and British Grand Prix, Phil Hill the Belgian and Italian, and Giancarlo Baghetti the French). One

Car: **Ferrari 156**
Maker: **Ferrari**
Year: **1961**
Class: **Formula 1**
Engine: **65° V-6 or 120° V-6**
Bore × Stroke: **65°: 81 × 48.2 mm or 67 × 60 mm**
  120°: 73 × 58.8 mm
Capacity: **65°: 1,496.43 cc or 1,480.73 cc**
  120°: 1,486.60 cc
Power: **65°: 200 bhp at 10,500 rpm or 185 bhp at 9,500 rpm**
  120°: 190 bhp at 9,500 rpm

reason for Ferrari's marked superiority was that the new formula took British makers by surprise, and throughout 1961 they had nothing capable of matching the Ferrari 6-cylinder. Thanks to Coventry-Climax, however, matters changed rapidly. In 1962 the 156, which had a six-speed transmission, 120° V-6 engine with four valves per cylinder, failed to win a race. In 1963, with Bosch direct injection and a monocoque hull, John Surtees drove it to victory in Germany, and in 1964 Lorenzo Bandini won with it in Austria.

Like Ferrari, BRM has always built its cars, including the engines, entirely within its factory. The success it has enjoyed, however, is in no way comparable with the Italian firm's. After the failure of the V-16, which was to have been used in Formula 1 in 1950–51, the only car that has given BRM good results has been the V-8 P 56. This was the single-seater with which Graham Hill won the 1962 World Championship. Peter Berthon, who had been chiefly responsible for the 16-cylinder 1500, also designed this car. He chose a 90° V-8 with a markedly greater bore than stroke (68.5 × 50.8 mm), resulting in high engine speeds (10,250 rpm in 1962 and 11,500 rpm in 1963). There were twin overhead camshafts for each bank of cylinders and five main bearings. Another feature unusual for the time was the Lucas transistorized ignition (also used by Coventry-Climax). It had a tubular chassis, and the magnesium wheels and the brakes were supplied by Dunlop. The fuel tanks had a total capacity of 142 liters (31.2 gal),

Car: **BRM P 56**
Maker: **BRM**
Year: **1962**
Class: **Formula 1**
Engine: **90° V-8**
Bore × Stroke: **68.5 mm × 50.8 mm**
Capacity: **1,498 cc**
Power: **188 bhp at 10,250 rpm**

were situated on either side of the driver's seat and, as in aircraft, were made of rubber.

The P 56's first victory was won by Graham Hill in the Glover Trophy at Goodwood on Easter Monday, 1962; Hill also won the International Trophy at Silverstone. Its first success in the World Championship came when Hill won the Dutch Grand Prix. This success was followed by victories in the German and Italian Grand Prix and finally the South African, which clinched the title.

89

Among the vast production of sports cars that has marked the rise of the Stuttgart marque, Formula 1 single-seaters were a brief and not very successful digression. The relatively modest capacity of the 1961–65 Formula 1 (1,500 cc) induced Porsche to enter the top formula. It began, in 1959, with a flat 4-cylinder Formula 2 that derived from the RSK sports car. With it Bonnier won the Modena Grand Prix in 1960, and Stirling Moss won at Aintree and Zeltweg. In 1962 an 8-cylinder engine was selected, with the boxer configuration retained. This engine, naturally, was air-cooled and had twin overhead camshafts, four Weber carburetors, and two valves per cylinder. Initially, the 8-cylinder engine, designated the 753, developed 180 bhp; this was increased to 204 bhp at 9,300 rpm at the end of the season. The 8-cylinder was known as the 804.

Two cars were entered in the Dutch Grand Prix of 1962 (Gurney and Bonnier), which was the opening race of that year's Grand Prix season. Bonnier came

Car: **Porsche F 1**
Maker: **Porsche**
Year: **1962**
Class: **Formula 1**
Engine: **8-cylinder boxer**
Bore × Stroke: **66 × 54.6 mm**
Capacity: **1,494 cc**
Power: **180 bhp at 9,200 rpm**

in seventh and Dan Gurney retired. At Monaco Bonnier came in fifth and Gurney again retired. Having missed the Belgian Grand Prix, Gurney surprisingly won the French Grand Prix, Bonnier coming in tenth. This victory, with the exception of Gurney's third place in the German Grand Prix, was the only good result achieved by the German single-seater. The lack of success attained by this expensive venture caused Porsche's management to abandon Formula 1 at the end of 1962 on the pretext that races for single-seaters fell outside the factory's program. The Porsche F 1 had a gearbox with five forward speeds.

Lotus-Climax 25 - 1963
Lotus-Climax 33 - 1964

It is commonly believed that the inventor of the monococque hull for racing cars was Colin Chapman, the head of Lotus. In actual fact, as Chapman himself has admitted, a similar solution had previously been used by De Tomaso on a Formula 3 car. It is certain, however, that the Lotus 25 of 1962 was the first Formula 1 single-seater to have a monococque hull. Colin Chapman, who has always devoted a great deal of his time as a designer to developing lighter cars, believed that a monococque would serve his purpose even though it would be more expensive. He felt the design would improve road holding and eliminate flexing and twisting and the breakages that often resulted.

The monococque hull, which was a feature of the Lotus 25, was immediately christened the "bathtub." It made its debut at the 1962 Dutch Grand Prix with Jim Clark at the wheel, and though he was eventually forced to retire by clutch trouble, he held the lead for quite some time. In the same year, however, Clark did win the Belgian, British, and United States Grand Prix, losing the World Championship on the last race, the South African. In 1963 the Lotus 25, which by then had Lucas injection, enabled Jim Clark to dominate the season. The Scotsman won the Belgian, Dutch, French, British, Italian, Mexican and South African Grand Prix, amassing a total of 73 points in the World Championship, of which 54 counted toward the title. With the 25, Chapman had a car that was not only very rigid but notably lighter than its predecessors. The monococque

weighed 6 kg (13 lb) less than a tubular structure, and eliminating the aluminium fuel tank saved another 25 kg (55 lb). Though De Tomaso's idea had only a single follower, the version produced by Chapman had quite a few.

The Lotus 33 was a development of the celebrated 25 and wàs first used at the 1964 German Grand Prix at Nürburgring. Jim Clark drove it on that occasion but failed to complete the race. The engine, an 8-cylinder Coventry-Climax, remained unaltered; the differences lay in the suspension and the steering and were intended to accommodate larger-section tires. It weighed only slightly more than the lower limit of 450 kg (992 lb). Two 33s were entered for the Austrian Grand Prix, which followed the German; one was driven by Clark and the other by Mike Spence. Both retired. In the Italian Grand Prix, still in 1964, Clark returned to driving a 25 while Spence, who came in sixth, continued to drive a 33. There were three 33s in the United States Grand Prix; those driven by Clark and Spence retired but the third, which was driven by the American Walt Hangsen, came in fifth. Finally, in Mexico Jim Clark was forced to retire, though he still finished fifth, and Moises Solana came in tenth. The 33's first success came in the first race of the following season. This was the South African Grand Prix, in which Jim Clark's win and Spence's fourth place confirmed that the car's many faults had been eliminated. Driving a 33, Clark also won the Belgian, French, British, Dutch, and German Grand Prix. But 1966 was a disastrous

1963 - Lotus-Climax 25 GB

year for the 33, which failed to win a single race. The following year Lotus brought out the 49. The 33 nevertheless made occasional appearances, taking Graham Hill to second place in the Monaco Grand Prix and Fisher to eleventh in the Canadian. The car's best year was thus 1965, and though it won many victories, the 33 had one of the shortest careers of any Lotus model.

Car: **Lotus-Climax 25**
Maker: **Lotus**
Year: **1963**
Class: **Formula 1**
Engine: **90° V-8 Coventry-Climax**
Bore × Stroke: **63 × 60 mm**
Capacity: **1,498 cc**
Power: **195 bhp at 8,200 rpm**

Car: **Lotus-Climax 33**
Maker: **Lotus**
Year: **1964**
Class: **Formula 1**
Engine: **V-8 Coventry-Climax**
Bore × Stroke: **68.4 × 50.8 mm**
Capacity: **1,492 cc**
Power: **200 bhp at 9,800 rpm**

1964 - Lotus-Climax 33

The 158 is the only Ferrari single-seater, apart from the ex-Lancia D 50, to have been powered by an 8-cylinder engine. The technical staff of the Modena factory, particularly at the time of Aurelio Lampredi and Carlo Chiti, displayed great eclecticism and imagination, but they had never seriously considered an 8-cylinder. The 158, which had a monocoque hull, was an attempt to resist the English offensive, the 156 no longer proving to be an effective competitor. In its initial version the engine developed 190 bhp at 10,700 rpm. When modified, the bore being increased and the stroke reduced, the power output rose to 210 bhp at 11,000 rpm.

Pointed, elegant, and sharply cut, the 158 was not a successful car. Despite this, John Surtees won his only World Championship with it in 1964. The English driver, who was later to leave Ferrari under unpleasant circumstances, succeeded in doing so while winning only two races, the German and Italian Grand Prix. The crucial points that gave Surtees

Car: **Ferrari 158**
Maker: **Ferrari**
Year: **1964**
Class: **Formula 1**
Engine: **V-8**
Bore × Stroke: **67 × 52.8 mm**
Capacity: **1,489.23 cc**
Power: **210 bhp at 11,000 rpm**

the title came through a generous act by his teammate Lorenzo Bandini, who in the last race, the Mexican Grand Prix, gave him second place by slowing down.

In 1965, the final year of the 1,500 cc formula, Ferrari failed to win a single race. Surtees finished second in South Africa, fourth in Monaco, retired in Belgium, third in France, third in Britain, seventh in Holland, retired in Germany and Italy, and didn't compete in the United States and Mexican Grand Prix. He won 17 points in the World Championship table to Bandini's 13.

Honda, who specializes in the building of motorcycles, has participated in a very limited way in the Drivers World Championship. However, the company's involvement has been impressive considering its lack of experience with four wheels and the distance of its base from the circuits. The Japanese firm chose a 60° V-12, which obviously owed much to Honda's experience with motorcycles. Its originality lay mainly in the fact that it was mounted transversely, behind the driver. A similar solution had been adopted in 1954 by Gioacchino Colombo for the Bugatti Type 251, though in that instance he used an 8-cylinder.

The Japanese single-seater, designated the RA 271, was hurriedly tuned by the American Ronnie Bucknum and made its debut in the 1964 German Grand Prix, acquitting itself well. The first important modification was made for the Italian Grand Prix of the same year, the six twin-choke Keihin motorcycle carburetors being replaced with direct injection. The following year the car was en-

Car: **Honda RA 271**
Maker: **Honda**
Year: **1965**
Class: **Formula 1**
Engine: **60° V-12**
Bore × Stroke: **58.1 × 47 mm**
Capacity: **1,495 cc**
Power: **230 bhp at 12,000 rpm**

trusted to the skill of another American, Ritchie Ginther, who came from Ferrari. The initial power of 220 bhp at 11,000 rpm was raised to 230 bhp at 12,000 rpm. The results of Ginther's contribution rapidly became apparent; the only victory Honda has won in the World Championship, the 1965 Mexico Grand Prix, was due to his work. This race was the last of the 1,500 cc formula. In 1968 Honda returned to racing with the experimental 302, which had an air-cooled, 8-cylinder rear engine. However, the death of its driver, the Frenchman Jo Schlesser, led the Japanese firm finally to abandon car racing.

The 312 marked Ferrari's return to 12 cylinders after the V-6s and V-8s. The change in 1966 in Formula 1 that permitted engines up to a capacity of 3,000 cc gave Ferrari ample reason to return to one of its traditional layouts. Once again the English found themselves at a distinct disadvantage, lacking a suitable engine. On the eve of the Championship, Ferrari seemed to be in a strong position. Events, however, turned out very differently.

Ferrari began the season with a 12-cylinder which developed 360 bhp at 10,000 rpm and had a five-speed transmission. In the first race of the season, the Monaco Grand Prix, Bandini came in second, while Surtees retired because of clutch trouble. The Englishman won the second race, the Belgian Grand Prix, and Bandini came in third. This was the last race in which Surtees drove for Ferrari. He was replaced by his compatriot Mike Parkes and, from the German Grand Prix onward, by Ludovico Scarfiotti, a sports car specialist. He quickly made a major

Car: **Ferrari 312**
Maker: **Ferrari**
Year: **1966**
Class: **Formula 1**
Engine: **60° V-12**
Bore × Stroke: **77 × 53.5 mm**
Capacity: **2,989. 56 cc**
Power: **375 bhp at 10,000 rpm**

contribution by winning the Italian Grand Prix, with the selfless help of Parkes. For that occasion an important modification was made to the 312's engine. Each cylinder had three valves, two inlet and one exhaust, and the power output rose to 375 bhp at 10,000 rpm.

It was a poor season for Ferrari. But the question remains how much better it could have done if it had had the services of John Surtees, who among other things was an excellent test driver, for the entire season. The English driver immediately found a place with Cooper (12-cylinder Maserati engine), and he drove one to victory in the Mexican Grand Prix, demonstrating that his powers were undiminished.

Brabham-Repco – 1966
Brabham-Repco – 1967

When the new Formula 1, which is still in force, came into effect, many believed that the best prepared car was the Ferrari 12-cylinder. However, the Italian maker and quite a few of those familiar with the secrets of the World Championship reckoned without the thrifty and shrewd Jack Brabham. Having already become a driver-maker, the Australian, in collaboration with Repco, in 1966 took an Oldsmobile 8-cylinder and developed it to meet the requirements of Formula 1. The Australian engineers Phil Irving and Frank Hallam had already carried out such a conversion for a Formula Tasmania car and for a sports car.

The 8-cylinder Repco used by Brabham developed 315 bhp as opposed to the Ferrari 12-cylinder's 360 bhp. Nevertheless, it easily had the better of the more powerful Italian car. One of the reasons for this success lay in the tubular chassis that Brabham and his designer Tauranac, a fellow Australian, had chosen, believing it to be easier to build and to repair than a monocoque.

The first Brabham-Repco 3000 was designated the BT 19 and won four Grand Prix in a row (France, Great Britain, Holland, and Germany), with Jack Brabham driving in each case. The Ferrari 312 gained only one victory.

During 1966 Brabham also brought out the BT 20. The chassis and body of this car differed substantially from the BT 19. The first Brabham to win a victory was the BT 11 with which Dan Gurney won the 1964 French Grand Prix. Jack Brabham's first victory in one of his own cars was in the Mexican Grand Prix of the same year. In 1967 Brabham the driver failed to repeat his achievements of the previous year, but another Brabham driver, the New Zealander Dennis Hulme, was highly successful. After a brief interval the BT 20 with which Hulme won the Monaco Grand Prix was replaced by the BT 24, which was derived from a Formula 2 single-seater. The engine, again developed by Repco, was made more powerful (330 bhp at 8,000 rpm); in this version it was designated the 740, the previous one being known as the 620. The dimensions of the car also differed from the BT 20's (the front track was 3cm/1.2 in narrower and the rear one 2.5 cm/1 in broader). The BT 24 with the 740 engine weighed 500 kg (1,102 lb), compared with the BT 19's 568 kg (1,252 lb). The BT 24 was used for the first time in the 1967 Belgian Grand Prix. It was driven then by Jack Brabham, who also drove it to its first victory, in the French Grand Prix. Dennis Hulme won the German Grand Prix and Jack Brabham captured the Canadian. The BT 24 won a total of three victories that year while the BT 20 gained one. The Lotus 49 won four races, all through the skill of Jim Clark. However, Clark, though tied for the lead in victories, lost the title to Dennis Hulme because of the New Zealander's better placings. In 1967 the Ford-Cosworth engine had its debut, putting an end to the Brabham-Repco partnership. However, their separation did not take place until after 1968, with Brabham-Repco failing to win a single race that year. The Anglo-Australian marque's first win with a Ford-Cosworth was Jacky Ickx's victory in the 1969 German Grand Prix. The Belgian driver also won the Canadian Grand Prix.

Brabham-Repco - 1966

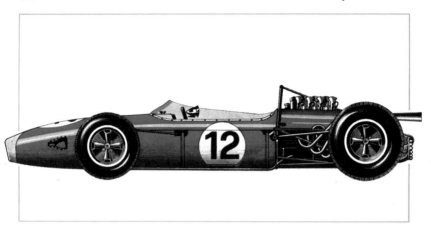

Car: **Brabham-Repco**
Maker: **Brabham**
Year: **1966**
Class: **Formula 1**
Engine: **V-8 Oldsmobile**
Bore × Stroke: **88.9 × 60.3 mm**
Capacity: **2,996 cc**
Power: **315 bhp at 7,800 rpm**

Car: **Brabham-Repco**
Maker: **Brabham**
Year: **1967**
Class: **Formula 1**
Engine: **V-8 Oldsmobile**
Bore × Stroke: **88.9 × 60.3 mm**
Capacity: **2,996 cc**
Power: **330 bhp at 7,800 rpm**

Brabham-Repco - 1967

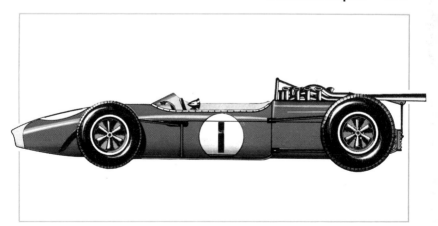

One of the most interesting American single-seater Formula 1 cars was built in England on the initiative of Dan Gurney. Gurney was, in fact, responsible for generating considerable interest in the United States in a type of sport racing that up until then had not had much success. Everything began when Gurney and his compatriot Carroll Shelby founded the All American Racers (AAR) in 1965, with the help of Goodyear. The AAR head office was in Santa Ana, California, though it operated from Rye, Sussex. Gurney engaged, for AAR, the famous designer Harry Weslake and, for the chassis, the no less well-known Len Terry, who was responsible for the Lotus 38. A very oversquare (bore 72.8 mm, stroke 60.3 mm) V-12 was selected; it had 48 valves, Locas injection, and transistorized ignition. Terry opted for a monocoque hull and, for the front and rear of the body, glass-resin. The chassis was ready long before the engine. As a result, in 1966, Gurney was often forced

Car: **Eagle-Weslake**
Maker: **Eagle**
Year: **1967**
Class: **Formula 1**
Engine: **60° V-12**
Bore × Stroke: **72.8 × 60.3 mm**
Capacity: **2,997 cc**
Power: **370 bhp at 9,500 rpm**

to use the Coventry-Climax as a substitute for the 12-cylinder.

After intense preparation in the winter of 1966–67, Gurney gained his first victory with his car by winning the 1967 Race of Champions at Brands Hatch. A second Eagle-Weslake, driven by Ritchie Ginther, who had joined Gurney, did well in the same event. The Anglo-American 12-cylinder never reached the heights that it promised on paper, but Gurney did go on to win the 1967 Belgian Grand Prix, recording the fastest lap in it as well. He nearly won the German Grand Prix but was forced to drop out, while in the lead, on the last lap.

The 3,000 cc V-12 prepared by Ferrari for the 1966 Formula 1 did not achieve great success despite its potential. Its initial 360 bhp were increased to 375 bhp for the Italian Grand Prix by the adoption of three valves per cylinder. During the period of inactivity over the winter the power was increased still further (385 bhp at 10,000 rpm); and in the course of the season another important modification, the adoption of four valves per cylinder, was made, raising the power to 390 bhp at 10,500 rpm. The 1967 season was one of the saddest and least successful in Ferrari's history. It failed to win a single Grand Prix. It didn't even enter the first race of the season, the South African Grand Prix; and Bandini was killed in the second, the Monaco Grand Prix, in a terrifying fire. Chris Amon made his debut in this race, coming in third. In the following race, the Dutch Grand Prix, he drove with Parkes and Scarfiotti, the three coming in fourth, fifth and sixth respectively. In the Belgian Grand Prix, Parkes was involved

Car: **Ferrari 312**
Maker: **Ferrari**
Year: **1967**
Class: **Formula 1**
Engine: **60° V-12**
Bore × Stroke: **77 × 53.5 mm**
Capacity: **2,989.56 cc**
Power: **390 bhp at 10,500 rpm**

in a serious accident that put an end to his career; this race was also Ludovico Scarfiotti's last for Ferrari. He reappeared in the Italian Grand Prix, but it was at the wheel of an Eagle-Weslake. From the French Grand Prix onward, Ferrari's only driver was Amon. By the end of the Championship, he had accumulated 20 points, far below the 51 points of the victor, Hulme. The 312's poor results in 1967 were undoubtedly the result of continual changes in the team caused by Bandini's death, Scarfiotti's departure, and Parkes's accident. The year before Ferrari had also lost Surtees, a driver of great talent.

The RA 302 made only a single appearance, the French Grand Prix in Rouen in 1968, an appearance marred by a serious accident in which its driver, the Frenchman Jo Schlesser, was killed. Although he was a good sports car driver, Schlesser had little experience in Formula 1 and was perhaps an ill-advised choice. On the third lap of the Grand Prix, which was run in pouring rain, the driver lost control of the Honda, crashing into an embankment. The car burst into flames, and Schlesser, trapped in the wreckage, died instantly.

Car: **Honda RA 302**
Maker: **Honda**
Year: **1968**
Class: **Formula 1**
Engine: **120° V-8**
Bore × Stroke: **88 × 61.4 mm**
Capacity: **2,987 cc**
Power: **380 bhp at 9,000 rpm**

The main differences between the RA 302 and the RA 271, which Honda had fielded earlier, lay in the engine. Instead of having a water-cooled 12-cylinder it had an air-cooled V-8 with a wide angle, 120°, to improve cooling. Another important difference lay in the position of the engine: in the 302 it was mounted longitudinally, whereas in the 271 it was mounted transversely. The load-bearing structure consisted of two caisson lateral members linked by a platform. The 8-cylinder engine was very oversquare. It developed 380 bhp at 9,000 rpm but, according to its makers, by the end of the planned period of trials and use it would easily have reached 430 bhp at 10,500. It had a five-speed transmission.

Another feature of the 302 was the driver's seat, placed very far forward—so much so that the pedals were in front of the front axle. It had a classical suspension, derived from the 1966–67 12-cylinder's. The RA 302 marked the end of Honda's involvement in motor car racing.

The English, by making possible the construction of much less costly cars than previously, have been responsible for opening the doors of motor racing. The change was due to the appearance of "assemblers," that is, the practice of putting together components manufactured elsewhere and not produced in-house as Ferrari and BRM have always done.

When the 1,500 cc Formula ended in 1965 the English once again found themselves lacking a suitable engine. Ford went to their rescue and financed the construction of a V-8 engine by Cosworth. The Lotus 49 was produced for this engine, which initially was made available only to Colin Chapman. The tuning was completed relatively quickly by Graham Hill. The 8-cylinder Cosworth made its debut at the Dutch Grand Prix on June 4, 1967. Hill recorded the fastest lap in practice, but in the race itself he was forced to drop out on the eleventh lap. The race, surprisingly, was won by Jim Clark in another Lotus 49. There were few precedents for an engine on its

Car: **Lotus-Ford 49**
Maker: **Lotus**
Year: **1968**
Class: **Formula 1**
Engine: **90° V-8 Ford-Cosworth DFV**
Bore × Stroke: **85.7 × 64.8 mm**
Capacity: **2,993 cc**
Power: **415 bhp at 9,500 rpm**

first outing dominating and winning a race.

Colin Chapman and his principal collaborator, Maurice Phillippe, knew the Cosworth engine well and designed the 49 around it. Keith Duckworth had designed his 8-cylinder to take up as little space as possible, and Chapman and Phillippe reduced the frontal area to a minimum. It had a five-speed ZF transmission, which was replaced by a Hewland in the 49 B of 1968. The 49 won a total of 13 World Championship races.

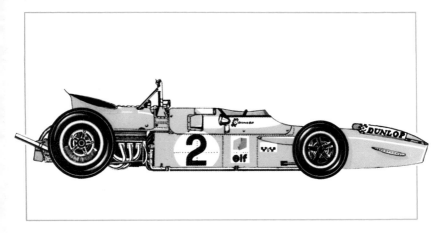

The MS 80 was the machine with which Jackie Stewart won his first World Championship. Matra began its involvement in Formula 1 in 1968, when it entered two cars. One, driven by Jean Pierre Beltoise, had its own 12-cylinder engine; but the other, driven by Stewart, had a Ford-Cosworth engine, since neither Stewart nor Ken Tyrrell had much confidence in the Matra engine.

The following year Matra's designer, Bernard Boyer, devised a new chassis. Both the French single-seaters had Ford-Cosworth engines. It was a triumphant year for Stewart. He began by driving the MS 80 to victory in the Race of Champions at Brands Hatch and went on to win the Spanish, Dutch, French, British, and Italian Grand Prix, totaling 63 points in the World Championship table compared to second-place Ickx's 37.

In addition to the Ford-Cosworth engine, the MS 80 had a five forward speed Hewland gearbox and a monocoque chassis that incorporated the fuel tanks.

This was the last year in which Stewart

Car: **Matra-Ford MS 80**
Maker: **Matra**
Year: **1969**
Class: **Formula 1**
Engine: **90° V-8 Ford-Cosworth**
Bore × Stroke: **85.7 × 64.8 mm**
Capacity: **2,993 cc**
Power: **430 bhp at 9,500 rpm**

raced for Matra. The split between the French marque and drivers Tyrrell and Stewart, a team that had given Matra such good results, was caused by Matra's insistence on using its own 12-cylinder engine. Tyrrell and Stewart did not believe that it could compete with the Ford-Cosworth, and they preferred instead to buy a March. Then, in the course of 1970, Tyrrell became a maker in his own right. Matra withdrew from racing after unsuccessful attempts in 1971 and 1972 with an entirely French car driven by Chris Amon.

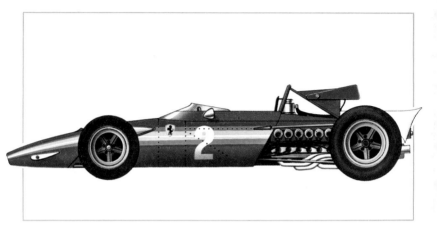

The B 70 represented another radical change in Ferrari's engineering. The engine, while remaining a 12-cylinder, was given a new layout, the V being replaced by a boxer, i.e., horizontally opposed cylinders. The boxer layout had previously been used by Ferrari on a 1,500 cc Formula 1 car and a twin-seater for the European Mountain Championship, the 212 E.

The boxer, which developed 445 bhp at 11,500 rpm, produced a turnaround in results. Although Jacky Ickx was forced to retire in the first race of the season (the South African Grand Prix) because of engine trouble, by the end of the season he declared himself satisfied with its performance. Ickx won the Austrian, Canadian, and Mexican Grand Prix while Regazzoni won the Italian Grand Prix. Quite a few Englishmen in the world of Formula 1 believed that the moment had arrived when Ferrari would regain its former glory and that the days of the Ford-Cosworth 8-cylinder were numbered. However, the new model was just

Car: **Ferrari 312 B**
Maker: **Ferrari**
Year: **1970**
Class: **Formula 1**
Engine: **180° 12-cylinder boxer**
Bore × Stroke: **80 × 49.6 mm**
Capacity: **2,991.80 cc**
Power: **445 bhp at 11,500 rpm**

a flash in the pan. Jacky Ickx failed to win the title even though his main rival that season, Jochen Rindt, was killed in practice at Monza on the eve of the Italian Grand Prix. By then Rindt had won the Monaco, Dutch, French, British and German Grand Prix, collecting a total of 45 points and winning the title posthumously.

The year 1970 was a tragic one for motor racing. Ignazio Giunti died in the 1,000 km (621 miles) race in Buenos Aires, Argentina; Bruce McLaren died while testing one of his own cars intended for Can-Am racing; and Piers Courage died in the Dutch Grand Prix. At the end of the year Jack Brabham, who was by then fully satisfied with his achievements, retired from racing.

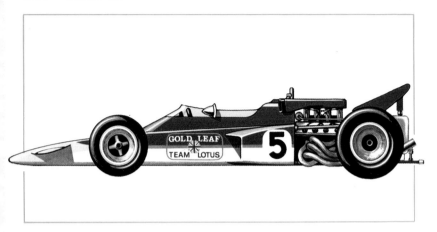

Among the many Lotus cars, the 72 stands out as the car used over the longest period (six seasons). Like all other Formula 1 single-seaters, it had its ups and downs. But overall, it was one of the most successful and versatile of cars, winning a total of 24 races, 19 of them in the World Championship circuit.

The principal new feature of the 72 was the positioning of the radiators on each side of the driving seat. The low-set nose gave the car excellent penetration with minimal wind resistance. Both the front and rear brakes were inboard with two ducts for cooling. The use of light-weight alloys, plus designer Maurice Phillippe's aeronautical experience, reduced the 72's weight to just above the permitted minimum. Another significant feature was the use of torsion bar suspension rather than coil spring. It had a five-speed Hewland DG 300 transmission. It made its debut in the Spanish Grand Prix on the Jarama circuit in Madrid and, on its fourth outing, captured its first victory when Jochen Rindt won the Dutch Grand Prix.

Car: **Lotus 72**
Maker: **Lotus**
Year: **1970**
Class: **Formula 1**
Engine: **90° V-8 Ford-Cosworth DFV**
Bore × Stroke: **85.7 × 64.8 mm**
Capacity: **2,993 cc**
Power: **430-440 bhp at 10,000 rpm**

Rindt went on to win the French, British, and German Grand Prix, but his run was broken in the Austrian Grand Prix. During practice for the Italian Grand Prix, Jochen Rindt was killed in an accident that happened just before the parabolic bend. The car's sudden swerve suggested that the crash might have been caused by a broken front left suspension. The Austro-German champion took the title posthumously, the first time that this had happened in the history of the World Championship.

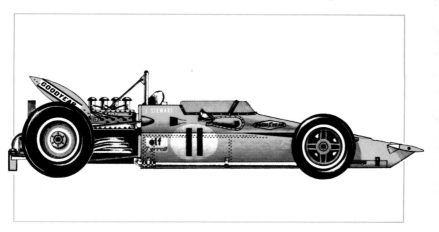

Ken Tyrrell has been involved in all aspects of motor racing—as driver, racing manager, talent scout, and maker. He began building his own cars when he became convinced he could no longer collaborate with either the French Matra, who was insisting on its own V-12 engine, or with March, a new company whose single-seater was rather unreliable.

Car: **Tyrrell**
Maker: **Tyrrell**
Year: **1971**
Class: **Formula 1**
Engine: **V-8 Ford-Cosworth DFV**
Bore × Stroke: **85.7 × 64.8 mm**
Capacity: **2,993 cc**
Power: **440 bhp at 10,500 rpm**

In order to build a car under his own name, Tyrrell turned to an unknown designer, Derek Gardner, who until then had worked with Ferguson. Gardner served him well, designing a simple and therefore reliable car, as Jackie Stewart's victories with the Tyrrell emphatically demonstrated. The new single-seater had a bathtub-shaped monocoque chassis, a five-speed Hewland FG-400 transmission, and, naturally, a Ford-Cosworth 8-cylinder engine. It made its debut at the Oulton Park Gold Cup Race in August, 1970, with Stewart setting a new lap record. The English driver also drove it in the Canadian and United States Grand Prix, doing well in both. In 1971 Tyrrell was sponsored by the French firm Elf, and he fielded an improved version of his car, the monocoque, the suspension, and the brakes being modified. Stewart came in second in the first Championship race of the season, the South African Grand Prix, then went on to win the Spanish and Monaco Grand Prix. Immediately afterward Tyrrell made further modifications to the body, and this new car was designated the 003. Stewart then won the French, British, and German Grand Prix with this car; and François Cévert came in second in France and Germany in the 002.

The good results achieved by the 312 B in 1970 gave rise to the hope that Ferrari would once again become a force to be reckoned with in the World Championship. The B2, however, which on paper was a marked improvement over the previous year's model, was actually a step backward. The engine was again increased in power, 470 bhp at 12,500 rpm; the chassis's rear suspension was modified; and the Girling disc brakes were replaced by Lockheed ones.

Two factors combined to neutralize the potential of the 312 B2. First, Jacky Ickx was unavailable for the exacting and indispensable task of tuning. Second, the B2 replaced the B too quickly. Mario Andretti won the season's first race, the South African Grand Prix, with a B while the B2 managed to win only a single race—Jacky Ickx's victory in the Dutch Grand Prix. The urge for improvement that has always driven Enzo Ferrari put his team and engineers in a difficult position; they were surrounded by problems and lacked a good test driver. The

Car: **Ferrari 312 B2**
Maker: **Ferrari**
Year: **1971**
Class: **Formula 1**
Engine: **180° V-12 boxer**
Bore × Stroke: **80 × 49.6 mm**
Capacity: **2,991.80 cc**
Power: **470 bhp at 12,500 rpm**

importance of test driving was demonstrated by Niki Lauda's essential contribution later on. Mario Andretti was an important addition to the Ferrari team. However, in order to meet his many commitments on both sides of the Atlantic, he was forced to shuttle back and forth between the United States and Europe. He competed in four Grand Prix for Ferrari—the South African, Spanish, German, and Canadian—winning one, coming in fourth in the German, and placing thirteenth in the Canadian. Ickx won the Dutch Grand Prix, came in second in Spain, third in Monaco, and eighth in South Africa and Canada. Regazzoni came in third in South Africa, Holland, and Germany, and sixth in the United States.

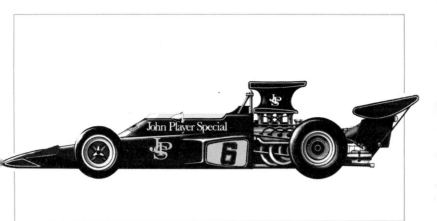

Born in 1970, the Lotus 72 proved itself in the same year, when the late Jochen Rindt won the World Championship posthumously. It then failed to win a single race in 1971 and was extensively rebuilt the following year. In that year, Lotus for the first time in its history renounced its own identity and agreed to display the initials of the tobacco firm that sponsored its racing. In 1972 the Lotus was simply known as the JPS (John Player Special), though to the world of racing it was still regarded as the Lotus.

For the 1972 season the aileron was moved further back and other details were also modified, regaining for the 72 its position as leader in both mechanical ideas and in results. With it Emerson Fittipaldi won five World Championship races—the Spanish, Belgian, British, Austrian, and Italian Grand Prix—and, at the age of 25, his first World Championship. In the same year the 72 also won four non-Championship races, two at Brands Hatch, one at Silverstone, and one at Vallelunga.

Car: **Lotus JPS 72**
Maker: **Lotus**
Year: **1972**
Class: **Formula 1**
Engine: **V-8 Ford-Cosworth**
Bore × Stroke: **85.7 × 64.8 mm**
Capacity: **2,293 cc**
Power: **440 bhp at 10,000 rpm**

In 1973 the 72 did even better, winning seven World Championship races. Emerson Fittipaldi won in Argentina, Brazil, and Spain, and Ronnie Peterson, who had replaced Wissel, won the French, Austrian, Italian and United States-East races. In 1974 Peterson drove the English car to victory in Monaco, France, and Italy; and Jacky Ickx, who had taken Fittipaldi's place after he had gone to McLaren, won at Brands Hatch. The 72 was used again in 1975, but by then it was no longer competitive. It had an exceptional record: six seasons, 19 World Championship wins, five in open Formula 1 races, two World Championships (Rindt and Fittipaldi), and three Formula 1 Constructor's Cups.

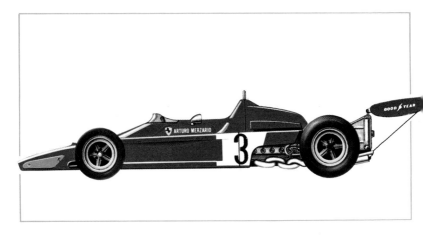

The year 1973 proved to be a dismal one for Ferrari; the firm failed to win a single victory and cut its season short. For the B3 various improvements were made to the engine (power raised to 485 bhp at 12,500 rpm) and to its general trim, with the water and oil radiators being placed in front of the rear wheels. At the end of the season, however, the radiators were restored to their original position. Relations between Jacky Ickx and Ferrari cooled still further, and the contract between them was terminated amicably before the end of the season. The B3's performance was so poor that Ferrari decided not to compete in the Dutch and German Grand Prix, and Ickx was allowed to compete in them driving a McLaren.

Ferrari's troubles were due more to the chassis than to the engine. As a rule, Ferrari engines have always been able to handle a situation, bearing out the principle that a reserve of power could compensate for deficiencies in the chassis. This principle, of which Enzo Ferrari was

Car: **Ferrari 312 B3**
Maker: **Ferrari**
Year: **1973**
Class: **Formula 1**
Engine: **180° V-12 boxer**
Bore × Stroke: **80 × 49.6 mm**
Capacity: **2,991.80 cc**
Power: **485 bhp at 12,500 rpm**

an ardent proponent, held good for quite a while. However, with the appearance of broad-sectioned tires, its worth has been greatly reduced. Instead the streamlining of the body, weight distribution, and the geometry of the suspension have become more important.

In 1974 Ferrari made the crucial decision to concentrate on the chassis while, in effect, neglecting the engine. From that year onward, Ferraris took on a completely different appearance from those of the recent and distant past. Without the disastrous season of 1973, Ferrari probably would not have had the courage to begin completely anew. The results amply justified the effort.

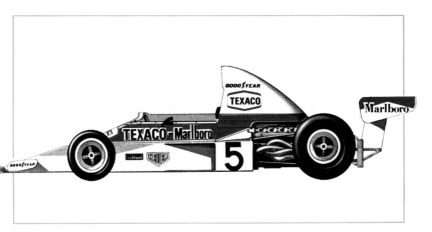

The M 23 had a long history behind it, stretching back to the day when Bruce McLaren, the marque's founder, followed the path blazed by Jack Brabham and set up his own business. Both of them had driven for Cooper. Bruce McLaren began as a constructor with a Formula 1 single-seater, the M2B, a car he drove in the new formula Drivers World Championship in 1966. This proved to be a difficult year and was marked by the vain search for a suitable engine. McLaren's success finally came in 1968 with a Ford-Cosworth in the Race of Champions at Brands Hatch. By then the car had become the M7A, designed by Robin Herd. In the course of the same year, the M7A won three World Championship races, McLaren taking the Belgian Grand Prix and Dennis Hulme the Italian and Canadian Grand Prix. By this time the company founded by McLaren was able to broaden its horizons, competing in the Indianapolis 500 and in Can-Am racing as well as in Formula 1.

The M 23 was derived from the M 16,

Car: **McLaren M 23**
Maker: **McLaren**
Year: **1974**
Class: **Formula 1**
Engine: **90° V-8 Ford-Cosworth DFV**
Bore × Stroke: **85.7 × 64.8 mm**
Capacity: **2,993 cc**
Power: **460 bhp at 10,250 rpm**

designed by Gordon Coppuck. Powered by an Offenhauser engine and driven by Mark Donohue, the M 16 won the 1972 Indianapolis 500. Like the Lotus 72, the M 16 had lateral radiators and a highly tapered nose. The M 23 had a Hewland gearbox, outboard front brakes, and inboard rear brakes. It quickly demonstrated its quality by winning the Swedish Grand Prix with Hulme at the wheel and, driven by Revson, the British and Canadian Grand Prix in 1973. The car was used again the following year, but the colors of its first sponsor, Yardley, were changed to those of Marlboro-Texaco. Besides Hulme, McLaren also employed Emerson Fittipaldi, who won his second World Championship that year.

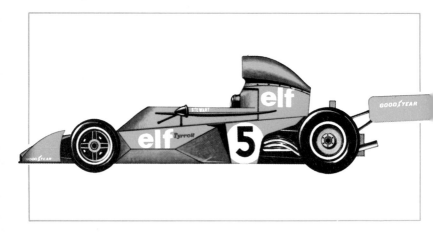

The departure of Jackie Stewart from racing at the end of 1973 was prompted, as is well known, by the death of his teammate François Cévert. In one blow Tyrrell had lost two of racing's best drivers. They were replaced by two young drivers, Jody Scheckter and Patrick Depailler, who had great potential but were rather inexperienced.

The 007 was designed and built with this factor in mind. Derek Gardner intended the car to be simple to avoid any special problems. To achieve his objective, Gardner abandoned the short wheelbase of the 006 and eliminated the broad front and massive air intake positioned on top of the roll bar. Ken Tyrrell clearly seemed to agree with his designer. The 007 was in certain ways a transitional car, verging on a single-seater trainer; but Jody Scheckter in particular was able to put it to good use, winning two races, the Swedish and British Grand Prix. Scheckter gained a further victory with the 007 in the 1975 South African Grand Prix.

Car: **Tyrrell 007**
Maker: **Tyrrell**
Year: **1974**
Class: **Formula 1**
Engine: **90° V-8 Ford-Cosworth**
Bore × Stroke: **85.7 × 64.8 mm**
Capacity: **2,993 cc**
Power: **460 bhp at 10,250 rpm**

The 007 was the last orthodox car that Derek Gardner designed while working for Tyrrell. After the 007 Gardner took a leap into the dark with the six-wheeled P 34 of 1976. This model was raced for two years. Clearly dissatisifed with his work, Gardner left his post at the end of 1977. Tyrrell had won 19 victories under his able technical direction. The 008 of 1978 and the later 009 model were the work of another well-known designer, Maurice Phillippe.

Like the Lotus 72, which was successfully raced for several seasons, the McLaren M 23 was active for several years (from the 1973 South African Grand Prix to the 1977 South African Grand Prix inclusive). It was continually being updated and improved, and it earned two World Championships, driven by Fittipaldi in 1974 and by Hunt in 1976.

The main modification made in 1975 was to the front suspension. This was a result of experience gained in Argentina at the start of that year's World Championship and took account of the fact that the M 23 consistently performed well on fast circuits but failed to do so on winding ones. Modifications made in 1976 also concerned the suspension geometry. In the same year, the M 23's poor showing between the Belgian and French Grand Prix (May 16 to July 4) was due to a modification that was imposed on McLaren. To comply with the rules, the oil radiators had to be moved from the sides of the car at its rear, beneath the aileron, and put back in their previous position.

Car: **McLaren M 23**
Maker: **McLaren**
Year: **1976**
Class: **Formula 1**
Engine: **V-8 Ford-Cosworth**
Bore × Stroke: **85.7 mm × 64.8 mm**
Capacity: **2,993 cc**
Power: **470 bhp at 10.500 rpm**

The other more important innovations made to the M 23 in 1976 concerned the transmission (six forward speed Hewland) and the streamlining of the body. The total weight was reduced by 15 kg (33 lb). Overall the M 23 won 16 victories in the World Championship, 6 of them being gained by James Hunt when he took the 1976 World Championship, beating the unfortunate Niki Lauda (Ferrari) by a single point.

1976 - Tyrrell P 34 GB

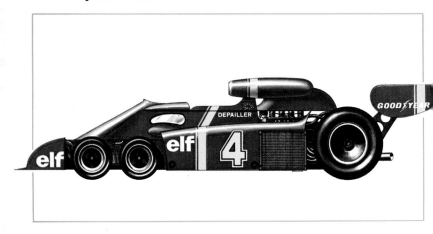

The P 34 (Project 34) was not in itself either a success or a failure; but its creator, Derek Gardner, did not achieve his objectives, the principal one being improved wheel grip in corners. Contrary to popular belief, the P 34's weak point was neither its six wheels, in particular the four smaller sectioned front wheels, nor the steering components. The real Achilles heel was the rear suspension's upper point of attachment.

The P 34 made its debut in the 1976 Spanish Grand Prix. While it couldn't be expected to achieve immediate results for its designer and maker, beginning with the Austrian and then with the Dutch Grand Prix, matters got worse. In addition Goodyear's special tires had been made with too hard a compound. Overall, however, the car had a favorable first year. Scheckter won the Swedish Grand Prix, and came in fourth in Belgium, third in Monte Carlo, sixth in France, second in Britain and Germany, fifth in Holland and Italy, fourth in Canada, and second in the United States-East. Depailler came in

Car: **Tyrrell P 34**
Maker: **Tyrrell**
Year: **1976**
Class: **Formula 1**
Engine: **V-8 Ford-Cosworth DFV**
Bore × Stroke: **85.7 × 64.8 mm**
Capacity: **2,993 cc**
Power: **475 bhp at 10,000 rpm**

third in Monaco, second in Sweden and France, seventh in Holland, sixth in Italy, and second in Canada and Japan. The P 34s were modified over the winter of 1976–77 and appeared to have been markedly improved, but their excessive weight and unstable trim made the task of their drivers (Scheckter had moved to Wolf and been replaced by Peterson) even more difficult. On top of everything else, the P 34s in Brazil were destroyed in accidents. The first good result did not come until the fourth race of the season, the United States-West Grand Prix, in which Depailler finished fourth. The French driver also came in fourth in Sweden, second in Canada, and third in Japan.

Ferrari 312 T, 312 T2, 312 T3, 312 T4, 312 T5 - 1975 - 80

The 312 T may be regarded as the first of a new generation of Ferrari single-seaters. There was only a single instance, the 246 of 1958, of the transverse gearbox being used before 1974–75. When it was used again, after a period of 15 years, it was highly successful, making a crucial contribution to improving the weight distribution around the driver's seat. By 1974 the shape of the Ferrari Formula 1 single-seater, the B 3, had already altered substantially, assuming the characteristic vertical form because of the bulky, flattened dynamic intake behind the driver. In that year the B 3 achieved good results, Lauda winning the Spanish and Dutch Grand Prix and Regazzoni the German. The B 3 was used again at the beginning of 1975 but with poor results, so the T was brought into service ahead of time for the South African Grand Prix, in which Lauda finished fifth. In the Spanish Grand Prix an irregular maneuver by Andretti (Parnelli) caused Lauda and Regazzoni to crash into each other. But from the Monaco Grand Prix onward, Lauda won an impressive series of victories, starting in Monaco and going on to win the Belgian, Swedish, French and United States Grand Prix and his first World Championship.

The superiority of Lauda and the T frequently enabled the Austrian driver to lead from the starting line, proving that his victories were not, as has been suggested, due to his infuriating use of tactics but instead to the outstanding quality of the car. Lauda himself had made a major contribution in tuning it.

The T2 of 1976 was very similar to the T, differing in its front section, which had the addition of a tubular structure, and its suspension (inverted wishbones). The wheelbase was lengthened to 2.56 m (8 ft 4.8 in), the track reduced to 1.40 m (4 ft 7.1 in) and its weight to 575 kg (1,268 lb). The T2 was used for the first time in the Spanish Grand Prix. Lauda came in second, but he was driving in poor physical shape, having fractured two ribs in an accident while driving a tractor in his garden. The World Champion then won the Belgian and Monaco Grand Prix and came in third in the Swedish Grand Prix. He dropped out in the French but was again victorious in the British Grand Prix. In the following race, the German Grand Prix, he had a dreadful accident, and it was uncertain whether he would survive. With an exceptional display of will and character, he resumed racing with the Italian Grand Prix, in which he came in fourth. Although he had missed the Austrian and Dutch Grand Prix, the large tally of points he had built up in the World Championship table seemed certain to win him his second world title. However, he came in eighth in the Canadian Grand Prix and fourth in the United States, and finished the season by withdrawing from the last race, the Japanese Grand Prix, because of appalling weather conditions. From the human angle his action was understood and excused, but it meant that he lost the Championship by a single point to James Hunt.

The T3 made its debut in the South

1975 - Ferrari 312 T

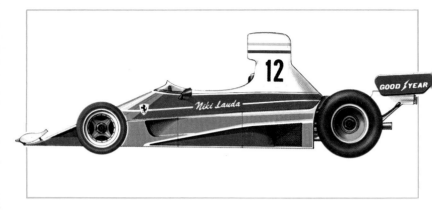

African Grand Prix. The general layout of the mechanical components was retained, but it differed from the T2 in wheelbase (2.70 m/8 ft 10.3 in), front tract (1.62 m/5 ft 3.8 in), rear track (1.58 m/5 ft 2.2 in), and weight (580 kg/1,278 lb). Another important change was the adoption of Michelin tires in place of Goodyears. The T3 won a total of four Grand Prix, Carlos Reutemann winning the United States-West, British, and United States-East, and Gilles Villeneuve

winning the Canadian. Reutemann also won the Brazilian Grand Prix, but he was driving a T2.

The T4 followed the lines of the T3, but it differed in its front track (1.70 m/5 ft 6.9 in), rear track (1.60 m/5 ft 3 in), overall length (4.46 m/14 ft 7.6 in versus 4.25 m/13 ft 11.3 in), and overall width (2.12 m/6 ft 11.5 in versus 2.13 m/6 ft 11.9 in). It was also to have been fitted with an electro-hydraulic gearbox as an alternative to the mechanical one, but the new

1976 - Ferrari 312 T

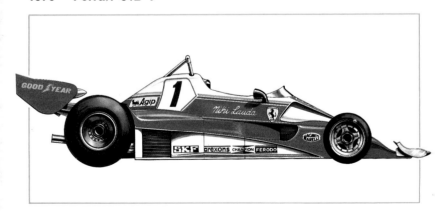

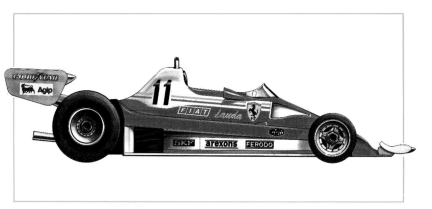

system was never used. Extensive research in the Pininfarina wind tunnel enabled Ferrari to adopt an internal flow solution that increased the negative lift by means of aerodynamic effects between the body and the ground.

In 1979 the T4 won six victories in the World Championship. Jody Scheckter won three of them—the Belgian, Monaco, and Italian Grand Prix—and the Championship. Gilles Villeneuve won the other three, the South African, United

Car: **Ferrari 312 T, T2, T3, T4, T5**
Maker: **Ferrari**
Year: **1975–80**
Class: **Formula 1**
Engine: **12-cylinder boxer**
Bore × Stroke: **80 × 49.6 mm**
Capacity: **2,991.8 cc**
Power: **T and T2: 500 bhp at 12,200 rpm**
  T3: 510 bhp at 12,200 rpm
  T4 and T5: 515 bhp at 12,300 rpm

Ferrari 312 T3 - 1978

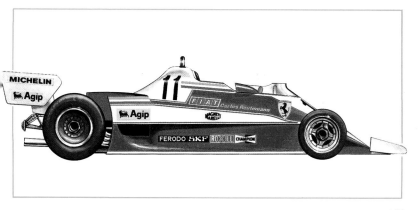

States-West, and United States-East Grand Prix, and came in second in the Championship.

The T5 is a further step toward a true "wing car". With this objective in mind, the cylinder heads were redesigned, gaining about 5 cm (2 in) of vertical space, in anticipation of a new, more compact boxer engine. Modifications were also made to the front suspension, the upper part of the wishbones being streamlined. The position of the steering gearbox was raised, which forced a partial restructuring of the chassis. Finally, its aerodynamic efficiency, the ratio of lift to drag, was improved to 1.3. The T5's dimensions were: length 4.53 m (14 ft 10.3 in), front track 1.75 m (5 ft 8.9 in), rear track 1.62 m (5 ft 3.8 in), width 2.14 m (7 ft 0.2 in), height 1.02 m (3 ft. 4.2 in), wheelbase 2.70 m (8 ft 10.3 in), and weight 595 kg (1,312 lb).

1980 - Ferrari 312 T5

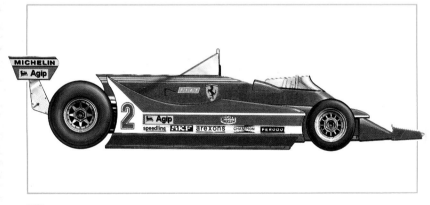

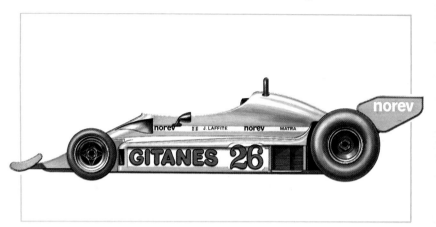

For three years Ligier was one of the small group of makers who remained faithful to the 12-cylinder. Picking up the pieces when Matra finally decided to pull out of racing, Ligier obtained permission to use Matra's 12-cylinder and also hired some of Matra's engineers.

Ligier's Formula 1 debut was in 1976, when with just one machine Jacques Laffitte managed to achieve some creditable results, a third in Belgium, a fourth in Sweden, and a third in Italy. In 1977 the JS 7 managed four good placings, including an unexpected victory in the Swedish Grand Prix. The marked progress made with the JS 7's chassis was offset by the engine's disappointing performance, a major cause of the car's numerous failures to finish. After a careful investigation, the defect was found to be deficient valve springs, probably the result of a poor batch of material. From that moment on the performance of the JS 7 improved, but not enough to make the French car one of the best in the Championship. The victory in the Swed-

Car: **Ligier JS 7**
Maker: **Ligier**
Year: **1976**
Class: **Formula 1**
Engine: **V-12 Matra (MS 76)**
Bore × Stroke: **79.7 × 50 mm**
Capacity: **2,993 cc**
Power: **520 bhp at 12,300 rpm**

ish Grand Prix greatly lifted morale, particularly since it was unexpected. Laffitte, driving brilliantly, was given the race when Andretti, who held a comfortable lead, ran out of fuel. In practice, however, both the engine and the chassis of Laffitte's car had shown themselves to be badly lacking. The Swedish Grand Prix has remained the only Formula 1 World Championship race to be won by a Matra engine.

The story of Wolf is without precedent in the annals of the Drivers World Championship. It was created by the Austro-Canadian multi-millionaire Walter Wolf with the help of a highly intelligent engineer, Harvey Postlethwaite, who had previously worked for Hasketh, and a team manager who had learned his trade with Lotus, Peter Warr. The Wolf won a Grand Prix, the Argentine, on its first outing. Such a feat had something of the miraculous about it, considering that Postlethwaite had just a few months in which to develop it. The car was, however, strictly orthodox, and it was powered by the inevitable Ford-Cosworth 8-cylinder. This first victory was won by the highly resourceful Jody Scheckter and proved to be no mere flash in the pan. The South African driver went on to win the Monaco Grand Prix, giving Cosworth its 100th success since 1967 in the Drivers World Championship, and the Canadian Grand Prix, Cosworth's 101st. He also came in second in South Africa, and third in the United States-West,

Car: Wolf WR 1
Maker: **Wolf**
Year: **1977**
Class: **Formula 1**
Engine: **V-8 Ford-Cosworth DFV**
Bore × Stroke: **85.7 × 64.8 mm**
Capacity: **2,993 cc**
Power: **470 bhp at 10,750 rpm**

Spanish, Dutch and United States-East Grand Prix.

Scheckter had good reason to say at the end of the season that the title had slipped out of his hand. He finished second overall, 17 points behind Niki Lauda.

This outstanding feat showed, once again, that in the Drivers World Championship anything was possible—even the establishment of a team that had been together for only a short time and a car that had been hastily built. Enzio Ferrari was not far off the mark when he asserted that the supremacy of the English manifested itself above all in the extraordinary flexibility of the "assemblers."

Brabham - Alfa BT 45-1976
Brabham - Alfa BT 46-1978
Brabham - Alfa BT 48-1979

The Brabham-Alfa Romeo twin name, a link between two illustrious sporting families from different periods, emerged in 1975 and was dissolved at the end of the 1979 racing season, before the conclusion of the World Championship. Even if Alfa Romeo had not decided to become directly involved in Formula 1 with a car built entirely by Autodelta, the collaboration with Brabham would still have been terminated. There were a multitude of reasons for the separation, but in essence they boiled down to two: the strong personality and business sense of Brabham's chief, Bernie Ecclestone, and the poor reliability of the Alfa Romeo 12-cylinder.

The first fruit of the agreement between the two organizations was the BT 45 designed by Gordon Murray. Work began in 1975, and the car made its debut with Carlos Pace and Carlos Reutemann in the 1976 Brazilian Grand Prix. In it Pace came in tenth while Reutemann retired after running out of fuel. The Alfa Romeo 12-cylinder boxer was immediately condemmed as too heavy, bulky and thirsty. The 1976 season concluded disastrously: Carlos Pace managed two fourths, a sixth, a seventh, two eighths, two ninths, and a tenth and was forced to drop out in four Grand Prix. Reutemann never finished higher than fourth and retired in ten Grand Prix. Reutemann, convinced that the Brabham-Alfa would never achieve greatness, secretly reached an agreement with Ferrari, and by the Italian Grand Prix of 1976, where he came ninth, he was driving for them. In Canada, Ecclestone replaced him with Larry Perkins, an Australian and winner of the 1975 Formula 3 Europa Cup. A revised and improved version of the BT 45, which was 5 kg (11 lb) lighter and had the oil coolers at the side, on a level with the engine, was driven in Canada by Pace.

For the 1977 season the car was greatly improved, particularly in regard to its streamlining, and it was much more competitive than the previous year. Even so, the results at the end of the season were again disappointing, despite the fact that Reutemann's replacement, John Watson, came close to victory in more than one race. On at least one occasion, the French Grand Prix, Watson was truly unlucky, running out of fuel in the last half mile while in the lead. On that occasion he came in second, his best position that year; he dropped out in eleven other Grand Prix. Hans Stuck achieved much better results. Starting with the United States-West Grand Prix, he took Carlos Pace's place after Pace was killed in an air crash. Pace had begun the 1977

Championship well, with a second place in Argentina. Stuck came in third in Germany and Austria, sixth in Spain and Belgium, and seventh in Holland and Japan.

The BT 46 was prepared over the winter of 1977 and was used in 1978, the year in which Niki Lauda joined Brabham-Alfa. It also had a new sponsor in Parmalat. The engine cooling system of radiant cells or panels on the sides was considered revolutionary, but it later had to be abandoned as too complicated, and the radiators were readopted. Niki Lauda won two races with the BT 46, the Swedish and Italian Grand Prix, but in both cases special circumstances lessened the achievement. In Sweden the car's road holding was improved by the use of a fan at the rear of the car. Jim Hall had done the same on his Chaparral. However, the device had to be removed after the race as it was no longer permitted. In Italy, Andretti and Villeneuve were each given one-minute penalities for false starts, lowering them from first and

second, respectively, to sixth and seventh. This meant that Lauda, who was third, became the winner.

Like the vast majority of the 1979 Formula 1 single-seaters, the BT 48 was a wing car or ground effect car. In order to achieve this effect, Autodelta altered the layout of its 12-cylinder from a boxer to a 60° V. This tricky operation was completed in the record time of five and a half months. However, the BT 48 hasn't changed matters much. In the 1979 season Niki Lauda came in fourth, sixth, and seventh in three races and dropped out in eleven. Nelson Piquet, who replaced Watson, managed a fourth, a seventh, and an eighth and retired 12 times. The collaboration between Alfa Romeo and Brabham ended with the Italian Grand Prix, and in the last two races Ford-Cosworth engines were used. Before announcing his retirement from racing Niki Lauda won the Imola Grand Prix (this race did not count toward the World Championship), using 12-cylinder Alfa Romeo for the last time.

Car: **Brabham-Alfa BT 45 and BT 46**
Maker: **Brabham**
Years: **1976 (BT 45) and 1978 (BT 46)**
Class: **Formula 1**
Engine: **180° V-12 (Boxer) Alfa Romeo**
Bore × Stroke: **77 × 53.6 mm**
Capacity: **2,995 cc**
Power: **500 bhp at 11,500 rpm**

Car: **Brabham-Alfa BT 48**
Maker: **Brabham**
Year: **1979**
Class: **Formula 1**
Engine: **69° V-12 Alfa Romeo**
Bore × Stroke: **78.5 × 51.5 mm**
Capacity: **2,991 cc**
Power: **520 bhp at 12,200 rpm**

Brabham-Alfa BT 48 - 1979

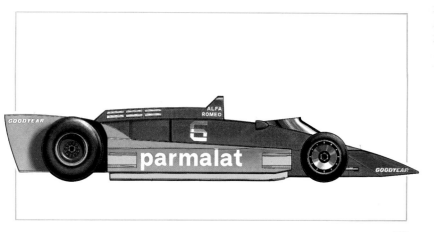

Designated the 79, this model's number was unconnected with the year, being merely one of the series of numbers used to distinguish the various Lotus models. The Lotus 79 sparked a genuine revolution in Formula 1 and in doing so gave Mario Andretti an easy victory in the World Championship.

Ironically, when the 79 made its debut during practice for the Monaco Grand Prix, Andretti dismissed it, preferring instead the 78. Nobody in Monaco noticed its new features, but in the following Grand Prix, the Belgian, it created astonishment when Andretti came in first and Peterson second. The Italian-American driver also won in Spain, France, Germany, and Holland, averaging a second's advantage over each lap.

What was the cause of the 79's superiority when there were so many other cars with similar engines? It lay in better road holding, achieved by channeling air beneath the car and the rear, while preventing air from escaping at the sides. The air entered at the front

Car: **Lotus 79**
Maker: **Lotus**
Year: **1978**
Class: **Formula 1**
Engine: **V-8 Ford-Cosworth DVF**
Bore × Stroke: **92.5 × 55.5 mm**
Capacity: **2,983.7 cc**
Power: **480 bhp at 10,500 rpm**

through a slit 7-8 cm (about 3 in) from the ground and 140 cm (56 in) wide (the maximum allowed by the regulations). As it passed below the car it was held in by skirts which almost touched the ground. Since the gap through which the air emerged was appreciably larger than the one through which it entered, a vacuum was created beneath the car that sucked it down, allowing it to enter bends and accelerate out of them faster.

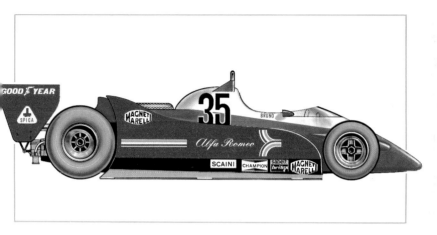

Begun in 1979, the Alfa Romeo was ready by June and on July 7 had its first outing on the Alfa Romeo circuit at Balocco. In September it made its World Championship debut in the Italian Grand Prix, and it would have done well had driver Bruno Giacomelli not ended up in the sand and been unable to get out.

A distinctive feature of the new car was its driver's seat, which like the 33 TT 12's was placed well forward. It was a typical wing or ground effect car. Various aeronautical techniques were used in its construction. One of these was the use of a sandwich panel chassis (aluminum walls, plus a honeycomb structure of resin, the whole being riveted and 25 mm/1 in thick), which meant a considerable saving of weight and greater stiffness.

The fuel tank's central position was determined by the need to make room for the Venturi and to achieve the best conditions for it. This was also the reason the 180° V-12 was replaced by the new 60° one, which was about 40 cm (16 in) nar-

Car: **Alfa Romeo 179**
Maker: **Autodelta**
Year: **1979**
Class: **Formula 1**
Engine: **60° V-12**
Bore × Stroke: **77 × 53.6 mm**
Capacity: **2,993 cc**
Power: **520 bhp at 12,300 rpm**

rower and, at 175 kg (386 lb), 8 kg (17.6 lb) lighter than the 180°. The 60° had four overhead camshafts and four valves, angled at 60° per cylinder. Depending on the circuit, the car could be fitted with a gearbox with five or six forward speeds and a reverse.

In 1979 this car failed to finish in any of the four Grand Prix it entered: the Italian, the Dino Ferrari at Imola, the Canadian, and the United States-East.

The F6A, though a ground effect car, was both orthodox and conventional in general conception. It was the third single-seater to bear the name Copersucar since Emerson Fittipaldi had left McLaren at the end of 1975 and accepted the sponsorship of a large firm of sugar refiners from his native Brazil. He and his brother have been responsible for the preparation and tuning of the Copersucars. Fortunate in establishing himself as a driver of international standing (at 25 he was the youngest winner of the World Championship), Emerson Fittipaldi has not been as fortunate as a maker.

The F6A, used from the 1979 South African Grand Prix onward (one point in the world table), has been even less successful than the F5A, with which Fittipaldi won 17 points in 1978, or the FD04, with which he won 11 in 1977 and 3 in 1976.

The ill-fated Copersucar project involved no less than five engineers who were well known in the racing world:

Car: **Copersucar F6A**
Maker: **Fittipaldi**
Year: **1979**
Class: **Formula 1**
Engine: **V-8 Ford-Cosworth**
Bore × Stroke: **92.5 × 55.5 mm**
Capacity: **2,982 cc**
Power: **480 bhp at 10,500 rpm**

Ricardo Divila, Jo Ramirez, Dave Baldwin (ex Ensign), Ralph Bellamy (ex Lotus) and Giacoma Caliri (ex Ferrari), the latter with specific responsibility for the body.

The Copersucar project as originally conceived by Fittipaldi and his sponsors has been a complete failure. For the 1980 season the Brazilian driver took over all the material from Wolf, who was no longer involved in racing, and re-christened it.

The letters JS, which have been retained over the years, were a homage to the memory of a close friend of Guy Ligier, Jo Schlesser, who was killed in the 1968 French Grand Prix at Dijon. The JS 11 is in itself clear evidence of the founder's passion for racing. An ex-driver, Guy Ligier had to start literally from scratch, producing a series of cars that finally commanded the attention of the public and the engineers.

The JS 11 was a ground effect car with a double wing section. Like all wing cars it was clearly inspired by the 1978 Lotus 79, but the small French team was extraordinarily quick to learn the lessons of that revolutionary car and to act upon them. Furthermore the rounded and smoothly blended shapes of the JS 11 indicated that Ligier, even in the process of imitation, attempted to be original rather than merely copy others' designs.

Another major break with the past was the replacement of the Matra 12-cylinder with the Cosworth 8. After a magnificent beginning at the start of the season, with

Car: **Ligier-Gitanes JS 11**
Maker: **Ligier**
Year: **1979**
Class: **Formula 1**
Engine: **90° V-8 Ford-Cosworth**
Bore × Stroke: **92.5 × 55.5 mm**
Capacity: **2,993 cc**
Power: **490 bhp at 10,500 rpm**

victories in the 1979 Argentine and Brazilian Grand Prix, the JS 11 seemed to be the car to beat. Although the actual potential of the car later had to be reappraised, the French team's performance was greatly affected by Patrick Depailler's deltaplane accident during a break in the World Championship.

"Compared to the 80 the 79 will seem like a double-decker bus." It was with these words that Colin Chapman unveiled his latest creation in December 1978. The astonishing successes of the 79, the fact that it had been imitated by nearly everyone, and the resources of Lotus's new principal sponsor (Martini) all suggested that the 80 would create a sensation. Never have such high hopes been dashed more completely: of the two cars, it was the 80 and not the 79 that turned out to resemble a double-decker bus.

The major difference between the 80 and the 79 lay in the application of the ground effect concept. The bottom of the 80 had been completely streamlined to provide two separate channels through which the air could flow unimpeded to the rear. For this reason even the passage holes of the lower members of the rear suspension were reduced significantly.

Driven exclusively by Andretti, who was attempting to defend his 1978 title in the 1979 Championship, the Lotus 80

Car: **Lotus 80**
Maker: **Lotus**
Year: **1979**
Class: **Formula 1**
Engine: **V-8 Ford-Cosworth**
Bore × Stroke: **92.5 × 55.5 mm**
Capacity: **2,993 cc**
Power: **490 bhp at 10,500 rpm**

was entered in only three Grand Prix— Spain, Monaco, and France. On its debut it came in third, but it dropped out in the other two races. From the British Grand Prix onward, the 80 was withdrawn from racing. It was not the first time that a new car had been an utter disappointment, but Colin Chapman had to suffer the double mortification of seeing the much praised 79 fail to live up to its previous year's renown.

For the record, the Lotus 80 had a wheelbase of 2.74 m (8 ft 11.9 in), a front track of 1.70 m (5 ft 6.9 in), a rear track of 1.63 m (5 ft 4.2 in), an overall length of 4.63 m (15 ft 2.3 in), an overall height of 0.96 m (3 ft 1.8 in), and weighed about 575 kg (1,267.6 lb).

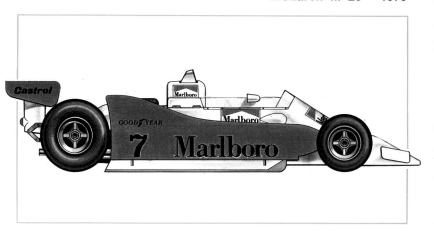

The M 28 was another of Gordon Coppuck's creations. Coppuck's combativeness at the heart of McLaren has defied all the misfortunes that have dogged the Anglo-New Zealand marque.

The M 28 was born in the winter of 1978–79. Incorporating the principles of a ground effect car, its unique feature was its body, which consisted of two sheets of aluminum with a layer of expanded resin in between. However, this construction turned out to be both heavy and fragile. It made its debut in the 1979 Argentine Grand Prix, in which John Watson did well, coming in third, while Patrick Tambay was forced to drop out after an accident. The subsequent disappointing results compelled Coppuck to run for cover. In Spain John Watson drove a revised and improved version, the 28 B, which had a shorter wheelbase, new suspension, and a new body. An engine breakdown stopped the car on the twenty-second lap.

In the following Grand Prix, the Belgian, Watson came in sixth while Tam-

Car: **McLaren M 28**
Maker: **McLaren**
Year: **1979**
Class: **Formula 1**
Engine: **V-8 Ford-Cosworth**
Bore × Stroke: **92.5 × 55.5 mm**
Capacity: **2,993 cc**
Power: **480 bhp at 10,500 rpm**

bay, driving the first version of the M 28, failed to qualify. He suffered the same disgrace in the next race, the Monaco Grand Prix. In Monaco another version of the M 28 appeared, the M 28 C, which was narrower and more pointed than the B. Finally, in the British Grand Prix, Watson drove yet another version, the M 29. Had it not been for a puncture the Irishman would have come in third; as it was he had to be content with fourth. The M 29 with its pressed and riveted body marked a return to traditional construction.

Renault's efforts to win a place in the front rank of Formula 1 began to pay off in 1979 with the victory of Jean Pierre Jabouille in the French Grand Prix at Dijon. Such a success had been in the air after the French marque's two drivers (René Arnoux being the other) had recorded the fastest times in practice and had gained places on the front row of the starting grid.

From the 1979 Spanish Grand Prix onward they had been driving the RS 10. This car was a ground effect single-seater designed by François Castaing, with fiberglass bodywork and a light alloy monococque in which the engine formed an element.

In 1979 Renault was alone in using a V-6 turbocharged engine. That year's version developed 500 bhp at 11,000 rpm and could, without risk, run at 12,000 rpm. Its maximum torque was 38 kgm (275 ft lb) at 9,600 rpm. It had the advantage of a regulation capacity, 1,500 cc, that was as high as half a normally aspirated Formula 1 engine's, as well as

Car: **Renault RS 11**
Maker: **Renault**
Year: **1979**
Class: **Formula 1**
Engine: **Turbocharged V-6**
Bore × Stroke: **86 × 42.8 mm**
Capacity: **1,492 cc**
Power: **500 bhp at 11,000 rpm**

the handicap of a turbocharged engine's sluggish response to the driver. It is to Renault's credit that it took the plunge. Renault made a further step forward when, from the Monaco Grand Prix onward, it used two turboblowers, reducing the speed at which the engine delivered its power by 1,000 rpm (6,500 rpm).

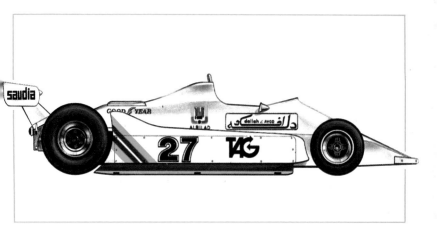

The Williams FW 07 was designed by Patrick Head, a young engineer who was virtually unknown until the 1979 season. Some insinuated that its strongest point lay in its being a faithful copy of the 1978 Lotus 79. Even if this were true, the fact that Head's cars were almost unbeatable at the end of the 1979 season would compel one to admit that Head had added something to it.

The Williams FW 07, it is generally agreed, is both simple and practical in its construction, successfully reconciling light weight in its mechanical components (the car weighed only 10 kg/24 lb more than the permitted minimum) with clean aerodynamic lines.

It had a poor debut when both Jones and Regazzoni had to retire because of mechanical trouble. The same happened in the following race, the Belgian Grand Prix. Finally, on its third outing, Regazzoni crossed the finish line a few meters behind the winner Scheckter in a Ferrari. It was in the course of the Monaco Grand Prix that this car revealed its potential. In

Car: Saudia Williams FW 07
Maker: Williams
Year: **1979**
Class: **Formula 1**
Engine: **V-8 Ford-Cosworth**
Bore × Stroke: **92.5 × 55.5 mm**
Capacity: **2,993 cc**
Power: **490 bhp at 11,400 rpm**

France Jones came in fourth and Regazzoni sixth. In Britain Regazzoni gained the car's first victory while Jones retired. Jones then won three victories in a row—Germany, Austria and Holland—and a fourth, the Canadian, after Jody Scheckter had won the Italian Grand Prix and secured the World Championship. In 1979 the Williams had the shortest wheelbase (2.29 m/7 ft 6.2 in) of any Formula 1 single-seater.

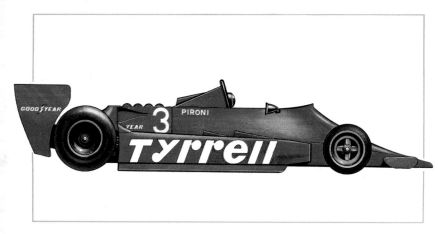

The year 1979 marked the third phase in the life of the Tyrrell racing organization. The first phase coincided with the creation of a car bearing the founder's name and designed by Derek Gardner. Jackie Stewart's acclaimed victories made Ken Tyrrell a celebrity. The second phase involved the experimental six-wheeled car, the P 34, and the breakup, after its failure, of the partnership between Tyrrell and his designer. The third phase began after the departure of Gardner with the arrival of Maurice Phillippe, an ex-collaborator of Colin Chapman.

Despite Phillippe's illustrious past, this third period began quietly, as shown by the fact that Ken Tyrrell started the 1979 season without a sponsor. Later on, the Italian firm Candy came to his rescue. However, its name standing out in large letters on the bare sides of the 009s emphasizes Tyrrell's difficult position and highlights the absence of other backers.

In the 1979 season, drivers Didier Pironi and Jean Pierre Jarier (who was inactive for a period because of viral

Car: **Tyrrell 009**
Maker: **Tyrrell**
Year: **1979**
Class: **Formula 1**
Engine: **V-8 Ford-Cosworth**
Bore × Stroke: **92.5 × 55.5 mm**
Capacity: **2,993 cc**
Power: **490 bhp at 11,400 rpm**

hepatitis) managed only 14 points apiece and tied for tenth place in the World Championship. Each came in third in two races: Pironi in South Africa and Britain, and Jarier in Belgium and United States-East.

Although nominally a ground effect car, the 009 remained a classical car overall. Its producers can be credited only for having built it in time to make the first race of the season.

4

Sports Cars – Rallies From 1926 to the Present

At the beginning of the century, cars were divided into two general categories: touring and racing. Sports cars were defined as cars intended for normal use but which had better performance, mainly because of modifications to the engine. The form of the body and the preparation of the cab also became important features for differentiating sports cars from the touring cars from which they originated.

It was with the Le Mans 24 Hour that specific requirements began to be established and that sports cars acquired a status of their own. However, competitors in that race, which later was to have an enormous influence on the progress of technology, had a completely free hand over compression ratio, weight, shape and material of the connecting rods and pistons, valve diameter and lift, transmission, brakes, type and make of the electrical equipment, capacity of the fuel and lubricant tanks, and type of cooling fluid for the engine.

The Le Mans 24 Hour regulations were extended to cover all other sports car events. It was specified that the body of a sports car must be completely finished without any temporary parts, that there must be a cab capable of taking at least two seats with the backs 25 cm (10 in) high, a space for the driver's feet of at least 25 cm (10 in) in breadth, and a stiff door 40 cm (1 ft 4 in) in width with a hinging and closing mechanism. In this way the structure, form and essence of a competition car were specifically outlined, clearly distinguishing the sports car from a true racing car. The primary feature differentiating them was and is the uncovered front wheels of the racing car, though occasionally the wheels have been faired when it was permitted.

Modern regulations governing sports car racing stipulate that for a race to count toward the Marque's World Championship it must last between 6 and 12 hours—another indication of the grueling tests these cars go through. They are certainly worthy of such legendary races as the Le Mans 24 Hour, the Targa Florio, the Tourist Trophy, and the Mille Miglia. *(continued on page 135)*

Maserati 26 1926: 8 cylinders, 1,492.6 cc, 125 bhp at 5,300 rpm

Lancia D 24 Carrera 1954: 8 cylinders, 3,284 cc, 265 bhp at 6,500 rpm

AC Cobra Ford 1963: 8 cylinders, 4,942 cc, 260 bhp

Gulf Ford GT 40 1968: 8 cylinders, 4,736 cc, 306 bhp

Porsche 908/3000 1969: 8 cylinders, 2,997 cc, 320 bhp

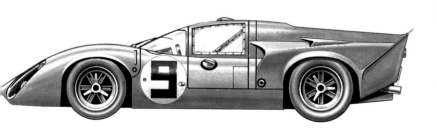

Lola T 70 S 1970: 8 cylinders, 4,992 cc, 500 bhp at 6,600 rpm

Fiat Abarth 3000 1970: 8 cylinders, 2,966 cc, 350 bhp at 8,200 rpm

Porsche 917/30 1973: 12 cylinders, 5,400 cc, 1,100 bhp

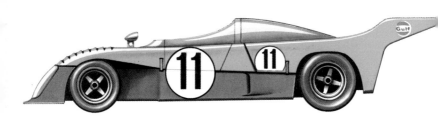

Gulf GR 8 1975: 8 cylinders, 2,995 cc, 370 bhp

The developments in bodywork and the search for improved aerodynamic coefficients have made sports cars faster and much more economical than Formula 1 single-seaters. It is significant that the most important recent innovation made on Formula 1 cars, the turbocharged engine, was initially tried out on sports cars (Renault and Porsche). Reducing fuel consumption has been one of the more important rules to which sports cars have been subjected, particularly at Le Mans. The celebrated French race has also been instrumental in seeking the solution to various fundamental problems in the use of cars, such as lighting at night and the effective operation of windshield wipers.

The series of prescriptions put into effect at Le Mans over the years (modified, sometimes abandoned and later, no less often, reinstated) constitute, in effect, a rule book for the makers of sports cars. For the post-war period it is sufficient to mention the admission of turbocharged engines since 1953; a limitation on the capacity of fuel tanks; the requirement to cover a specified number of laps before being allowed to top off with oil and water; and the insistence on a proper windshield, on a minimum width of the cab, a minimum height of the car off the ground and a minimum turning radius.

Marko-Van Lennep's average of 222.304 km per hour (138.163 mph) in the 1971 Le Mans, which is still unsurpassed, is particularly impressive. Not only was it achieved in a race of such length, but it has only rarely been exceeded in the much shorter Formula 1 races.

Without a doubt, technical progress has been due more to sports cars than to Formula 1 cars.

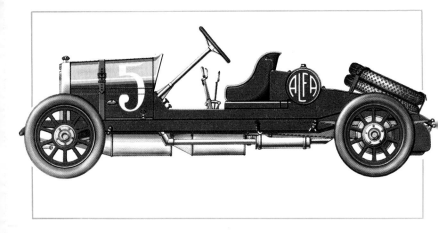

The 24 HP was the foundation of what was later to become Alfa Romeo. The company that produced the A.L.F.A. (Anonima Lombarda Fabbrica di Automobili) had very different aims from those that would later typify Alfa Romeo. It had been founded, with a base in Naples, to assemble the French Darracq cars. This company subsequently moved to Milan, but commercially it was a failure. The Società Italiana Automobili Darracq would almost certainly have disappeared had not a group of partners and the Banca Agricola Milanese, which guaranteed the capital (500,000 lire), continued the business under a new name, A.L.F.A.. As its badge it chose the cross of Milan and the snake of the Visconti. Giuseppe Merosi was placed at the head of its technical office even though he was not an engineer, but a surveyor. His technical competence, however, was beyond dispute, a fact he had amply demonstrated in other factories.

The first A.L.F.A. was the 24 HP, which had a monobloc engine and shaft drive.

Car: **A.L.F.A. 24 HP**
Maker: **A.L.F.A.**
Year: **1910**
Class: **Sports-Tourer**
Engine: **4-cylinder in-line monobloc**
Bore × Stroke: **100 × 130 mm**
Capacity: **4,084 cc**
Power: **42 bhp at 2,200 rpm; 45 bhp at 2,400 rpm; 49 bhp at 2,400 rpm**

Although in its most highly tuned version it developed 49 bhp at 2,400 rpm, it had not been designed for sporting purposes. However, since in those days races were the best means of publicity, it was inevitable that the 24 HP should be entered in competitions. Its racing debut was in the 1911 Targa Florio, and it only just missed a sensational victory. A.L.F.A.'s chief test driver, Nino Franchini, led for two of the race's three laps, and he was forced to drop out only because he was blinded by a spray of mud. Production of the 24 HP continued, with no significant variations, until 1913.

The Super Sport was one of the many variations of tourers built on the RL chassis that entered production in 1920. The Super Sport and the Sport were fairly similar. In fact the manufacturers designated the cars produced from the first to the fifth series as Sports and those of the sixth and seventh series Super Sports. Luigi Fusi, the highly informative historian of Alfa, provides even more precise details for identifying the two types of car. He states that from the first to the sixth series the leaf spring support was rigid with the axle. In addition, there were no front brakes on cars of the first and second series, only expansion band rear brakes. From the third series (September 1923) onward, there were internally expanding front and rear brakes. From the seventh series (1926) onward, the diameter of the front and rear brake drums increased from 360 mm (14.17 in) to 420 mm (16.54 in).

The Sport and the Super Sport (both made in torpedo, berline, and spyder versions) were powered by the same

Car: **Alfa Romeo RL Super Sport**
Maker: **Alfa Romeo**
Year: **1922**
Class: **Sport**
Engine: **6-cylinder in-line, cast-iron monobloc**
Bore × Stroke: **76 × 110 mm**
Capacity: **2,994 cc**
Power: **83 bhp at 3,600 rpm**

6-cylinder as the standard RL (up to and including the fifth series). However, they had an increased capacity (2,994 cc), achieved by slightly expanding the bore (from 75 to 76 mm). It developed 71 bhp at 3,600 rpm and had a top speed of 130 km per hour (80.8 mph).

A combined total of 537 units of both types was produced. The chassis sold for 36,000 lire and the complete car for 56,000 lire. The lines of the bodywork (the torpedo version is illustrated), with the V radiator, were among the most attractive of the period and helped to make the RL a popular and sought-after model.

Alfa Romeo has concentrated mainly on sports models. The RL, which was begun in 1920 in answer to the 3,000 cc, 800 kg (1,764 lb) minimum weight formula, is one of the most famous of its many products. The new formula came into force in 1921 and lasted just one year. The RL, which ought to have suffered a no less rapid demise, continued to be built until 1927, with a record production for that time of 2,640 units.

The first version of the RL appeared in 1921; and two types, the normal and the sport, went into production simultaneously. It had a straight-6, cast-iron monobloc engine that developed 56 bhp at 3,200 rpm in the normal version and 71 bhp at 3,500 rpm in the sports model. In 1923 a number of special RLs were prepared for the fourteenth Targa Florio; they achieved excellent results, coming in first, second, and fourth. By slightly increasing the bore, the capacity was raised from 2,994 cc to 3,154 cc and the power output reached 95 bhp at 3,800 rpm.

Car: **Alfa Romeo RL Targa Florio**
Maker: **Alfa Romeo**
Year: **1923**
Class: **Sport**
Engine: **6-cylinder in-line, cast-iron monobloc**
Bore × Stroke: **78 × 110 mm**
Capacity: **3,154 cc**
Power: **95 bhp at 3,800 rpm**

The success of 1923 led Alfa Romeo to prepare an even more powerful car for 1924. It had a 3,620 cc engine that developed 125 bhp at 3,800 rpm. Four of these cars were produced; all were two-seater racing style spyders, and two of them had 2,994 cc engines. A feature of the 1924 RL was its V radiator. The cars performed brilliantly. Antonio Ascari would have won his race had he not braked sharply a hundred yards from the finish, stalling his engine. He was unable to restart it, and the car was pushed over the finishing line—but too late. Alfa Romeo had to be content with second, third, fifth, and tenth places.

The Bentley 4500 began as a racing car to replace the then obsolete 3000, which was no longer able to compete with the Sunbeam of the same capacity.

Announced in June 1927, it was a re-working of the 3000 and had a top speed of 136 km per hour (84.5 mph). Its engine was derived from the 6-cylinder, 6,500 cc, retaining the same layout—minus two cylinders—with the same bore and stroke. It developed 110 bhp at 3,500 rpm. There was also a version with a supercharged engine (240 bhp at 4,200 rpm), but it was not built by the factory since William Owen Bentley was op-posed to the supercharger. The Bentley 4500 was the work principally of Sir Henry Birkin, and it was intended above all for the Le Mans 24 Hour. Despite the power of its engine, it never won a race. A unique feature of this car was that the supercharger was installed at the front, just behind the radiator.

Between 1928 and 1931, 733 of the 4500s were built, 273 of them in the first year. Although mainly intended for rac-

Car: **Bentley 4500**
Maker: **Bentley**
Year: **1928**
Class: **Sport**
Engine: **4-cylinder in-line**
Bore × Stroke: **100 × 140 mm**
Capacity: **4,398 cc**
Power: **110 bhp at 3,500 rpm**

ing, the 4500 was fitted with various body styles to adapt it for other uses.

Its place in history was secured mainly by its victory at the 1928 Le Mans 24 Hour. Wolf Barnato and Bernard Rubin beat the American Stutz of Brisson-Bloch by a narrow margin, and Birkin came in fifth. That year's Le Mans was of particu-lar interest because four American cars had entered, a Stutz and three Chryslers.

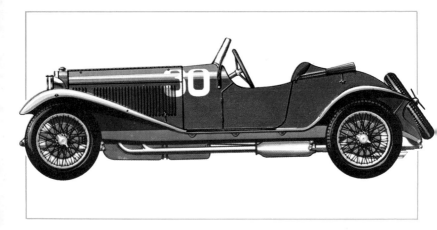

The birth of this car was the direct consequence of the successes, indeed triumphs, achieved by the P2. Vittorio Jano, who had only recently joined Alfa Romeo, had created the P2, whose exceptional performance had reasserted the factory's name in the sporting field. He then persuaded the Milanese firm to produce a sports car that combined a modest capacity, for its period, with brilliant performance. Jano did not choose a 4-cylinder engine but a 1,487 cc straight-6 with overhead valves. In the standard version the engine developed 44 bhp at 4,200 rpm with a compression ratio of 5.75:1. Initially it was designated the N.R. and was unveiled in April 1925 at the Motor Show, held that year in Milan. Deliveries to the public began in 1927. In 1928 the company produced the 6C 1500 Sport (54 bhp at 4,500 rpm) and the 6C 1500 Super Sport, which had a fixed cylinder head (84 bhp at 5,000 rpm). In 1929 the Super Sport appeared (76 bhp at 4,800 rpm with supercharger, 60 bhp without).

Car: **Alfa Romeo 6C 1500 Super Sport**
Maker: **Alfa Romeo**
Year: **1929**
Class: **Sport**
Engine: **6-cylinder in-line**
Bore × Stroke: **62 × 82 mm**
Capacity: **1,487 cc**
Power: **60 bhp without supercharger; 76 bhp with supercharger at 4,800 rpm; 84 bhp with fixed cylinder head at 5,000 rpm**

The 6C 1500 Super Sport began what was to become an outstanding career by taking Campari-Ramponi to victory in the second Mille Miglia (1928). This car, with bodywork built by Zagato, covered the 1,600 km (994 miles) of the race at an average of 84.128 km per hour (52.286 mph), a considerable improvement over the average of Minoia-Morandi in an O.M. in 1927.

A feature worth mentioning in all of the 6C Super Sport versions was the favorable power-to-weight ratio. The 6C Super Sport with a fixed cylinder head weighed 860 kg (1,896 lb), including the two spare wheels.

As always happens, a successful model becomes the basis for a series of variations and adaptations. The 6C gave rise to the 1750, in all its many versions. This car in its turn achieved considerable success, establishing itself as the best car in its class of that period. Jano's skill lay in extracting a greater amount of power from the 6-cylinder through a relatively modest increase in capacity and with little or no increase in the car's weight. The range of variations began with the Tourer (46 bhp at 4,000 rpm), which weighed a total of 1,250 kg (2,756 lb), inclusive of two spare wheels. Next in line were the Grand Tourer and the Grand Sport (85 bhp at 4,500 rpm), which weighed 920 kg (2,028 lb) with two spare wheels, and the Super Sport and Grand Sport with fixed cylinder head (95 bhp at 4,800 rpm). There was also a supercharged Grand Tourer (80 bhp at 4,400 rpm) as well as a 6C 1900 Grand Tourer Sixth Series (1933).

Jano moved from one model to the next in a whirl of innovations and updat-

Car: **Alfa Romeo 6C 1750 GS**
Maker: **Alfa Romeo**
Year: **1929**
Class: **Sport**
Engine: **6-cylinder in-line**
Bore × Stroke: **65 × 88 mm**
Capacity: **1,752 cc**
Power: **85 bhp at 4,500 rpm; 95 bhp at 4,800 rpm with a fixed cylinder head**

ing. Incredibly, the 1750 made its debut in the 1929 Mille Miglia, just one year after the 6C 1500 had won the same race. Perhaps not even today could sports car makers equal Jano's feats.

Alfa Romeo produced a total of 1,075 of the 6C 1500 and 2,579 of the 6C 1750 models. These two cars earned such a reputation for performance and reliability that Alfa Romeo's factory was flooded with orders from all over the world.

The 8C 2300 was the natural development of the 6C, prompted by the need to improve performance in a sector, that of sports cars, where it was continually climbing. When using a successful model as a starting point, it is usual to increase rather than to decrease the capacity (Alfa Romeo went from the 1500 to the 1750).

The close relationship between the 1500–1750 and the 2300, even though the latter had a straight-8 engine, is shown by the fact that the 2300 adopted the same bore and stroke as the 6C 1750. The capacity was increased by adding 2 extra cylinders to the 6 plus a centrally driven valve gear. The cylinder block consisted of two light-alloy half blocks, with the cylinder head also divided in two. The supercharger was placed on the right-hand side. As was then normal practice for Alfa Romeo, the 8C 2300 was built in numerous versions (short and long chassis, spyder, racer, Monza, Le Mans). It began with a power output of 142 bhp at 5,000 rpm and rose to a maximum of 180 bhp at 5,400 in the

Car: **Alfa Romeo 8C 2300**
Maker: **Alfa Romeo**
Year: **1931**
Class: **Sport**
Engine: **8-cylinder in-line**
Bore × Stroke: **65 × 88 mm**
Capacity: **2,336 cc**
Power: **142 bhp at 5,000 rpm**

Le Mans. The single-seater Monza 8C developed 165 bhp and later 178 bhp at 5,400 rpm.

Like its parent, the 8C was highly successful despite a disappointing debut in the 1931 Mille Miglia. However, it went on to prove itself immediately afterward by taking Tazio Nuvolari to victory in the Targa Florio and Howe-Birkin in the Le Mans 24 Hour.

The SSKL did not originate as a sports car but as a tourer and, as such, was the first Mercedes model to have a super-charged engine. However, it had been used by Rudolf Caracciola as far back as 1925 in sprint and endurance races. In 1926 Mercedes produced a sports ver-sion with a shortened chassis (wheel-base 3.34m/l0 ft 11.5 in), four doors, an open top, and a windshield divided in half. It was designated the 24/100/140 K. Various modifications to the engine were tested in racing and from 1927 onward were incorporated in production. The power output without a supercharger rose to 110 bhp at 2,800 rpm and with one increased to 160 bhp at 3,000 rpm. The S (Sport) version also came into production in the same year. It had the same wheelbase and track as the K; but the chassis was totally altered, the en-gine being moved back more than 30 cm (1 ft). The engine itself was also modified (bore 98 mm, stroke 150 mm, and a capacity of 6,789 cc). It developed 120 bhp at 2,800 rpm and 180 bhp at 3,000

Car: **Mercedes SSKL**
Maker: **Mercedes**
Year: **1931**
Class: **Sport**
Engine: **6-cylinder in-line, supercharged and not**
Bore × Stroke: **100 × 150 mm**
Capacity: **7,069 cc**
Power: **140–160 bhp at 2,800 rpm (normally aspirated); 200 bhp at 3,000 rpm (super-charged)**

rpm. When fueled by benzene and with a higher compression ratio, the power out-put rose to 220 bhp. In 1928 the engine was further modified: bore 100 mm, stroke 150 mm, capacity 7,069 cc, com-pression ratio 4.7:1 and 5.2:1, power output 140 bhp and 160 bhp without supercharger and 200 bhp with. In 1931 it was made still lighter (125 kg/275.6 lb) and more powerful (170 bhp at 3,200 rpm, 225 bhp with supercharger at 3,000 rpm and 275 bhp with a larger super-charger becoming the SSKL). In that year Caracciola won the Tourist Trophy and the Spa 24 Hour, and came in second in the Le Mans 24 Hour. With Sebastian he captured the Mille Miglia at Ayus and won twice at Nürburgring.

Officially classified as a Grand Sport by the Molsheim factory, the 55 replaced the 43. It was powered by a Type 51 racing car engine, while its chassis was derived from the Type 54. However, the twin overhead camshaft engine developed 135 bhp instead of the 51's 180 bhp and had a maximum speed of 180 km per hour (112 mph). It could go from zero to 100 km per hour (62 mph) in 13 seconds and hit 160 km per hour (99 mph) in the space of 400 meters (437 yards).

Together with the Alfa Romeo 2300, the Bugatti 55 was regarded as one of the most brilliant sports cars of its period. Yet even the most devoted admirers of the 55 and of Bugattis in general were forced to admit that the Alfa Romeo 2300 was tougher, more adaptable, with superior road holding. The 55 was an extremely beautiful car; the two-tone color scheme and lack of doors emphasized its long, elegant lines. The 55's color scheme was inspired, perhaps unwittingly, by the celebrated American Duesenberg.

Car: **Bugatti 55**
Maker: **Bugatti**
Year: **1932**
Class: **Sport**
Engine: **8-cylinder in-line**
Bore × Stroke: **60 × 100 mm**
Capacity: **2,270 cc**
Power: **135 bhp at 5,000 rpm**

Most 55s were built as spyders, but a few had cabriolet bodies. In any case only a limited number were built, partly because the car was launched in the markets of Europe when economic times were hard. It is estimated that only 38 were produced. The most highly regarded historians of Bugatti mentioned this car only briefly, not so much because of its limited production but because it did not rank among the firm's most successful models.

The Pescara was named after the city on Italy's Adriatic Coast and, more specifically, after the 24 Hour which took place in 1934 on its circuit. The 6C achieved a resounding success in it, sweeping the first three places.

This year was a fertile period for ideas and products. The Alfa Romeo technical department also undertook a more direct development of the 6C 1750 (a special 1,900 cc version had already been produced) than the one which led to the 8C. In the 8C version the bore and particularly the stroke of the 6C's engine were increased.

The 6C Pescara had a cast-iron crankcase with a single cylinder block that had 6-cylinder bores and a light alloy cylinder head. Other prominent features of the car, which was unveiled in Milan in April 1934, were the synchromesh third and fourth speeds of the gearbox and the free wheel. It was produced as an extra light four-seater berline (Touring). It weighed 1,280 kg (2,822 lb), had a top speed of 145 km per hour (90 mph), and the en-

Car: **Alfa Romeo 6C Pescara**
Maker: **Alfa Romeo**
Year: **1934**
Class: **Sport Grand Tourer**
Engine: **6-cylinder in-line**
Bore × Stroke: **70 × 100 mm**
Capacity: **2,309 cc**
Power: **95 bhp at 4,500 rpm**

gine developed 95 bhp at 4,500 rpm.

The car's tremendous success in the Abruzzan 24 Hour in which Cortese-Severi, Tadini-Barbieri, and Rosa-Comotti took the first three places encouraged Alfa Romeo to produce a small run (60) of the cars. While the six-seven seater Castagna berline (225 were produced) cost 44,500 lire and the Alfa berline cost 41,500 lire, the Pescara was sold at 50,500 lire. The 6C was also produced in semirigid (Touring) and cabriolet (Castagna) versions, which sold for 42,500 lire and 45,000 lire, respectively.

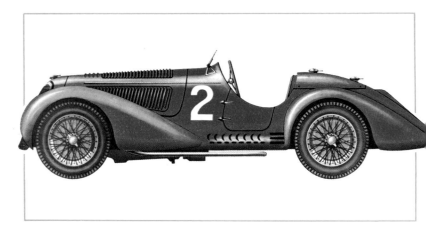

There were three successive stages to the 8C. It began with a 2,300 cc engine (bore 65 mm, stroke 88 mm, and a total capacity of 2,336 cc). The capacity was then raised to 2,556 cc (bore 68 mm, stroke 88 mm) and in 1934 raised again to 2,905 cc (bore 68 mm, stroke 100 mm). The engine was fed by two superchargers and by two up-draft carburetors; it developed 180 bhp at 5,200 rpm.

There were essentially two kinds of body, the spyder and the coupé. The spyder was built by both Touring and Pininfarina while only Touring built the coupé. The wheelbases of the spyder and the coupé differed by 20 cm (7.9 in) (2.80 m to 3 m/9 ft 2.2 in to 9 ft 9.9 in), respectively, giving rise to the 8C 2900 Corto (short) and 8C 2900 Lungo (long) models. These two models were begun in 1936 and built between 1937 and 1939, benefiting from experience gained in the field of superchargers (the Type B single-seater of 1934) and in the field of suspension and brakes (1935 racing cars, which continued to be built until

Car: **Alfa Romeo 8C 2900**
Maker: **Alfa Romeo**
Year: **1936**
Class: **Sport**
Engine: **8-cylinder in-line**
Bore × Stroke: **68 × 100 mm**
Capacity: **2,905 cc**
Power: **180 bhp at 5,200 rpm**

1937). In 1934 an 8C 2900 Corsa, designated the A, had been designed. It provided the inspiration for the 8C 2900 Corto and the 8C 2900 Lungo, the latter two also being designated 2900 Bs. In the A of 1934 the power output was 220 bhp at 5,300 rpm and the compression ratio 6.5:1, as opposed to 5.75:1 for the others. The 2900 A made its debut in 1936 by winning the tenth Mille Miglia. The drivers were Varzi and Bignami. Eventually, two variations of the A were built. The one used in Grand Prix racing had the fuel tank in the tail and the spare wheel at the side. The other version had the fuel tank in the tail and a rear-mounted spare wheel, a solution used in Touring's spyder.

The 6C 2300 Mille Miglia was born out of the participation of a 6C 2300 B, with a new Touring bodystyle, in the 1937 running of the famous Brescian race. The car came in fourth overall, winning the Tourer category. The B was begun in the wake of the successes gained by the 2300 right from its first appearance. The B differed from the 2300 in having a mechanical rather than electrical fuel pump; synchromesh third and fourth gears; and silent, constant mesh second, third, and fourth gears. Further modifications were made to the transmission (new flexible couplings) and to the rear axle. The Mille Miglia was alone in having spoked wheels. Two series were built.

The 6C 2300 is probably the Alfa Romeo that has been successful in the greatest number of models. Its most everyday version was a six/seven-seater berline with a body built by Alfa Romeo itself. There was also a Grand Tourer constructed entirely at Portello. All the best-known coachbuilders of the period (the Farina, Castagna, and Touring

Car: **Alfa Romeo 6C 2300 Mille Miglia**
Maker: **Alfa Romeo**
Year: **1937**
Class: **Sport**
Engine: **6-cylinder in-line**
Bore × Stroke: **70 × 100 mm**
Capacity: **2,309 cc**
Power: **95 bhp at 4,500 rpm; 105 bhp at 4,800 rpm**

workshops) produced their own versions based on the 6C 2300 chassis. They created highly compact and elegant cars. Today these are among the most sought-after models in the highly active period-car market. The version illustrated above is a magnificent example of the close relationship between the 2300 and its intended use. This version, the Mille Miglia, was one of its most successful models. Note the spoked wheels and the streamlined shaping of the mudguards; this foreshadows the continuous, pontoon-side type of the immediate post-war period.

The 6C 2500 constitutes the link between the pre-war models and those of the immediate post-war period. Work on it had begun in 1939 with the intention of producing a replacement for the 6C 2300 by slightly increasing its capacity (the bore was raised from 70 to 72 mm) and improving the feed (a single twin-choke, down-draft carburetor in place of two carburetors). As was traditional for Alfa Romeo, several versions of the 2500 were produced. First came the five-seater Tourer and the six/seven-seater Tourer with a wheelbase of 3.25 m (10 ft 8 in) and bodywork built by Alfa Romeo itself. This version was followed by a five-seater Sport with a body built by outside coachbuilders and a wheelbase of 3.00 m (9 ft 10 in), and by the Super Sport with custom-built coachwork and a wheelbase of 2.70 m (8 ft 10 in).

In the two berlines the engine developed 87 bhp at 4,600 rpm; in the Sport, 95 bhp at 6,400 rpm; and in the Super Sport 110 bhp at 4,600 rpm. The SS Racer (Corsa) was prepared for the 1940

Car: **Alfa Romeo 6C 2500 SS**
Maker: **Alfa Romeo**
Year: **1940**
Class: **Sport**
Engine: **6-cylinder in-line**
Bore × Stroke: **72 × 100 mm**
Capacity: **2,443 cc**
Power: **110 bhp at 4,600 rpm**

Mille Miglia; the power output was raised to 125 bhp at 4,800 rpm. In that year, the Mille Miglia was raced over a special course (Brescia-Cremona-Mantua) and was won by a BMW. The Alfa 6C 2500 SS Racer (Corsa) acquitted itself very well, coming in second, fourth, seventh, and eighth overall. This racing version had bodywork built exclusively by Touring, one constructed as a berline and the others as spyders.

The production of the Sport and Super Sport models, and later the Tourers, was resumed after the war, when they were known as Golden Arrows. The principal difference between these cars and the pre-war models was that the Golden Arrows had the gearshift set beneath the steering wheel.

The 125 S was the first product of the Modena firm to bear the name Ferrari. It was designed by Gioacchino Colombo and made its racing debut on May 5, 1947 at Piacenza, with Franco Cortese at the wheel. It was in the lead when a broken fuel pump forced it to drop out. It made good some time later by winning the Rome Grand Prix on the Caracalla circuit, with Cortese again at the wheel.

The 125 was powered by a 12-cylinder (1,500 cc) engine, which developed 72 bhp at 5,600 rpm and had a compression ratio of 8:1. The engine was a light alloy monobloc with a single chain-driven camshaft, hemispherical combustion chambers, seven main bearings, two valves per cylinder, and three Weber 30 DCF carburetors. The five-speed transmission had synchromesh third and fourth gears. The chassis had tubular side members, independent front suspension with a lower transverse leaf spring, and a rigid rear axle.

Already before the end of 1947 the 125 had a sister, the 159 S, a 12-cylinder of

Car: **Ferrari 125 S**
Maker: **Ferrari**
Year: **1947**
Class: **Sport**
Engine: **60° V-12**
Bore × Stroke: **55 × 52.5 mm**
Capacity: **1,496.77 cc**
Power: **100 bhp at 7,000 rpm**

about 2,000 cc. The numbers of the two cars reflected the individual cylinder capacities of their engines (124.73 cc in the first case and 158.57 cc in the second). This system of nomenclature was retained for a period of time and then replaced by one based upon the number of cylinders and the capacity divided by 100. For example, 625 had 6 cylinders and a capacity of 2,500 cc, and the 312 had a capacity of 3,000 cc and 12 cylinders.

The 166 was the first of Ferrari's vast number of products to make the Modena marque's name known the world over. It gained a number of prestigious victories, beginning with Clemente Biondetti's in the 1948 Mille Miglia. The same car and driver won the following year's Mille Miglia; and the 166, driven by Luigi Chinetti and Lord Selsdon, also won a Le Mans 24 Hour, the first one after the war.

The 166, like its older sisters, took its distinguishing number from the capacity of the individual cylinders of the engine, a 12-cylinder of just under 2,000 cc. Although it was derived from Gioacchino Colombo's first 12-cylinder, there were already structural differences between it and the 12-cylinder 159 of about the same capacity. The 159 was virtually square (bore 59 mm, stroke 58 mm) while the 166 was oversquare (bore 60 mm, stroke 58.8 mm).

Another important feature of the 166 was the existence of various diverse types (S, F 2, Inter, MM, FL), each intended for a particular use. The S was

Car: **Ferrari 166 S**
Maker: **Ferrari**
Year: **1948**
Class: **Sport**
Engine: **60° V-12**
Bore × Stroke: **60 × 58.8 mm**
Capacity: **1,995.02 cc**
Power: **150 bhp at 7,000 rpm**

used principally for sports car racing. The F 2 was Ferrari's first "cadet" single-seater. The Inter took its name from the annual race held at Monza, the MM from its double victory in the Mille Miglia, and the FL from the open formula (formula libre) races in which it competed. The engines of the various types differed substantially in terms of engine speeds (the lowest being the Inter's 6,000 rpm and the highest 7,000), compression ratios (8:1 in the Inter and 8.5:1 in the others) and power outputs (from 115 bhp of the Inter to 310 bhp of the FL).

This car, which has left a permanent impression on the history of the English marque, was born almost by chance. With an eye to launching the Mark VII, Sir William Lyons, Jaguar's founder, had a number of extra chassis built. A sports version, called the XK, was produced for the purposes of publicity or promotion. The venture was intended to be only a minor part of the Jaguar production program, but the public's enthusiastic welcome of the XK 120 led Sir William to change his plans. The public was attracted not only by the inspired lines of the car but also by its finishings and outstanding performance, due principally to the twin overhead camshaft engine. Another attraction was its ability to reach 200 km per hour (124 mph) at a time when the vast majority of production cars could achieve only 130 km per hour (81 mph).

Production continued for six years and reached a total of about 12,000 cars. The XK 120 was then followed by the 140 and the 150, which were gradually updated,

Car: **Jaguar XK 120**
Maker: **Jaguar**
Year: **1951**
Class: **Sport**
Engine: **6-cylinder in-line**
Bore × Stroke: **83 × 106 mm**
Capacity: **3,442 cc**
Power: **160 bhp at 5,000 rpm**

particularly with regard to the brakes. Jaguars, as is well known, were the first production cars to have disc brakes. This development was the result of a favorable experience at Le Mans.

The XK 120 was not a true racing car. However, it did enable quite a few amateurs to engage in their favorite sport with a car which, at the same time, was perfectly suitable for more ordinary driving.

Production ceased in 1961. It was replaced by the E Type, which also earned a good reputation and opened up export markets to Jaguar.

Briggs Cunningham, a multi-millionaire, was responsible for building this car, in addition to others bearing the same name. He became known in racing circles when, in 1950, he entered two Cadillacs for the Le Mans 24 Hour. One, a spyder, was driven by· himself and Walters; the other, a berline, was driven by Sam and Miles Collier. Both were powered by a 5,439 cc, 8-cylinder. The berline came in tenth and the spyder eleventh, each having covered more than 3,000 km (1,865 miles). In the following year Cunningham came to Le Mans with three sports cars powered by 5,425 cc Chrysler V-8 engines. These were driven by Walters-Fitch, Rand-Wacker, and by himself and Huntoon. Cunningham had in fact become a maker, and these cars bore his name.

He returned to Le Mans in 1952, this time with three C4Rs, which had tubular chassis and De Dion rear axles. They were driven by Walters-Carter, Fitch-Rice, and Cunningham-Spear. The latter pair did well, coming in fourth overall.

Car: **Cunningham C4R**
Maker: **Cunningham**
Year: **1952**
Class: **Sport**
Engine: **Chrysler V-8**
Bore × Stroke: **96.8 × 92.1 mm**
Capacity: **5,425 cc**
Power: **300 bhp at 5,200 rpm**

Walters and Fitch came in fourth with the C5R in the 1953 Le Mans, and Spear and Johnson came in fourth in the same race in the following year with a C4R. In that year Cunningham and Bennett, who were also driving a C4R, came in fifth.

Although Cunningham was particularly loyal to the French race, he never managed to reach the front rank. However, he did gain an overall victory in the 1953 Sebring 12 Hour with a C4R driven by Fitch-Walters. He always used Chrysler engines, but for the C6R changed to a 3,000 Meyer & Drake 4-cylinder. The C6R competed in the 1955 Le Mans 24 Hour but was forced to retire in the thirteenth hour because of engine failure.

Begun in 1952, this car was derived from the prototype 6C 3000 C 50 prepared for the 1950 Mille Miglia. The engine capacities differed substantially, having been increased from 2,995 cc to 3,495 cc and the power output rising from 168 bhp at 6,200 rpm to 246 bhp at 6,500 rpm. The 1953 car, incorrectly classed as a 3000, was also intended for sports car racing. Three were entered in that year's Mille Miglia, and one of them came in second. In the same year Juan Manuel Fangio drove another one to victory in the Supercortemaggiore Grand Prix at Merano.

The 6C 3000 has an important place in Alfa Romeo's history as it marked the end of the Milan factory's direct involvement in racing. After a long break, in 1964, Alfa Romeo resumed activity with the designing of the 33.2. This resumption was the start of a new policy by the Milan factory, one that saw its return to Formula 1. Between the 6C 3000 and the 33.2 a number of sports car prototypes were produced but never got beyond the

Car: **Alfa Romeo 6C 3000**
Maker: **Alfa Romeo**
Year: **1953**
Class: **Sport**
Engine: **6-cylinder in-line**
Bore × Stroke: **87 × 98 mm**
Capacity: **3,495 cc**
Power: **246 bhp at 6,500 rpm**

experimental stage. At that time Alfa Romeo was committed to mass-produced cars. Among the lost sports cars were the 2000 Sportivo (sports) of 1954 (138 bhp at 6,500 rpm) and the Prototipo 750 Competizione (prototype 750 competition), a 1,500 cc machine (145 bhp at 8,000 rpm). A peculiar feature of both these cars was that they were powered by a 4-cylinder engine. The Milan factory had not used such an engine since the Alfa 20/30 ES of 1921. The marked supremacy of mass production over sports design and manufacture in the post-war period led to the predominance of the 4-cylinder engine.

First of all, the long and seemingly obscure name of this car deserves an explanation. "A" probably stood for the beginning of the series, "6" for the number of cylinders (in line), "G" for ghisa (cast iron), which was the metal that the monobloc engine was made of, "C" for Competizione (competition/racing), and "S" for Sport. The A 6GCS appeared in April 1947, and deliveries to customers began in 1948. The long delay was attributed to the uncertainties caused by the departure of the Maserati brothers from the Modena factory. Initially, the Orsi were inclined to cease sports car manufacture; but Omer managed to convince his father, Adolfo, of the advantage of such production.

The first A 6GCS, a coupé, was entrusted to Luigi Villoresi and made its debut in the 1947 Mille Miglia. On that occasion a broken valve forced it to retire. Later in the same year its body, which was the work of Fantuzzi, acquired its final shape with classic bicycle style mudguards that wrapped around the wheels.

Car: **Maserati A 6GCS**
Maker: **Maserati**
Year: **1953**
Class: **Sport**
Engine: **6-cylinder in-line**
Bore × Stroke: **72 × 80 mm**
Capacity: **1,978 cc**
Power: **130 bhp at 6,000 rpm**

The fact that the mudguards could be removed easily led to speculation that Maserati intended to use the A 6GCS as both a sports car and a Formula 2. This was not in fact the case, and the car appeared as a Formula 2 in only a single race, at Reims in 1948. In its proper guise as a sports car, the A 6GCS was introduced at the Circuito di Modena (Modena Circuit) in 1947 and, driven by Ascari and Villoresi, it came in first and second. Substantial modifications were made in 1950, and in 1952 the A 6GCSM single-seater version was produced. The cars won several victories in both classes, considerably boosting the morale and fortunes of Maserati.

One of the many models built by Porsche, the RS 1500 has an unusual history. The engine was intended for a racing car and was called the "spyder" to distinguish it from other engines, already in production, which had the same capacity. The name did not refer to a model with an open-topped body, but indicated instead that it was a four overhead camshaft engine. The car that it powered was designated the 550. This model had a tubular chassis, two seats, a light alloy body, a four-speed transmission, and torsion bar front suspension.

The 550 was presented to the public at the 1953 Paris Motor Show after having been tested, with a disguised body, in the trials that took place that year at Nürburgring for a sports car race that preceded the German Grand Prix. Hans Herrmann was the driver on its first outing. Herrmann, an American importer of Porsches, wanted the car to have a name as well as a number; he decided that "spyder" would be suitable. In time, the name "spyder" no longer applied just to

Car: **Porsche RS 1500**
Maker: **Porsche**
Year: **1953**
Class: **Sport**
Engine: **4-cylinder boxer**
Bore × Stroke: **85 × 66 mm**
Capacity: **1,498 cc**
Power: **135 bhp at 7,200 rpm**

the model's engine but to the whole car; and together they passed into history.

It was first raced in the 1954 Mille Miglia. Driven by Hans Herrmann and Hubert Linge, the car won the 1500 class and came in sixth overall—marking the start of a brilliant career. A version of the RS 1500 with a lengthened body, ending in a fin, was also built. This model was intended for the faster circuits, such as the one used for the Le Mans 24 Hour.

Among those English sports cars sold to the public, the Aston Martin DB3S, along with the Jagaur XK 120, has probably left the best memory, thanks to some outstanding results in prestige races such as the Le Mans 24 Hour.

A DB3S came in second overall in the celebrated French race in both 1955 and 1956. Admittedly, in 1955 the results were significantly affected by Mike Hawthorn's hazardous maneuver in his Jaguar, involving Pierre Levegh (Mercedes) and Lance Macklin (Austin-Healey) in a three-car collision. The other two Mercedes (Fangio-Moss and Kling-Simon) were retired at two in the morning. For the record Frere-Collins covered a total of 4,073.020 km (2,531.398 miles) at an average of 169.709 km per hour (105.475 mph). Their average speed just beat the overall record, which had been set the year before by the Ferrari 4,954 cc of Gonzales-Trintignant.

In 1956 the DB3S again came in second, this time driven by Moss-Collins, at

Car: **Aston Martin DB3S**
Maker: **Aston Martin**
Year: **1954**
Class: **Sport**
Engine: **6-cylinder in-line**
Bore × Stroke: **82.5 × 89 mm**
Capacity: **2,922 cc**
Power: —

an average of 167.443 km per hour (104.067 mph).

The DBS was a shorter version of the DB3S. It had a straight-6 engine of about 3,000 cc, disc brakes, and a self-locking rear axle. The overall balance of the car was further endorsed when the regulations for the 1955 Le Mans 24 Hour stipulated that refueling could only take place every 32 laps (432 km/268.5 miles) instead of 30 and that the capacity of the fuel tank was to be limited to 200 liters (44 gal). In 1956 refueling stops were spaced further apart (every 34 laps), enforcing a consumption of no more than 26 liters for every 100 km (10.87 mpg).

The D-Type is the most famous of this English marque's sports car racers. Jaguar became involved in racing after considerable hesitation, but it never regretted having taken the step. The firm had set its sights on winning the Le Mans 24 Hour, which, according to the founder of the marque, Sir William Lyons, was a race that best showed off the qualities of the car.

Jaguar won its first victories (1951 and 1953) in the French race with the XK 120. The XK 120 was actually sold to customers, so its successes were that much more important and appreciated. However, Jaguar soon realized that the XK 120 would be unable to achieve much more. They quickly began work on the D-Type, emphasizing the sporting characteristics; it was ready by 1954. In that year it managed only a second place at Le Mans. In fact, victory eluded Rolt-Hamilton, whose main opponents were Gonzales-Trintignant driving a Ferrari 4,954 cc, by a mere hair's breadth. The

Car: **Jaguar D-Type**
Maker: **Jaguar**
Year: **1954**
Class: **Sport**
Engine: **6-cylinder in-line**
Bore × Stroke: **83 × 106 mm**
Capacity: **3,442 cc**
Power: **250 bhp at 6,000 rpm**

English car then took the first three places in the Reims 12 Hour; and a revised and improved version of the D-Type won the Le Mans 24 Hour in 1955, 1956, and 1957. The D-Type stood out because of its engine power (250 bhp) and its monocoque chassis as well as its body, whose streamlined look was greatly admired.

The D-Type was also set apart from the C-Type by its lower weight (about 75 kg/165 lb). The characteristic shape of the body, which has remained a symbol of the Jaguar, was the work not of a stylist but an expert in aerodynamics (Malcolm Sayer). By repeated studies in a wind tunnel he created a minor masterpiece.

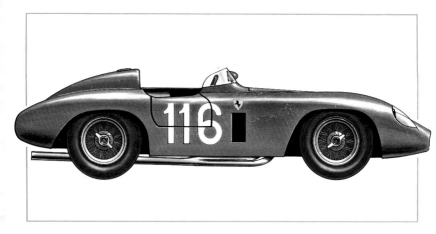

The 750 Monza was one of the most controversial and abused of all Ferrari's cars. It was while driving one of these cars that Alberto Ascari was killed at Monza on May 26, 1955. The circumstances surrounding this accident have never been cleared up and are unlikely to be since there were no witnesses. Only four days before the tragic accident at Monza, Ascari had escaped with nothing more than a bruised nose when his Lancia D 50 spectacularly left the road on the Monte Carlo circuit and plunged into the sea. The short space of time between this nerve-wracking experience and his death is regarded as one of the more likely causes behind his fatal accident. On the other hand, the Belgian driver Olivier Gendebien leveled a strong accusation against the 750 Monza itself. Gendebien had also been in a serious accident while driving this car, during practice for the 1956 Tourist Trophy. According to him, it was very understeered—or at least this was the case with some 750s that had been built be-

Car: **Ferrari 750 Monza**
Maker: **Ferrari**
Year: **1954**
Class: **Sport**
Engine: **4-cylinder in-line**
Bore × Stroke: **103 × 90 mm**
Capacity: **2,999.62 cc**
Power: **260 bhp at 6,400 rpm**

fore modifications were made.

This ill-fated car was powered by a 4-cylinder of about 3,000 cc. It first appeared in 1954, a period when the Modena factory was using 4-cylinder engines. The 750 Monza may be regarded as a twin sister to the 735 S of 1952, which was also powered by a 4-cylinder of about 3,000 cc. The two engines had almost identical bores (735 S: 102 mm, 750 Monza: 103 mm) and the same stroke (90 mm).

The Mercedes racing policy of 1954–55 saw the SLR as a development of the Formula 1 single-seater and, at the same time, a worthy successor to the celebrated SSKL. The German marque's return to racing turned out to be shorter than planned. The cause was a bolt from the blue—the tragedy at Le Mans on June 11, 1955. The Mercedes driven by Pierre Levegh was directly involved in a three-car collision with Mike Hawthorn (Jaguar) and Lance Macklin (Healey).

The 300 SLR used the same engine as the W 196 but with an increased capacity of 2,982 cc. It developed 282 bhp at 7,700 rpm in 1954 and 302 bhp at 7,500 rpm in 1955. The engine was angled at 33° to give a better frontal section and weighed about 232 kg (512 lb). The coupé version of this car featured gull wing doors, which had already been adopted on the 300 SL 6-cylinder.

In the opinion of the drivers and in particular Stirling Moss, this car was both manageable and indestructable at the same time. Moss and Denis Jenkinson

Car: **Mercedes 300 SLR**
Maker: **Mercedes**
Year: **1954**ˋ
Class: **Sport**
Engine: **8-cylinder in-line**
Bore × Stroke: **78 × 78 mm**
Capacity: **2,982 cc**
Power: **282 bhp at 7,700 rpm**

won one of the most important of the 300 SLR's victories, the 1955 Mille Miglia, establishing a new record average that has never been beaten. The version used at Le Mans reached 93 km per hour (58 mph) in first gear, 122 (76 mph) in second, 167 (104 mph) in third, 222 (138 mph) in fourth, and 288 (179 mph) in fifth. At Le Mans and the Swedish Grand Prix at Kristianstad, the 300 SL used air brakes. In the 1955 Mille Miglia the 300 SLR of Moss got less than 3 km per liter of fuel (8.5 mpg).

The 290 MM was another Ferrari to win glory in the Mille Miglia with Castellotti's victory in 1956 and Taruffi's in 1957. In both these years the Brescian race was run under unusual circumstances. In 1956 it took place in appalling weather, and the 1957 race proved to be the last one. It also marked the end of driver Piero Taruffi's career. A 3500 Ferrari of the same type won the 1956 Sebring 12 Hour (Fangio-Castellotti) and the 1,000 km (621.5 miles) at Buenos Aires in 1957 (Gregory-Musso-Castellotti).

On the technical side, the 290 MM marked Ferrari's return to 12-cylinder engines after a brief experiment with 4- and 6-cylinder in-line engines, which were even used on some sports cars. The MM, in its turn, gave rise to the S. This version had the same capacity but developed slightly more power (330 bhp versus 320 bhp) because of an increase in engine speed (8,000 rpm versus 7,300 rpm). Like all its sisters—the second generation 12-cylinders—the 290 was powered by an oversquare engine, the

Car: **Ferrari 290 MM**
Maker: **Ferrari**
Year: **1956**
Class: **Sport**
Engine: **60° V-12**
Bore × Stroke: **73 × 69.5 mm**
Capacity: **3,490.61 cc**
Power: **320 bhp at 7,300 rpm**

bore being much greater than the stroke (73 × 69.5 mm). It took its name from the capacity of the individual cylinders (290.88 cc). Interestingly enough, though a large number of engines with widely different characteristics were built, the 290 MM and S were the only 3500s put in the field by Ferrari. The one exception was the 354 S of 1956, but this car had a 4-cylinder engine (280 bhp at 6,000 rpm). Its two victories in the Mille Miglia made the 290 one of the most famous of Ferrari's sports cars.

Lotus, which boasts a racing record of the highest rank, has never devoted much of its time to sports cars. However, it did spend some time on sports models at the beginning. The 11, pictured above, was one of the most successful versions. Its best points included a highly streamlined body and the arrangement of the mechanical components. The body was the work of Mike Costin, a well-known expert in the field, who was later to join with Keith Duckworth to produce the celebrated Cosworth. Colin Chapman, who was responsible for the mechanical side, used two different engines, the Ford and the Coventry-Climax, the latter angled at 10°.

Quite a few first-rate drivers relied on the 11. One of these was Colin Chapman who, before he concentrated solely on design and the management of his company, was an excellent driver. Driven by Bicknell-Jopp the 11 came in seventh overall and first in the 1100 class in the 1956 Le Mans 24 Hour. In 1957 another 11, this time driven by McKay-Frazer-

Car: **Lotus 11**
Maker: **Lotus**
Year: **1956**
Class: **Sport**
Engine: **4-cylinder in-line Coventry-Climax**
Bore × Stroke: **72.4 × 66.6 mm**
Capacity: **1,098 cc**
Power: **75 bhp at 6,500 rpm**

Chamberlain, came in ninth overall and first in the 1100 class in the same race. Again in 1957, a Lotus-Climax 11 powered by a 744 cc engine reached the top of the special performance table, establishing a new record. It was an extremely good year for Lotus in the French race; four cars started and four finished. In the same year ten Ferraris started but only two finished, Maserati had only one finisher out of five, Porsche one out of six, Panhard one out of four, and Aston Martin one out of four. Jaguar, however, kept pace with Lotus: five cars out of five finished the race.

This car made its debut on January 20, 1957 in the Buenos Aires 1,000 km (621.5 miles). Driven by Stirling Moss and Juan Manuel Fangio, the 450 S demonstrated its superiority by taking a sizeable lead; but then Fangio left the road and ended up in the haybales that marked the roadside. Its steering was damaged, and the car subsequently developed clutch trouble and was retired. On March 23 of the same year Fangio and Jean Behra won the Sebring 12 Hour convincingly. For the Mille Miglia the 450 S was improved by the adoption of a two-speed overdrive mounted behind the clutch, which raised the top speed to 304 km per hour (188.9 mph). One of the overdrive speeds was for the faster stretches and the other for the turns. Maserati prepared two cars for the Brescian race, one intended for Jean Behra, the other for Stirling Moss whose co-driver, as in 1955, was Jenkinson. Behra, however, had an accident during practice, and only Moss's 450 S started. This fastest of cars seemed fated not to do

Car: **Maserati 450 S**
Maker: **Maserati**
Year: **1957**
Class: **Sport**
Engine: **90° V-8**
Bore × Stroke: **93.8 × 81 mm**
Capacity: **4,477 cc**
Power: **400 bhp at 7,000 rpm**

well in the Mille Miglia. Just 10 kilometers into the race, the brake pedal broke and forced the two Englishmen to give up. Things went no better at Le Mans. There Moss-Schell had a 450 S coupé with a body designed by Mike Costin. Moss's victory in the Swedish 1,000 km (621.5 miles) reawakened hopes that Maserati could win the Marque's World Championship. Only one race remained, at Caracas, Venezuela; Maserati entered in force despite its lack of financial means. The result was a disaster. All four Maseratis, including the three 450 Ss, either left the road or collided with one another.

The 250 TRS is a car that Ferrari designers fondly remember as one of the most glorious and best balanced in its range. Not surprisingly, the designation 250 stood for the capacity of the individual cylinders. The TRS stood for Testa Rossa Sport (Red Cylinder Head Sports Car), a nickname whose origins are shrouded in mystery. The first TRSs actually had cylinder heads painted red, a feature with no technical significance. The red paint was probably the result of some mechanic's initiative or imagination. There is no doubt, however, that the 250 TRS achieved a great record.

It made its debut in the Buenos Aires 1,000 km in 1958 and came in first, driven by Peter Collins and Phil Hill. The same combination repeated their success in the Sebring 12 Hour, followed shortly by the victory of a 250 TRS driven by Musso-Gendebien in a prestigious Italian race, the Targa Florio. The same car won another important victory in 1958 when Gendebien-Hill came in first in the Le Mans 24 Hour.

Car: **Ferrari 250 TRS**
Maker: **Ferrari**
Year: **1958**
Class: **Sport**
Engine: **60° V-12**
Bore × Stroke: **73 × 58.8 mm**
Capacity: **2,953.21 cc**
Power: **290 bhp at 7,500 rpm**

Although 1959 was a bad year for Ferrari in the Marque's World Championship, the 250 TRS once again dominated the Sebring 12 Hour, driven by three Americans (Hill, Gurney, and Daigh) and the Belgian Gendebien. Gendebien and Daigh, who formed a team, had to retire in the eighth hour because of a broken differential. However, they made themselves available and gave the other Ferrari team a great deal of help. The Italian marque had also entered a third car, driven by Behra-Allison. This entry came in second, a lap behind the leaders, and underlined the brilliant achievements of the 250 TRS.

Aston Martin competed for some time in both sports car and Formula 1 races, and the 1/300 was one of its most successful products. It began very well, taking first and second places in the 1957 sports car Grand Prix at Spa. The winning driver was Tony Brooks. Fifteen days later, with Noel Cunningham and Reid as co-drivers, Brooks won the Nürburgring 1,000 km (621.5 miles).

The 1/300 was derived from the 1/250, which had competed in the 1956 Le Mans 24 Hour. This car featured a trans-axle layout (gearbox at rear, engine at front), which greatly reduced the frontal section and enabled the car to achieve, for its capacity, a high top speed (between 270 and 285 km per hour/168–177 mph). The DBR 1/300 also handled excellently, the result of good weight distribution.

In 1959 this car's best results were the victory of Moss-Fairman in the Nürburgring 1,000 km (621.5 miles), Salvadori-Shelby's victory in the Le Mans 24 Hour, Trintignant-Frère's second in the

Car: **Aston Martin DBR 1/300**
Maker: **Aston Martin**
Year: **1959**
Class: **Sport**
Engine: **6-cylinder in-line**
Bore × Stroke: **83 × 90 mm**
Capacity: **2,922 cc**
Power: **265 bhp at 6,400 rpm**

same race, and finally the victory of Shelby-Fairman-Moss in the Tourist Trophy. With three victories out of five in that year, Aston Martin won the Marque's World Championship, beating Ferrari by two points and Porsche by three. The 1/300's outstanding results in 1959 can, with hindsight, be seen to have depended to a great extent on the major contribution made by Stirling Moss. He was then 30 years old and in superb form. In the same year he also won the Italian and Portuguese Grand Prix in a Cooper.

The 246 P is very important in Ferrari's history, for it was the first rear-engined sports car. It had a 2,417.33 cc, 65° V-6 engine, with two spark plugs per cylinder and double overhead camshafts for each bank of cylinders. It owed much of its technical conception to the rear-engined F 2, even though it was launched after the F 2 appeared. The 246 P was contemporary with the 156 F1, and both made their debut in 1961.

The 246 P's first race was the Sebring 12 Hour (1961), where it was driven by Von Trips-Ginther. Unfortunately Von Trips, who was leading in the race, left the road when his steering broke. Ferrari entered two 246 Ps in that year's Targa Florio, driven by Gendebien-Phil Hill and Von Trips-Ginther. On the day of the race the papers were muddled and Gendebien was paired with Von Trips and Hill with Ginther. This enfuriated Hill, and he immediately left the road. Even though he resumed the race, a similar accident forced him to retire shortly afterward. The other 246 P, masterfully driven, particu-

Car: **Ferrari 246 P**
Maker: **Ferrari**
Year: **1960**
Class: **Sport**
Engine: **65° V-6**
Bore × Stroke: **85 × 71 mm**
Capacity: **2,417.33 cc**
Power: **280 bhp at 8,500 rpm**

larly by Von Trips, won the race after Moss-Graham Hill were eliminated by a broken transmission.

On the third outing, the Nürburgring 1,000 km (621.5 miles), Von Trips-Phil Hill and Gendebien-Ginther again drove the 246 P. Von Trips, who was well behind with his own car, placed himself at the wheel of Ginther-Gendebien's and through brilliant driving pulled it up to third place. Ginther-Von Trips, again in a 246 P, were leading in the Le Mans 24 Hour when they were forced to retire after running out of fuel. In the Pescara 4 Hour, the last race of the season, Ginther-Baghetti went into the lead; but the 246 P was forced to retire yet again, this time because of a broken spoke in the steering wheel.

It was Enzo Ferrari's intention that the Ferrari Superamerica should be merely a large Grand Tourer primarily aimed at the American market. However, it was later also used as a sports car and gave rise to a highly successful series of two-seaters known as the 330/P, 330/P2, 330/P3, and 330/P4. All were powered by the same 3,967.44 cc, 12-cylinder engine, with steadily increasing power outputs.

An important feature of the 400 Superamerica's 12-cylinder was the marked difference between the bore and the stroke (77 × 71 mm), making it classically oversquare. In its Superamerica version, it developed 340 bhp at 7,000 rpm and had a compression ratio of 8:1. Its weight, 1,280 kg (2,822 lb), underlined that it was intended for the American market.

Enzo Ferrari decided to enter the American Grand Tourer market by offering a large capacity car in stages. He began with the 1951 340 America, powered by a 4,101.66 cc, 12-cylinder engine (also used in the 340 F1), which de-

Car: **Ferrari 400 Superamerica**
Maker: **Ferrari**
Year: **1960**
Class: **Sport**
Engine: **60° V-12**
Bore × Stroke: **77 × 71 mm**
Capacity: **3,967.44 cc**
Power: **340 bhp at 7,000 rpm**

veloped 230 bhp at 6,000 rpm and had a compression ratio of 8:1. This car was not a great success; and two years later, in 1953, it was replaced by the 375 America. This version also had a 12-cylinder engine taken from a Formula 1 car, this time a 375 F1. It had a capacity of 4,522.94 cc, developed 300 bhp at 6,500 rpm, and had a compression ratio of 8.4:1. Finally, before the 400 Superamerica, Ferrari brought out the 410 Superamerica of 1956, which had a 4,961.57 cc, 12-cylinder engine, developing 340 bhp at 6,500 rpm and with a compression ratio of 8.5:1. This was the same engine, though with reduced power, as the one used in Umberto Maglioli's car, which won the last Carrera Panamericana.

The then chief designer at Maserati, Giulio Alfieri, believed that a chassis composed of a network of small diameter tubes was preferable to a monocoque structure. His belief gave this car its most prominent structural feature, a large number of tubes. Among the many nicknames quickly coined for the Maserati 60/61, as it was known in the factory, the most popular and enduring one was the "Birdcage." The car began with a 2,000 cc front-mounted engine and was completed in the spring of 1959. It had a brilliant debut on July 12, 1959 in a race preceding the French Grand Prix at Rouen. The race was won easily by Stirling Moss. The Orsi intended the 60 for private drivers; but the programs changed rapidly, and the 60 became the 61 with the adoption of a 2,890 cc engine that developed 250 bhp at 6,500 rpm. The 61's excellent handling, due to its low weight, prompted an American, Lucky Casner, to form a Maserati team in the United States called Camoradi USA (CAsner, MOtor RAcing DIvision).

Car: **Maserati 60/61 Birdcage**
Maker: **Maserati**
Year: **1960**
Class: **Sport**
Engine: **4-cylinder in-line**
Bore × Stroke: **60: 93.8 × 72 mm; 61: 100 × 92 mm**
Capacity: **60: 1,989 cc; 61: 2,890 cc**
Power: **60: 200 bhp at 7,800 rpm; 61: 250 bhp at 6,500 rpm**

Thanks to Casner the 61 won numerous victories in America and sold well in the U.S. market. According to that profound student of racing cars Jim Hill, the 60/61 must be considered the most advanced front-engined sports car ever built. Amid the declining fortunes of Maserati, the 60/61 was beaten only by rear-engined cars; and even against these it fought hard before yielding.

The Milanese factory was famed in the past both for the excellence of its products and the speed with which they were brought into being. However, development of the TZ (Tubolare Zagoto) series of cars offered convincing proof of the changes gradually overtaking Alfa Romeo.

The TZ was designed in 1959 as a replacement for the SZ, using, as far as possible, mass-produced mechanical components. In 1960 the construction of a prototype actually began, but the first road trials did not take place until the following year. It was finally available on the market in 1963. It had the same engine as the SS (Sprint Special). After the engine had been reworked to take part in Grand Tourer class races, the TZ won a series of victories worthy of Alfa. In 1963 these were the Sebring 12 Hour, the forty-eighth Targa Florio, the Nürburgring 1,000 km (621.5 miles), the Le Mans 24 Hour, the Tour of France, and the Alpine Cup. In 1964 the TZ won the Tour of Corsica and in 1965 the Sebring 12 Hour and

Car: **Alfa Romeo TZ 2**
Maker: **Alfa Romeo**
Year: **1963**
Class: **Sport**
Engine: **4-cylinder in-line**
Bore × Stroke: **78 × 82 mm**
Capacity: **1,570 cc**
Power: **112 bhp at 6,500 rpm**

the Targa Florio for a second time. A total of about 120 of these cars were produced; a feature of the last ten was the earliest use of plastic in the bodywork. It should be noted, in connection with this, that the TZ was already very light at the time it was first made available to sportsmen, weighing 660 kg (1,455 lb). For its relatively modest capacity it had a high top speed (215 km per hour/134 mph) and, like the Giulia berline, a long stroke (78 × 82 mm) engine.

The TZ in particular reasserted the importance of the truncated tail on sports car bodies. Although visually ugly, it was highly functional.

The technical problem posed by the gas turbine engine was in vogue during a period roughly spanning the years 1953 to 1963. Rover finally accepted the invitation of the Automobile Club de l'Quest, the organizers of the yearly Le Mans 24 Hour, to enter a car powered by such an engine. It did so in association with BRM. The latter prepared the car, using the chassis of its current Formula 1 model as a basis and enlarging it. It also offered its drivers, Graham Hill and Ritchie Ginther. The ACO set up a prize of 25,000 francs if the car covered a minimum of 3,600 km (2,237 miles).

Despite the handicap of being without a heat exchanger, the Rover-BRM did much better than expected. At the end of the 24 hours it had, with great consistency, covered 4,172.910 km (2,593.480 miles) at the highly respectable average of 173.346 km per hour (107.735 mph). Had the Rover-BRM been regularly classified (it was not competing for a place in the main table), it would have come in eighth overall.

Car: **Rover-BRM**
Maker: **BRM**
Year: **1963**
Class: **Sport**
Engine: **Rover gas turbine**
Bore × Stroke: —
Capacity: —
Power: **150 bhp**

In 1965 the experiment was repeated with the Mk II, which on this occasion was a full competitor in the race and was driven by Graham Hill and Jackie Stewart. The car was fitted with a heat exchanger and was much less thirsty than its sister (a consumption of 20 liters per 100 km/14.13 mpg versus 45 per 100/6.28 mpg in 1963); however, it was also much slower. Even so the Rover-BRM managed to achieve a good position (tenth) and do better than all the other English cars. The most noticeable feature about the Rover-BRM, as in 1963, was its consistency. It improved its position in the table every hour, with the exception of the third hour when it fell from thirty-second to thirty-third place.

The Ferrari 250 was produced in various versions; it was first talked about in 1952 as the S and finished eleven years later as the P. Officially, that is, according to the table listing the specifications of all the main types of Ferrari engines, the 250 was still powered by a 2,953.21 cc 12-cylinder engine. In fact, however, the capacity of its engine had been raised to about 3,300 cc, like the 275/P (3,285.72 cc).

A feature of the car, which had a closed top, was its rear-mounted engine. Pininfarina had to solve several problems in order to make it a berlinetta. However, the proof of the 250 LM's complete mechanical and aerodynamic success was its victory in the 1965 Le Mans 24 Hour. The race was won by Jochen Rindt-Masten Gregory. They were driving on behalf of Luigi Chinetti's Nart (North American Racing Team), which had entered the car with no particular expectations. The race was a disaster for the official Ferrari team. Pedro Rodriguez-Vaccarella came in seventh in a 365/P2;

Car: **Ferrari 250 LM**
Maker: **Ferrari**
Year: **1964**
Class: **Sport**
Engine: **60° V-12**
Bore × Stroke: **77 × 58.8 mm**
Capacity: **3,285.72 cc**
Power: **320 bhp at 7,700 rpm**

Guichet-Parkes in a 330/P2 retired, as did Surtees-Scarfiotti in a 330/P2 and Bandini-Biscaldi in a 275/P2.

In the eighth hour Rindt-Gregory were fourteenth, by the eleventh they were third, by the twelfth second, and by the twenty-first hour they had gained the lead, where they remained until the finish. On the strength of this victory the 250 LM, which was also known as the 275 LM because of its 3,300 cc engine, competed in several races under the colors of Nart. This move was a clear protest by Ferrari for the fact that type-approval of its GTO in the Grand Tourer class still hadn't been given.

The 904, or Carrera, is regarded as one of the most stylistically successful competition models that Porsche has ever produced. Butzi Porsche, the son of Ferry and the nephew of the great Ferdinand Porsche, was responsible for the design of the body. Butzi was just 28 when he assumed responsibility for the styling department of the Stuttgart marque. Though he himself was not interested in racing, he succeeded in impressing a highly sporting appearance on his creations. The 904 was the first Porsche to have a glass resin body. It weighed about 90 kg (198 lb).

The new 2,000 cc engine had four overhead camshafts and was designated the 587/3. Porsche produced 100 of the engines in order to obtain immediate type-approval for the car. Officially it was claimed to develop 180 bhp at 7,200 rpm. A particularly original feature of the 904 was the position of its engine, which was behind the driver's seat but in front of the rear axle. It had a five-speed transmission and disc brakes on all four wheels.

Car: **Porsche 904 GTS Carrera**
Maker: **Porsche**
Year: **1964**
Class: **Sport**
Engine: **4-cylinder in-line**
Bore × Stroke: **92 × 74 mm**
Capacity: **1,996 cc**
Power: **180 bhp at 7,200 rpm**

The car was officially unveiled in November 1963 at the Circuito della Solitude (Solitude Circuit). Although it bore the number 904, it was more widely known as the GTS Carrera. The price was 29,700 marks, a third of which had to be paid on ordering. Porsche was careful to assure prospective clients that a 6-cylinder engine would not be used in any of the first 100 units to be built. The first 904 was sold to an American customer, and its first race was the Daytona 2,000 km (1,243 miles) on February 16, 1964. It was driven by Chuch Cassell and Augie Pabst but was forced to retire. The 904's other early appearances on the circuits were mainly used by Porsche to tune the car, given the short time that had been devoted to its preparation.

The 330/P2 was one of the group of Ferrari sports cars to carry the letter P, standing for prototype, in its designation. The first of the line was the 250/P of 1963, which was powered by a V-12, 2,953.21 cc engine with a power output of 300 bhp at 7,800 rpm and a compression ratio of 9.8:1. The car's number, as was customary for a Ferrari, referred to the capacity of the individual cylinders (246.10 cc). The 250/P was followed by the 330/P (cylinder capacity 330.62 cc), a 3,967.44 cc, 12-cylinder that developed 370 bhp at 7,300 rpm. The next car in the P series was the 275 (cylinder capacity 273.81 cc), another 12-cylinder, with a capacity of 3,285.72 cc. This engine developed 320 bhp at 7,700 rpm and had a compression ratio of 9.7:1. In 1963 the 365/P (cylinder capacity 365.86 cc) appeared with a capacity of 4,390.35 cc, a power output of 380 bhp at 7,300 rpm, and a compression ratio of 9:1. It was then the turn of the 330/P2. This version had the same individual cylinder and engine capacities as the 330/P, but the

Car: **Ferrari 330/P2**
Maker: **Ferrari**
Year: **1965**
Class: **Sport**
Engine: **60° V-12**
Bore × Stroke: **77 × 71 mm**
Capacity: **3,967.44 cc**
Power: **410 bhp at 8,200 rpm**

power output was raised to 410 bhp at 8,200 rpm and the compression ratio to 9.8:1. At the same time, the 275/P2 appeared, having the same individual cylinder and engine capacities as the 275/P but developing 350 bhp at 8,500 rpm, with a compression ratio of 9.8:1.

Between 1962 and 1965 Ferrari fielded six different, though related, sports cars. Such extraordinary vitality did not end with the P2; it was followed by the P3 and the P4 as well as by the Dino. The continuous succession of sports cars at this time demonstrated Ferrari's determination to oppose Ford with every means at its disposal. In Ferrari's case, the means was inventiveness rather than a seemingly inexhaustible supply of capital, as in the American marque's case.

The number 40 by which this Grand Tourer was designated has probably caused many budding historians to rack their brains for its meaning. The answer is fairly straightforward. It stands for the height in inches from the ground to the top of the car and was intended to emphasize the car's low-slung build.

Car: **Ford GT 40**
Maker: **Ford**
Year: **1966**
Class: **Sport**
Engine: **8-cylinder Cosworth**
Bore × Stroke: **108 × 96 mm**
Capacity: **6,997 cc**
Power: **475 bhp**

The GT 40, and similarly the Cosworth 8-cylinder, testify to Ford America's strong commitment to racing at this time. After Ford tried but failed to reach an agreement with Ferrari, Ford decided to proceed on its own and quickly. Cosworth was commissioned to provide the 8-cylinder engine. For the GT 40 Ford turned to the British firm Lola and bought the prototype of a sports car that had just been finished by Eric Broadley. Initially, the engine had a capacity of 4,200 cc, later raised to 4,700 cc and then 7,000 cc.

Success was slow to come; but from 1966 onward Ford made the full weight of its powerful organization felt, winning at Le Mans, Daytona, and Sebring. It won again at Le Mans in 1967, 1968, and 1969. It should be noted that McLaren-Amon's victory in the 1966 24 Hour was achieved with a 7,000 cc engine as was Gurney-Foyt's in 1967, while the successes of Rodriguez-L. Bianchi in 1969 and Ickx-Oliver in 1969 were achieved with 5,000 cc (4,942 cc) engines, as stipulated by the regulations.

After having made a full-scale effort, Ford decided to put an end to its direct sporting activity. Its participation had brought the company enormous publicity. Henry Ford II himself maintained that the Monday papers, with the results of the races, had more effect than a full-page advertisement.

The Chaparral name (after a swift Texas bird) came into being in 1961 under the initiative of Jim Hall, an amateur driver and mechanical enthusiast. In that year he commissioned a number of sports cars with tubular chassis and front engines from the firm of Trout and Barnes of Culver City, California. They were powered by 8-cylinder Chevrolets. With them Hall won the 1962 Road America 500 and a number of sprint races. In the same year Hall, together with James Sharp, founded Chaparral Cars, based at Midland, Texas. The financial resources of the two even enabled them to build a two-mile test track. It was at Midland that Hall began to prepare the first true Chaparrals, which had semi-monocoque chassis, rear-mounted 8-cylinder Oldsmobile engines, and glass resin bodies. The Oldsmobile engine was later replaced by a Chevrolet. The first victory by a true Chaparral came at Pensacola in April 1964. In the meantime the car had been fitted with automatic transmission. In 1965 Hall and Sharp won the Sebring

Car: **Chaparral 2F**
Maker: **Chaparral**
Year: **1967**
Class: **Sport**
Engine: **V-8 Chevrolet**
Bore × Stroke: **107 × 95.5 mm**
Capacity: **6,997 cc**
Power: **525 bhp**

12 Hour, the first time an American team and car had done so since Walters and Fitch in 1953 with the Cunningham C4R. The 2F was produced for races in Europe and, like the 2D, was powered by a 5,360 cc 8-cylinder Chevrolet. Phil Hill and Bonnier drove it to victory in the Nürburgring 1,000 km (621.5 miles). Its second triumph in Europe came at the hands of drivers Phil Hill and Mike Spence in the 1967 Brands Hatch 500 Mile. In the meantime the capacity of the engine was increased to 7,000 cc. A distinctive feature of the Chaparral, from the 2E (1966) onward was its high rear aileron 1.37 m (4 ft 6 in) from the ground.

It was during 1966 and 1967 that Ford America intervened in Le Mans in a truly massive way. In those years the firm was involved directly rather than working through Gulf-Mirage (the English team run by John Wyer) or other private stables. In 1966 the regulations of the French endurance race still permitted makers complete freedom regarding engine capacity. Ford entered its powerful Mk II (6,982 cc); and driven by McLaren-Amon it captured first place, covering 4,843.09 km (3,010 miles) at an average of 201.795 km per hour (125.416 mph). The winning car was followed by two other Mk IIs driven by Miles-Hulme and Bucknum-Hutcherson. For Ferrari the race was a disaster. The P3s of Bandini-Guichet, Pedro Rodriguez-Ginther, and Scarfiotti-Parkes were all forced to retire, as were the 365/P2s of "Beurlys"-Dumas, Mairess-Muller, and Gregory-Bondurant.

The feud between the two marques was resumed in 1967. Ford fielded the Mk IV (6,980 cc) and Ferrari the 330/P4.

Car: **Ferrari 330/P4**
Maker: **Ferrari**
Year: **1967**
Class: **Sport**
Engine: **60° V-12**
Bore × Stroke: **77 × 71 mm**
Capacity: **3,989.56 cc**
Power: **450 bhp at 8,200 rpm**

Ferrari managed to do infinitely better with this car than it had done the year before. The Ford Mk IV of Gurney-Foyt won; but Scarfiotti-Parkes and Mairess-"Beurlys," who were both driving P4s, came in second and third, respectively. The fact that the first, second, and third placed cars all easily exceeded the previous year's winning average shows how well the Ferraris performed. The 218.038 km per hour (135.511 mph) of Gurney-Foyt was beaten in 1971 only by the Porsche 917 K of Marko-Van Lennep (222.30 km per hour/138.160 mph). The Ferrari P4 made a brilliant debut in 1967 by finishing first and second in the Daytona 24 Hour, while a P3/4 came in third. A P4 also won the Monza 1,000 km (621.5 miles).

Except for the 512, which because of the war never reached the track, the 33.2 was the first Alfa Romeo to have a rear-mounted engine, and as such it marked a turning point in the firm's history.

The 33.2 had a V-8 engine of about 2,000 cc, which developed 270 bhp at 9,600 rpm and had a compression ratio of 11:1. It was begun in 1964, and the first car underwent preliminary trials at the end of 1965 with the engine of the TZ 2. In addition to the 90° V-8 engine, which the Milanese marque had never used before, and the engine's position, the 33.2 also had a highly original chassis. It was composed of three 200 mm (7.87 in) diameter tubes in the shape of an asymmetrical H, which enclosed the synthetic rubber fuel tank. The structure was completed by two members, one placed at the front to support the steering and pedals, and the other at the rear, supporting the engine and the water and oil radiators as well as the seats and the body. The latter was made of acrylic resin and weighed 55 kg (121.25 lb).

Car: **Alfa Romeo 33.2**
Maker: **Alfa Romeo**
Year: **1968**
Class: **Sport**
Engine: **90° V-8**
Bore × Stroke: **78 × 50.4 mm**
Capacity: **1,995 cc**
Power: **270 bhp at 9,600 rpm**

The 33.2 made its racing debut in the hill climb at Fleron in Belgium on March 12, 1967, coming in first. In 1969, after being fitted with a new body, it took part in the Daytona 24 Hour, coming in first and second in the 2,000 class. As a consequence of this victory, the car was christened "Daytona."

The 33.2 was also produced in a Stradale (Road) version. This car had the same specifications as its sister with the exception of its power output (230 bhp at 8,800 rpm) and weight (700 kg/1,543 lb versus 580 kg/1,278 lb). A total of 30 racing 33.2s and 18 Stradales were produced, the latter being put on the market between 1967 and 1969 at a price of about ten million lire.

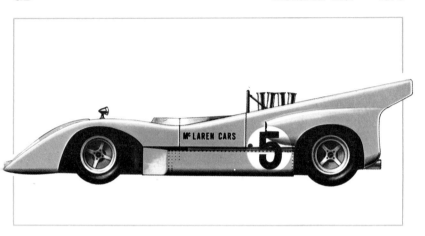

This car is intimately linked with the history of McLaren and still more with that of its creator, Bruce McLaren. It was at the wheel of an M8F, during trials on the Goodwood circuit, that McLaren lost his life on June 2, 1970. The accident happened when the rear-mounted engine cover suddenly came off. The car did an about-face and left the road out of control. There was nothing the 32-year-old driver could have done.

The M8F paid tribute to the memory of its creator and builder by displaying an overwhelming superiority in that year's Can-Am races. Dennis Hulme won at Watkins Glen, Edmonton, Mid-Ohio, Donnybrooke, Laguna Seca, and Riverside. Gurney, in an identical car, came in first both at Mosport and Mont Tremblant. Gethin won the Road America. Out of the ten Can-Am races, nine were won by McLarens. Dennis Hulme ended the season with the enormous advantage of 132 points to 65 for the second-placed driver. McLarens took the first three places in the Can-Am table, and Hulme alone won

Car: **McLaren M8F**
Maker: **McLaren**
Year: **1970**
Class: **Sport**
Engine: **V-8 Chevrolet**
Bore × Stroke: **107 × 95.5 mm**
Capacity: **6,997 cc**
Power: **625 bhp**

a total of $150,000 in prizes.

The M8F was powered by a Chevrolet engine of about 7,000 cc and had a monocoque chassis. Besides demonstrating an enviable state of tuning and a reliability rarely found among racing cars, it was, as the illustration clearly shows, striking in appearance. A large part of the fortunes of McLaren, still active even after the death of its founder, has rested on its impressive number of Can-Am wins and the rich prizes that have always been a feature of these races.

Apart from the 612/CA of 1969 (6,222.16 cc, 640 bhp at 7,700 rpm), the 512 S had the largest engine capacity of any Ferrari. A 500, the 500 SA of 1964, had already been produced by the Italian marque. It is unlikely that such a capacity would have been included again in Ferrari's programs; however, the Commission Sportive Internationale inopportunely decided to raise the maximum capacity to 5,000 cc for cars eligible for the Marque's World Championship, provided that at least 25 units were built. Ferrari was on the point of withdrawing from this championship, since building 25 units would be a heavy financial commitment. In the end it decided to go ahead, having taken care to place the maximum number of cars with private organizations—the quickest way to dispose of them.

The specifications of the 512 S were virtually the same as those of the 500 S, differing only in capacity (4,993.53 cc for the 512 S and 4,961.57 cc for the 512). The claimed power output was 500 bhp at 8,500 rpm with a compression ratio of

Car: **Ferrari 512 S**
Maker: **Ferrari**
Year: **1970**
Class: **Sport**
Engine: **60° V-12**
Bore × Stroke: **87 × 70 mm**
Capacity: **4,993.53 cc**
Power: **500 bhp at 8,500 rpm**

11.5:1. It weighed 820 kg (1,807.8 lb).

The car had a successful debut when Giunti, Andretti, and Vaccarella won the 1970 Sebring 12 Hour. However, that year's Le Mans 24 Hour witnessed a stunning victory for Porsche. The Ferrari, driven by Posey-Bucknum and Walker-De Fierlandt, could do no better than fourth and fifth positions. A new version, the SM, was driven to victory in the Kyalami 9 Hour by Ickx and Giunti. In 1971 the SM took part in the Le Mans 24 Hour, coming in third and fourth with Posey-Adamovicz and Craft-Weier.

The 33.3 marked Alfa Romeo's return in strength to racing and the resumption of a tradition that had been interrupted by the war. Making use of experience gained with the 33.2, the 33.3 had a rear-mounted engine but a box structure chassis (Avional) with titanium members. It was powered by a 90° V-8, with four valves per cylinder and an electronic ignition, that developed 400 bhp at 9,000 rpm. The six-speed gearbox projected behind the rear wheels. It had a spyder body style. Designed in 1968, the 33.3 made its debut in 1969 by winning at Zeltweg in Austria and at Enna. In 1970 it was second overall in the Imola 500 km (310.8 miles) and at Zeltweg.

As time passed the car continually evolved. In 1971 the power output of the engine was raised to 420 bhp, the transmission reduced to five speeds, and the total weight brought down to 650 kg (1,433 lb) from the 700 kg (1,543 lb) of the previous year's model. In that year the 33.3 won at Brands Hatch, the Targa Florio, and Watkins Glen.

Car: **Alfa Romeo 33 TT 3**
Maker: **Alfa Romeo**
Year: **1971**
Class: **Sport**
Engine: **90° V-8**
Bore × Stroke: **86 × 64.4 mm**
Capacity: **2,998 cc**
Power: **400 bhp at 9,000 rpm; 440 bhp at 9,800 rpm**

In terms of design, the true 33 TT 3 was born in the winter of 1970, when it was given a tubular chassis (TT stands for telaio tubolare/tubular chassis) and the driver's seat was moved well forward. The 2.16 m (7 ft 1 in) wheelbase was increased to 2.24 m (7 ft 4 in); and the gearbox, while remaining five speed, was placed between the engine and the differential. The power output of the engine rose to 440 bhp at 9,800 rpm. In 1972 the 33 TT 3 came in second overall in the Marque's World Championship, with five third places (Buenos Aires, Daytona, Sebring, Brands Hatch, and Nürburgring) and one second place (the Targa Florio), as opposed to the ten victories of the season's actual winner, Ferrari.

Like the Ferrari 512 S, the Porsche 917 was built in compliance with the rules laid down by the Federation Internationale de l'Automobile concerning sports cars that came into force in 1969. The car represented a heavy investment for the German marque. It has been calculated that each of the required 25 cars cost Porsche between $50,000 and $80,000. The increase in the permitted engine capacity (up to 5,000 cc) prompted the German marque to choose a 12-cylinder, air-cooled boxer by stretching the 8-cylinder boxer used on the 908. The engine capacity was 4,494 cc, and it developed 580 bhp with a compression ratio of 10.5:1. The year 1969 was not a good one for the 917. However, in 1970 the management of the car was entrusted to the English specialist John Wyer; and the 917 took the Marque's World Championship with victories by Rodriguez-Kinnunen in the Daytona 24 Hour, the Brands Hatch 1,000 km (621.5 miles), the Monza 1,000 km, and the Watkins Glen 6 Hour. Driven by

Car: **Porsche 917 K**
Maker: **Porsche**
Year: **1971**
Class: **Sport**
Engine: **12-cylinder boxer**
Bore × Stroke: **85 × 66 mm**
Capacity: **4,494 cc**
Power: **580 bhp**

Attwood-Herrmann, the 917 also won the Le Mans 24 Hour while Siffert-Redman won the Austrian 1,000 km. In the winter of 1971 the car underwent various modifications that increased the power output to 600 bhp. In 1971 the German car, still carrying the colors of John Wyer, won the Daytona 24 Hour (Rodriguez-Oliver); the Sebring 12 Hour (Elford-Larrousse); the Le Mans 24 Hour (Marko-Van Lennep); the Buenos Aires 1,000 km (Siffert-Bell); the Monza 1,000 km (Rodriguez-Oliver); the Spa-Francorchamps 1,000 km (Rodriguez-Oliver); and the Austrian 1,000 km (Rodriguez-Attwood). In three years of competition, 1969-71, the 917 won 15 of the 24 World Championship races.

The first boxer engine built by Ferrari was used in a Formula 1 car, the 512 F1 of 1964. This innovation passed virtually unobserved. The engine first appeared in a sports car in 1969, the year in which Ferrari won the European Mountain Championship with Peter Schetty. The third boxer was installed in the 312 or, more precisely, the 312 B F1, which was produced at the end of 1969. This last engine (capacity of 3,000 cc) was selected for a prototype sports car, the 312 P. The car was unveiled at the end of 1970 and competed in the 1971 Marque's World Championship.

Driven by Ignazio Giunti in the Buenos Aires 1,000 km (621.5 miles), it proved to be more than a match for the Porsche 917 and the Ferrari 512 M, both of which had much larger capacities. After having taken the lead at Buenos Aires, Giunti came out of a fast turn to find the road blocked by Jean Pierre Beltoise's Matra-Simca, which had run out of fuel. Giunti smashed into the car and was killed. Only a miracle prevented Beltoise,

Car: **Ferrari 312 P**
Maker: **Ferrari**
Year: **1972**
Class: **Sport**
Engine: **12-cylinder boxer**
Bore × Stroke: **77 × 53.5 mm**
Capacity: **2,989.56 cc**
Power: **430 bhp at 9,800 rpm**

who was pushing his car toward the pits, from being crushed between the two vehicles. The 312 competed in a large number of other races that year but failed to finish in any of them. There were a variety of reasons, mostly trivial, for this failure.

In 1972 the car came into its own. Its body was slightly modified and the chassis was greatly strengthened in compliance with a rule that came into force that year stipulating a minimum weight of 650 kg (1,433 lb). The 312 P won ten of the eleven races of the Marque's World Championship. The decisive contribution came from Jacky Ickx who, driving sometimes with Andretti and sometimes with Redman, won four races.

The MS 670 was an outcome of the firm's withdrawal from Formula 1 racing. At the end of 1972, after a season virtually without success, Matra decided to abandon Formula 1 and to concentrate exclusively on the Sports Car World Championship. In the past the only sports car race it had competed in was the Le Mans 24 Hour; but from then on it would compete in all such races listed in the calendar.

The 670 was directly derived from the 660, which had been used in the 1972 Le Mans 24 Hour. It was powered by a 60° very oversquare (79.7 × 50 mm) 2,999 cc, V-12 engine mounted in a mid-rear position. It had a monocoque structure, a load-bearing engine, and a glass resin spyder body style. The version of the car used in 1,000 km (621.5 miles) had a total weight of 650 kg (1,433 lb), while the version used in 24 Hour races weighed 670 kg (1,477 lb). A Hewland DG 300 gearbox was used for 1,000 km races and a ZF 5 DS25 for 24 Hour races; both were five speed.

For the driving team Matra engaged

Car: **Matra-Simca MS 670**
Maker: **Matra**
Year: **1973**
Class: **Sport**
Engine: **60° V-12**
Bore × Stroke: **79.7 × 50 mm**
Capacity: **2,999 cc**
Power: —

four Frenchmen ("l'équipe de France"): François Cévert, Jean Pierre Beltoise, Henri Pescarolo, and Gerard Larrousse plus Jabouille, Jaussaud, Depailler, and Wollek for races where four cars were entered. The 1972 car was lighter in weight and underwent various small modifications, mainly concerning the streamlining and the suspension geometry.

Matra-Simca's concentration on sports car racing bore fruit in the form of the Marque's Championship and victories in the Vallelunga 6 Hour, the Dijon 1,000 km, the Le Mans 24 Hour, the Austrian 1,000 km, and the Watkins Glen 6 Hour.

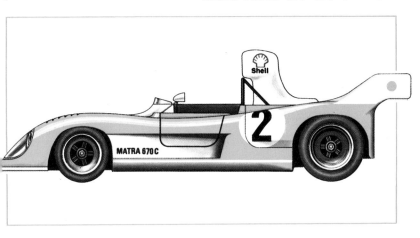

Matra-Simca plundered the 1974 Marque's World Championship with a car almost identical to the previous season's, though this time it also bore the colors and emblem of Gitanes cigarettes, a generous sponsor. Ferrari, however, had completely withdrawn from the Championship, doing the opposite of Matra-Simca the year before and concentrating all its efforts on Formula 1.

The 670 C started badly. It was soundly beaten in the first race of the season, the Monza 1,000 km (621.5 miles), when its two teams (Pescarolo-Larrousse and Beltoise-Jarier) were forced to retire. It recovered in the following race, the Spa-Francorchamps 1,000 km, with drivers Ickx and Jarier. It continued on a high note by also winning the Nürburgring 1,000 km (Beltoise-Jarier); the Imola 1,000 km (Pescarolo-Larrousse); the Austrian 1,000 km (Pescarolo-Larrousse); the Le Mans 24 Hour (Pescarolo-Larrousse); the Watkins Glen 6 Hour (Beltoise-Jarier); the Paul Ricard 1,000 km (Beltoise-Jarier); in the Brands

Car: **Matra-Simca MS 670 C**
Maker: **Matra**
Year: **1974**
Class: **Sport**
Engine: **60° V-12**
Bore × Stroke: **79.7 × 50 mm**
Capacity: **2,999 cc**
Power: **—**

Hatch 1,000 km (Beltoise-Jarier); and the Kyalami 6 Hour (Pescarolo-Larrousse).

At the end of the season the French marque had won the title with a total of 140 points against 81 points for Gulf-Ford (its main rival), 76 for Porsche, and 65 for Alfa Romeo.

The end of this triumphant season also saw the departure of Matra from racing after a ten-year involvement, five of them with Simca. Jean Luc Lagardere, its general manager, justified the decision by saying that the firm had achieved all the goals it had set for itself.

1975 - Alfa Romeo 33 TT 12

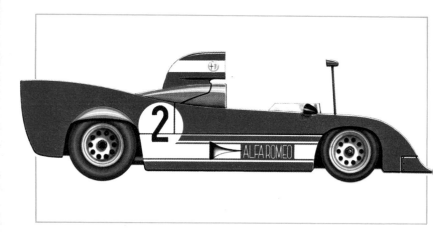

The 33 TT 12 (the TT stood for telaio tubolare/tubular chassis) was preceded by the 33 2000 (debut in 1967) and the 33 3000 (used from 1969 on). The car underscored Alfa Romeo's original decision to become directly involved in racing again—a decision made primarily to oppose Ferrari. Ferrari's reaction was to enter into collaboration with Fiat.

The first 12-cylinder boxer engine was ready at the beginning of 1973. It developed 470 bhp at 11,000 rpm, but by the end of the season this had risen to 500 bhp. The total weight of the car was 750 kg (1,653 lb).

The 33 TT 12 made a good start in the 1974 season by winning its first race, the Monza 1,000 km (621.5 miles). Soon after, it was virtually laid up because of financial problems. Over the winter of 1974–75 it was dusted off and updated. In 1975 it made an excellent showing, winning the Marque's Championship. Admittedly Alfa Romeo had no real opposition that year; Ferrari had retired at the end of 1973 and Matra-Simca at the

end of the 1974 season. One of the distinctive features of the 33 TT 12, regarded as one of the most successful 12-cylinders built by the Milanese marque, was the position of the driver's seat. It was placed well forward, a feature that appeared again in the 177 and 179 F1s. Prior to this last engine, a 12-cylinder had been used in 1931 with the linking of two 1,752 cc, 6-cylinders; in 1936 with the C; and in 1940 with the Type 512. The latter was a rear-engined single-seater that never got beyond the prototype stage.

Car: **Alfa Romeo 33 TT 12**
Maker: **Alfa Romeo**
Year: **1975**
Class: **Sport**
Engine: **12-cylinder boxer**
Bore × Stroke: **77 × 53.6 mm**
Capacity: **2,995 cc**
Power: **500 bhp at 11,500 rpm**

Committed on two racing fronts—the Sports Car World Championship and the Marque's World Championship—Porsche triumphed in both with cars powered by 6-cylinder turbocharged engines. It could not have demonstrated more eloquently its belief in the superiority of such engines, which also had the advantage of being much less polluting.

The conviction that they could win both championships led Porsche to make the daring move of entering only one car in the Marque's World Championship. Everything went smoothly, with Ickx and Mass easy winners at Mugello and at Vallelunga. However, matters became complicated after the technicians of the Commissione Sportiva Automobilistico Italiana (Italian Motor Sport Commission) served notice that the 935's rear aileron did not conform to the regulations. The Commission Sportive Internationale backed up this view, and Porsche was given six weeks to make the modifications. The decision, sharply contested by the German marque, cost it the Nürburg-

Car: **Porsche 935**
Maker: **Porsche**
Year: **1976**
Class: **Sport**
Engine: **Turbocharged 6-cylinder in-line**
Bore × Stroke: **92.8 × 70.4 mm**
Capacity: **2,857 cc**
Power: **630 bhp at 8,000 rpm**

ring 1,000 km (621.5 miles) and the Austrian 1,000 km, which were won by BMW. Porsche then regained the upper hand with victories by Stommelen-Schurti in the Watkins Glen 6 Hour, Ickx-Mass in the Dijon 6 Hour, and Ickx-Van Lennep in the Le Mans 24 Hour. Even though it was by a narrow margin, 95 points versus 85, Porsche captured this second title after having won the Sports Car World Championship by sweeping all seven races in the calendar with the 936. Ickx's victory in the 1976 Le Mans 24 Hour was his third; in 1977 he won his fourth, equaling the record of his compatriot Olivier Gendebien.

This car, as often happens in motor sport, was begun soon after a bitter defeat. In Renault's case the defeat was the one suffered in the 1977 Le Mans 24 Hour after its car had held the lead for 19.5 hours.

The experience of 1977 highlighted certain technical deficiencies, particularly in connection with the pistons and the gearbox, that it was possible to avoid in preparing the new car. The trials began as early as October that year and continued, at the Le Castelet circuit, throughout the winter. The search for a straightaway of the same length as the one at Le Mans (5 km/3.1 miles) led the French team to move to the Transport Research Center in the United States. There the car reached 320 km per hour (198.88 mph) and covered 2,200 km (1,367.3 miles) at an average of 270 km per hour (167.81 mph). Having returned to Le Castelet in February, it covered a further 7,000 km (4,350.5 miles) and then another 2,500 km (1,553.4 miles) in April. The A442B, which Pironi and Jaussaud drove to vic-

Car: **Renault A442B**
Maker: **Renault**
Year: **1978**
Class: **Sport**
Engine: **Turbocharged V-6**
Bore × Stroke: **86 × 57.3 mm**
Capacity: **1,997 cc**
Power: **500 bhp at 9,900 rpm**

tory, was powered by a 1,997 cc turbocharged 6-cylinder that developed 500 bhp at 9,900 rpm. The rotational speed of the Garrett turbocharger was 90,000 rpm. The car had a total weight of 715 kg (1,576 lb), and the body was completely streamlined, with antivortex disc wheels. The A442B underwent a total of more than 70 modifications, 30 of which involved the engine. The remainder were made to the gearbox, suspension, chassis, and body. At the same time that Renault was carrying out this program, it was progressing with the Formula 1 single-seater.

The Renault Alpine S of 1971 and the Lancia Stratos of 1974 have dominated the international rallies, gaining outstanding reputations. They have been assisted by the generosity with which the French and Italian firms have supported racing.

In 1971 the Rallies Championship was divided into two categories. The first was the Marque's Championship, over 8 races, and the second the European Championship, over 21 races. The Marque's Championship, considered more important, was dominated by the Renault Alpine S, with 36 points, followed by the Saab with 18 points.

The Stratos has been the worthy successor to the Fulvia HF. It was put forward by Bertone at the 1970 Turin Motor Show. It had the Fulvia HF's 1,600 cc engine positioned centrally. Later Lancia decided to fit it with the 2,418 cc, V-6 Ferrari Dino engine, a move made possible by the fact that both Ferrari and Lancia were part of the Fiat Group. Its racing debut came in the 1972 Tour of Corsica, and its first victory was Munari's in the 1973 Tour of France.

In 1974, the year in which it won type-approval as a GT car, the Stratos, driven by Munari, won the Sanremo Rally and the Rideaux Lakes in Canada.

▲
Car: **Renault Alpine S**
Maker: **Alpine**
Year: **1971**
Class: **Grand Tourer**
Engine: **4-cylinder in-line Renault**
Bore × Stroke: **77.8 × 84 mm**
Capacity: **1,596 cc**
Power: **160 bhp at 7,000 rpm**

Car: **Lancia Stratos**
Maker: **Lancia**
Year: **1974**
Class: **Grand Tourer**
Engine: **65° V-6 Ferrari Dino Transverse Central**
Bore × Stroke: **92.5 × 60 mm**
Capacity: **2,418 cc**
Power: **270 bhp at 7,800 rpm**
▼

5

Indianapolis Cars– From 1911 to the Present

After the inglorious end of the Targa Florio as a speed competition, the Indianapolis 500 became the race that had been held the greatest number of times (63 up until 1979). The 500 is still the richest motor race in the world; the most followed, with at least 300,000 spectators and millions who watch it on TV; and the most spectacular. Although the formula of this race has been accused of being static and excessively conservative, it can be considered as stimulating if one looks at the wide variety of cars that have competed between 1911 and today (classical, front-wheel drive, four-wheel drive, more than four wheels, gasoline, diesel, turbocharged, and gas turbine engines). However, it took Jack Brabham's daring attempt (1961) with the tiny Cooper to start the change from front- to rear-mounted engines.

The 500's organizers claim that it is also the safest race. In the first 50 years of its history, they maintain, only 27 drivers out of 2,201 competitors have lost their lives during practice or the race. The 500 is, however, infamous for the fatal accidents that occur there, which often involve members of the public. The long list of drivers, mechanics, and spectators who have lost their lives begins with Arthur Greiner's mechanic, Sam Dickson.

The fact that the 2.5-mile track has remained virtually unchanged makes it easier to compare the results achieved in the earlier races and in later ones. The only important change that the now celebrated oval has undergone took place after its inauguration in 1909 when, following numerous accidents, the owners of the track decided to pave it. A total of 3,250,000 bricks were required, and the operation was completed in the record time of 63 days. Because the paving is so slippery, even though over the years the bricks have been covered by asphalt, the Indianapolis 500 has never been run in the rain.

The first winner, Harroun driving a Marmon, averaged 120.041 km per hour (74.606 mph). By 1978 Al Unser had more than doubled this speed, achieving 259.689 km per hour (161.398 mph) in a Lola-Cosworth. (In 1979 the winner's average was lower.) There has been an average increase of 2 km per hour each year, confirmation of the progress made by racing cars over roughly three-quarters of a century.

Forty cars, including three Fiats, took part in the first 500 in front of nearly 80,000 spectators. The winner, Ray Harroun, who started in twenty-eighth position, received $14,000, of which $10,000 was the prize with the remainder being offered by various firms for publicity purposes. Harroun, satisfied with the success, announced his immediate retirement from racing. His car has passed into history as the first, so far as is known, to have a rear-view mirror. The Wasp was powered by a 7,816 cc, 6-cylinder Marmon engine.

USA

Mercer 35 - 1911

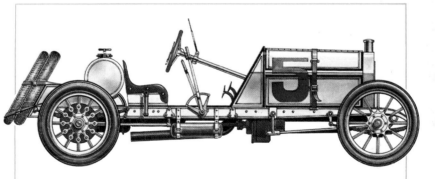

One of the most interesting cars to take part in the first Indianapolis 500 was the Mercer 35. The two that were entered came in twelfth and fifteenth and were driven by Hughie Hughes and Charles Bigelow, respectively. The 35 was powered by a 4-cylinder in-line twin block with a capacity of 4,940 cc, developing 60 bhp. It had a three-speed transmission and brakes only on the rear wheels. In its standard version (50 bhp at 1,600 rpm) the 35 could cover a standing mile in 51 seconds. Mercer itself was founded in 1911 and was based in Trenton, New Jersey.

1912 - National   USA

Twenty-four cars were entered in the second 500. The moral victor of the race was Ralph De Palma, who took the lead on the third lap and remained there, easily dominating the opposition, until the 197th lap, the third from the finish. Then the engine of his Mercedes broke down. Although at that point De Palma had a lead of five laps over the second car, all that he and his mechanic could do was to finish eleventh after pushing their car for two laps. The winner, a National driven by Joe Dawson, had a 4-cylinder with a capacity of more than 8,000 cc.

1913 - Peugeot GP   F

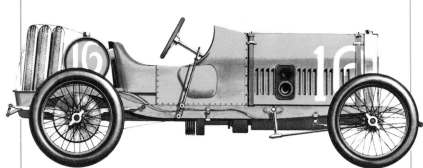

The Peugeot GP of 1912, with which Jules Goux won the 500 in 1913, remains one of the most outstanding racing cars ever built. It was designed by Ernest Henri in collaboration with the drivers Paul Zaccarelli, Georges Boillot, and Jules Goux. His main requirement was the 4-cylinder engine with four valves per cylinder, twin overhead camshafts, and a capacity of 7,600 cc, which developed 130 bhp at 2,200 rpm. In 1912 Georges Boillot drove it to victory in the Dieppe Grand Prix. The car weighed 1,400 kg (3,086 lb) and had a top speed of 160 km per hour (99.44 mph).

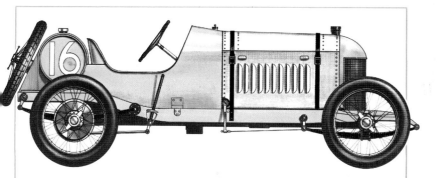

The year René Thomas won the 500 in a Delage at an average of over 132 km per hour (82 mph) was the European industry's most successful season. It turned out to be the worst year for the Americans. This race marked the first time that prizes were offered for the 100, 200, 300, 400 mile stages—all won by the French drivers. The Delage was built in 1913 and complied with the Grand Prix formula. It had a 7,032 cc, 4-cylinder engine that developed 110 bhp at 2,200 rpm. It weighed 1,036 kg (2,284 lb) and had a top speed of 170 km per hour (105.6 mph).

USA   **Stutz - 1915**

Victory nearly eluded Ralph De Palma once again when a connecting rod broke three laps from the finishing line. However, he still managed to win the race, beating Dario Resta in a Peugeot. Stutzes driven by Gil Anderson and Earl Cooper also came in third and fourth, respectively. The Stutzes had 4,839 cc, 4-cylinder engines that developed 120 bhp at 2,700 rpm. They also had four-speed transmissions, weighed 1,070 kg (2,359 lb), and had a top speed of 160 km per hour (99 mph). Like Mercer, Stutz built prestigious sports cars.

The regulations of the Indianapolis 500 imposed two further reductions in capacity, one in 1915 to 4,916 cc and one in 1920 to 3,000 cc. The intention was to penalize the European cars in particular. Ralph De Palma, for the third time, ran into serious trouble while in the lead just short of the finish. On the 187th lap his Ballot caught fire. His mechanic, Pete De Paolo, displayed great courage in extinguishing the flames with the means available in the car. Had he not done so the Ballot would not have finished. Shortly afterwards De Palma was forced to stop for a time by other problems, and he eventually finished fifth.

Victory went to Gaston Chevrolet, who was driving a Frontenac built by his brother Louis. Louis Chevrolet had emigrated to the United States from his native Switzerland. He had founded a car factory bearing his name but had sold it to General Motors and signed an agreement that forbid him to use his own name for other motoring enterprises. Having regained his full independence, he re-

Car: **Frontenac**
Maker: **Louis Chevrolet**
Year: **1920**
Class: **Indianapolis**
Engine: **4-cylinder in-line**
Bore × Stroke: **79 × 151 mm**
Capacity: **2,980 cc**
Power: **120 bhp at 4,200 rpm**

turned to designing racing cars, under the name of Frontenac, with 4- or 8-cylinder engines and overhead camshafts. The cars won several races, including the 1920 and 1921 Indianapolis 500s.

Gaston Chevrolet, who set a new record average of more than 144 km per hour (89.5 mph), finished ahead of René Thomas in a Ballot and Tommy Milton and Jimmy Murphy in Duesenbergs. Suspense rose when Chevrolet went into the pits three laps from the end to refuel, but he still managed to beat Thomas by a good margin.

Duesenberg shares with Ballot the credit for introducing the straight-8 engine to racing cars. Both marques decided on this step with the 1919 Indianapolis 500 in mind. In addition, both based their engines on one with similar specifications that had been built by Ettore Bugatti for the Allied Air Forces during World War I. Thus, the 1919 Indianapolis race can be regarded as one of the most stimulating 500s ever held. As for Bugatti, besides his many successes as a designer of racing cars, he must be given credit for having designed an engine that, while not intended for racing, became closely involved in it.

Both Duesenberg and Ballot had to reduce their cars' capacity to 3,000 cc in compliance with the regulations of the American race. The Duesenberg brothers, August and Frederick, reduced the bore and stroke by 12.5 and 16 mm, respectively. The 1921 Duesenberg was the first racing car to have hydraulic brakes (on the rear wheels only). When it was taken to Europe in the same

Car: **Duesenberg**
Maker: **Duesenberg**
Year: **1921**
Class: **Indianapolis**
Engine: **8-cylinder in-line**
Bore × Stroke: **63.5 × 117 mm**
Capacity: **2,964 cc**
Power: **115 bhp at 4,225 rpm**

year, the hydraulic control was extended to all four wheels. Another peculiarity of the 1921 Duesenberg was that it had the steering wheel on the left instead of the right as in most European cars of that period. It was not a single-seater, the driver being regularly accompanied by a mechanic. The Duesenberg's European expedition was the opposite of a tourist's jaunt. It ended with Murphy's victory in the French Grand Prix at Le Mans, with the American driver achieving an average speed of 127.202 km per hour (79.057 mph). This was the second time the great French race had been held at Le Mans.

1923 - Mercedes

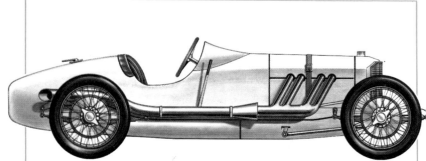

In 1923 the capacity at Indianapolis was lowered still further, to 2,000 cc. Millers swept the board, taking the first four places as well as sixth and seventh positions. The Mercedes of Max Sailer came in eighth; and another of the German firm's official entries, Christian Werner, came in eleventh. Between 1921 and 1925 Mercedes built three different racing cars; all were 2,000 ccs but each had a different engine (4-, 6-, and 8-cylinders). The one illustrated here had a 4-cylinder engine that developed 120 bhp at 4,500 rpm. It weighed 870 kg (1,918 lb) and had a top speed of 165 km per hour (102.5 mph).

1927 - Miller

In 1926 capacity was reduced yet again, to 1,500 cc, but superchargers were permitted. In 1927 Frank Lockhart's Miller was beaten by the Duesenberg of George Sauders. However, the record established by the Duesenberg of De Paolo in 1925 remained unbeaten and stood until 1932. Lockhart set a fast pace at the outset, and everyone thought he would repeat his previous year's success. At the end of his turn he handed the car over to his co-driver "Dutch" Bauman. Unfortunately Bauman was forced to retire by a broken differential, and the car came in eighteenth. The Miller had an 8-cylinder in-line engine that developed 154 bhp at 7,000 rpm.

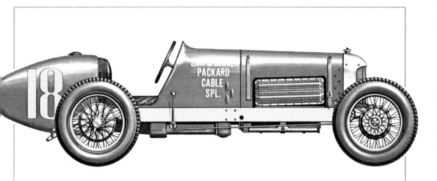

The Packard Cable, which in 1929 was driven by Leon Duray and came in twenty-second, was simply a front-wheel-drive Miller powered by a supercharged straight-8 engine. The name Packard on its sides had nothing to do with the American car manufacturer of the same name but referred to a maker of cables. It also displayed *Car & Driver*, the title of one of the top-selling American motoring magazines. Miller built a total of fifty 1,500 ccs, ten of them having front-wheel drive.

The Ford entry in the 1935 Indianapolis 500 was a particularly interesting car because of its front-wheel drive. It was built and entered by Henry A. Miller. Of the 33 starters that year, as many as nine had front-wheel drive. One, that of Mauri Rose, even had four-wheel drive. The Ford 8V (No. 43) was driven by Ted Horn, one of the best-known American racing drivers of the period. The Ford came in sixteenth overall, having dropped out on the 143rd lap because of steering trouble. The highest place achieved by a front-wheel-drive car was Wilbur Shaw's second.

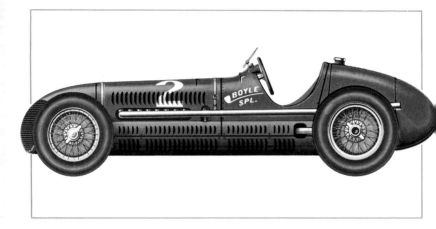

This is an historic car for two specific reasons. First, it won the Indianapolis 500 in 1939 *and* 1940 (and nearly won the 1941 race). Second, its construction coincided with the sale of Maserati to the Orsi, though Bindo, Ettore, and Ernesto Maserati continued to run the technical and design sides of the factory. The 3,000 was prepared for the new 1938–40 formula that specified a maximum capacity of 3,000 cc and a minimum of 769 cc for engines with superchargers and 4,500–1,000 cc for normally aspirated engines. The minimum weight varied between 400 and 800 kg (881.8 and 1,763.7 lb) in proportion to the capacity. There was no fuel limitation. The Maserati brothers, who had built an excellent voiturette with a 1,500 cc engine, produced the 3,000 cc by exactly doubling the 1,500 cc. The 4-cylinder engine became an 8-cylinder in-line, the single stage Roots supercharger became a twin stage, and the single choke Memini carburetor became a twin choke.

The car quickly showed itself to be well

Car: **Maserati Indy**
Maker: **Maserati**
Year: **1938**
Class: **Indianapolis**
Engine: **Supercharged 8-cylinder in-line**
Bore × Stroke: **69 × 100 mm**
Capacity: **2,992 cc**
Power: **(1938) 350 bhp at 6,000 rpm; (1939) 365 bhp at 6,400 rpm**

balanced but unreliable, managing to finish only a single race, the Italian Grand Prix at Monza (fifth place, Trossi). In 1938 the regulations of the Indianapolis 500 were altered and became virtually the same as those then in force in Europe. The American Mike Boyle ordered a Maserati 3,000. It was with this that Wilbur Shaw had a comfortable victory in the American race, the first European success since the Peugeot of Wilcox in 1919. An important detail was that Shaw retained the four-speed transmission (virtually useless at Indianapolis) and finished two minutes ahead of the second car. Shaw also won in 1940 and just missed victory in 1941, when a broken wheel forced him to retire.

The Sampson of 1939–40 is another car that can be cited to support the thesis that the Indianapolis 500 has played and continues to play a decisive role in technical progress, even though only a very small proportion of the solutions put forward have been taken up.

The Sampson made its debut at Indianapolis in 1939, when it came in thirty-first after having to retire on the nineteenth lap because of differential trouble. In 1940, driven by Bob Swanson as in the previous year, it came in sixth.

The original feature of the Sampson lay in its narrow angled V-16. This consisted of two paired straight-8 Miller engines. It had two centrifugal superchargers installed at the rear of the engine, with a single intake duct positioned in the center of the V.

The 16-cylinder layout of the engine was designed by Frank Lockhart for the Stutz Black Hawk, the car in which this front-rank American driver was killed during a record attempt in 1928. Another original feature of the Sampson was the

Car: **Sampson**
Maker: **Sampson Motor Inc.**
Year: **1940**
Class: **Indianapolis**
Engine: **V-16 (two paired Miller 8-cylinder in-line engines)**
Bore × Stroke: **55.5 × 76.2 mm**
Capacity: **2,956 cc**
Power: **385 bhp at 7,500 rpm**

De Dion rear suspension; and it also had front-wheel drive.

In 1939 and 1940 the 500 was dominated by Wilbur Shaw in the Maserati, but it is interesting to note that in 1940 Swanson completed 196 laps. The Sampson 16-cylinder also raced in 1942, when it finished twenty-second after retiring on the eighty-ninth lap because of low oil pressure.

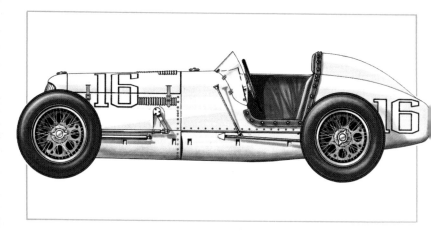

The years 1942–45 were one of the rare times when the Indianapolis 500 was not run. (It had also been suspended during 1917–18.) The first race after World War II was run in 1946. It was marked by the victory of George Robson, a 37-year-old driver racing at Indianapolis for his third time (he had previously competed in 1940 and 1941). Robson drove a Thorne Engineering Special (named after its sponsor Joel Thorne). This car was the first 6-cylinder to win the American race since the Marmon Wasp in 1911. The construction of these cars stems from 1937, the year in which Art Sparks prepared two cars on behalf of Thorne. These competed in the 1938 and 1939 Indianapolis 500, driven in the first race by Householder and Snyder and in the second by Snyder and Mays. The cars didn't compete in 1940; but they returned in 1941, and one of them, driven by Horn, came in third. During the war they were taken back to California and rebuilt. They were still competitive in 1946. Robson, who started in the fifth row, won with a

Car: **Thorne Engineering Special**
Maker: **Art Sparks**
Year: **1946**
Class: **Indianapolis**
Engine: **6-cylinder in-line**
Bore × Stroke: **81 × 95.3 mm**
Capacity: **2,946 cc**
Power: **5,400 rpm**

lead of 44 seconds over the second-place car, which bore the name of its driver, Jimmy Jackson.

One of the most interesting single-seaters in the 1946 Indy 500 was Paul Russo's Fageol Twin Coach Special. This twin-engined car had two Offen-hauser 4-cylinders with a total capacity of 3,000 cc and a power output of 320 bhp, one of the engines being mounted at the front and one at the rear. The driver's seat was in the center and the fuel tank in the tail. Another feature of the Fageol was four-wheel drive. Russo retired from the race on the seventeenth lap after an accident, but the car had excited great interest both because of its technical solutions and the excellent position its driver took at the start (front row).

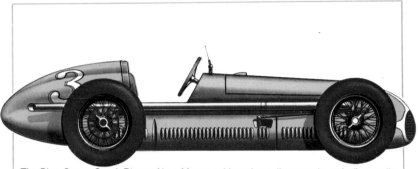

The Blue Crown Spark Plugs of Lou Moore achieved excellent results at Indianapolis during the four years, 1947–50, in which they were used. In 1947 and 1948 they came in first and second, driven by Mauri Rose and Bill Holland, respectively. In 1949 the cars took first and third places with Bill Holland and George Connor, and in 1950 came in second, sixth, and eighth with Holland, Connor, and Wallard. The Blue Crowns of 1947 and 1948 were all front-wheel drive, while in 1949 and 1950 only the one driven by Bill Holland had this feature. The engine was a 4-cylinder Offenhauser fed by just a single carburetor to limit fuel consumption.

The Novis, among the faster cars that have appeared at Indianapolis, also had front-wheel drive. They were powered by a V-8 engine with a centrifugal super-charger, a capacity of 3,000 cc, and a power output of 550 bhp at 8,000 rpm. Its Achilles heel was its high fuel consumption (between 70 and 92 liters per 100 km/3.07–4.04 mpg). To avoid this problem, which forced it to refuel more than once, it had a large fuel tank with a capacity of 523 liters (115 gal). The early Novis also needed to have the front tires changed frequently.

Contrary to what was and still is believed in Europe, the Indianapolis 500 has often encouraged the construction of highly specialized cars (four-wheel drive, front-wheel drive, gas turbine). One such car was the Cummins Diesel Special, which, as its name suggests, was powered by a diesel engine. It had a capacity of 6,751 cc, developed 350 bhp at 4,000 rpm, and had a supercharger driven by the exhaust gases, making it one of the earliest cars to have a turbocharged engine. The oil crisis and the anti-pollution standards have led to a recent revival of such engines.

At the time, this car cost $500,000, a considerable sum; and it was entrusted to a veteran of Indianapolis, Freddie Agabashian. The Cummins had torsion bar suspension and an unusual engine placement: in order to reduce the frontal section, the 6-cylinder was laid over on its right side. This car had a good chance at Indianapolis, as shown by Agabashian's excellent starting position, the front

Car: **Cummins Diesel Special**
Maker: **Cummins**
Year: **1951**
Class: **Indianapolis**
Engine: **6-cylinder diesel**
Bore × Stroke: **100 × 120 mm**
Capacity: **6,751 cc**
Power: **350 bhp at 4,000 rpm**

row. He had in fact recorded the best time in the qualifying trials.

However, the Cummins Diesel failed to finish the race for a simple, almost trivial reason: dust and rubber particles blocked the intake duct, starving the engine of air. The car's weight (1,240 kg/2,734 lb) caused excessive wear to the tires. This problem, which had also arisen during the qualifying trials, was probably due to poor weight distribution.

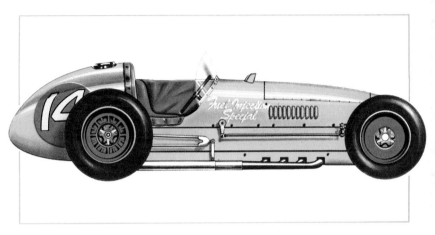

This car was no exception to the harsh laws of Indianapolis, that is, the cars that excelled in this race were traditional, the work of a proved mechanic, and meticulously tuned.

The victory of Bill Vukovich ("Vuky"), a Slovene by origin, driving in his fourth Indianapolis was due not only to his ability as a driver (he was a veteran of Midget races and was champion in 1950) but also to the extraordinary reliability of the Meyer & Drake 4-cylinder. This engine was better known under the name of Offenhauser, or Offy; this make, in actual fact, no longer exists.

The 1953 race, which was held in scorching heat, raised doubts about the durability of the old 4-cylinder. However, the Offy triumphed again, proving once more that its 20 years were not a handicap but a guarantee because of its continuous rejuvenation. That year the makers tried to maintain the engine speed between 5,700 and 6,100 rpm as opposed to the 5,200 rpm of 1952, despite

Car: **Fuel Injection Special**
Maker: **Howard Keck Co.**
Year: **1953**
Class: **Indianapolis**
Engine: **4-cylinder in-line Offenhauser**
Bore × Stroke: **109 × 117 mm**
Capacity: **4,428 cc**
Power: —

the fact that the 4-cylinder was guaranteed to sustain only 4,400 rpm.

Vukovich's car also had a traditional chassis, a Kurtis Kraft 500 A, with the engine mounted on it angled at 36° to the left. It had torsion bar front and rear suspension.

Vukovich's average of 207.187 km per hour (128.768 mph) was only the third time in the history of Indianapolis a driver had recorded an average of over 200 km per hour (124.301 mph), following the 203.172 km per hour (126.272 mph) of Wallard in 1951 and the 207.480 km per hour (128.950 mph) of Ruttmann in 1952.

1956 - John Zink Special   USA

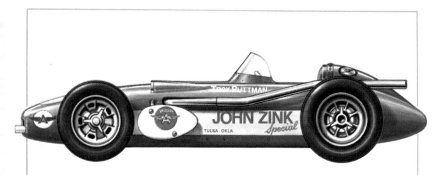

The John Zink was another veteran of Indianapolis, having competed many times and won once, in 1956. Like the vast majority of cars competing in the 500 during the 1950s, it had a 4-cylinder Offenhauser engine. In 1956, 33 cars took part, and all except one—Paul Russo's Novi, which had an 8-cylinder Novi engine—powered by the Offenhauser. Paul Russo was in the lead on the twenty-second lap, but a burst tire caused him to crash against a safety wall and put him out of the race. There were numerous accidents in 1956.

1957 - Dean Van Lines   USA

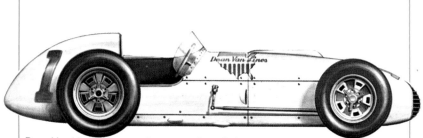

Dean Van Lines, a transport company, has tried on several occasions to win the 500. The cars it sponsored almost always did well and were driven by front-rank sportsmen such as Bob Sweikert, Jimmy Bryan, A. J. Foyt, and Mario Andretti. In 1957 the Dean Van Lines was driven by Jimmy Bryan and came in third. The 1957 race was much better balanced with the first eleven cars all finishing. The Dean Van Lines was powered that year by a 4-cylinder Offenhauser (a Ford V-8 from 1965 onward) and had a Kuzma chassis.

USA   **Agajanian Willard Battery Special - 1963**

The year 1963 was one to remember in the history of the 500 because of the participation of Lotus. Lotus entered two cars, one driven by Jim Clark and the other by Dan Gurney; both were powered by Ford engines. It was with these V-8 engines that the American marque began its assault on the 500. The race was won by Parnelli Jones, in an Agajanian Willard Battery Special with an Offenhauser engine, by an extremely narrow margin over Jim Clark. That year only 5 of the 33 starters, including the Lotuses, were rear-engined; but by the following year there were 12, and by 1965 there were 27.

USA   **Sheraton Thompson Special - 1964**

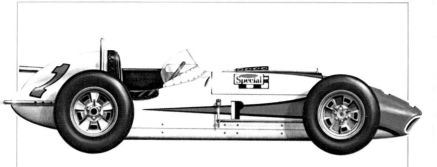

The year 1964 marked the last victory of an Offenhauser before the Ford V-8 gained the upper hand in its battle with the old but still effective 4-cylinder. The victor was A. J. Foyt, gaining the second of his four Indy wins. However, a great deal of luck was involved in his victory. The 1964 race was marked by several accidents and two deaths (drivers Eddie Sachs and Dave MacDonald). Clark was in the lead when he was eliminated in the forty-seventh lap by a broken suspension. Foyt was shrewd enough not to push too hard, which enabled him to set a new record average.

The technical advances made by Jack Brabham and later the Lotuses in the design of American single-seaters intended for the Indianapolis 500 have been so profound and radical as to constitute a revolution. It began in 1961 when Jack Brabham's 2,700 cc Cooper-Climax surprised everyone with its performance. In 1963 it was the turn of Colin Chapman with one of his cars powered by a 4,200 cc 90° V-8 Ford engine, which developed 375 bhp at 7,200 rpm and was fed by four twin choke Weber carburetors. This engine, which powered the Fairlane production car, was installed in a Lotus 25 that had been lengthened by 10 cm (4 in) and rechristened the Lotus 29. A feature of this car was its six fuel tanks with a total capacity of about 225 liters (49.5 gal). To counterbalance the centrifugal effects of the turns (which were all left-handed), the six fuel tanks were placed on the left side of the car. Two Lotus 29s were entered in the 1963 Indianapolis, one driven by Jim Clark and the other by Dan Gurney, whose Lotus was powered

Car: **Lotus 29 Indy**
Maker: **Lotus**
Year: **1963**
Class: **Indianapolis**
Engine: **90° V-8 Ford**
Bore × Stroke: **96.5 × 72.8 mm**
Capacity: **4,261 cc**
Power: **375 bhp at 7,200 rpm**

by an Offenhauser engine. Clark came in second because of inadequate refueling services in his pit, and Gurney came in seventh.

Lotus's second attempt, in 1964, with the 34 version was frustrated by the poor performance of the Dunlop tires; but its third try was a great success. Chapman returned to Indianapolis in 1965 with the 38, designed by Len Terry. This car had a monococque hull, with fuel tanks capable of holding more than 260 liters (57 gal) of a mixture based mainly on alcohol. The car won easily, holding the lead for all but ten of the race's 200 laps. In 1961 all the cars competing in the 500 had front-mounted engines, but by 1966 all but one were rear-engined.

The Ford engine's first victory at Indianapolis was in 1965 with Jim Clark at the wheel of a Lotus. In 1966 this engine gained its second success thanks to another British driver, Graham Hill, and a British chassis (built by Lola). Jackie Stewart almost won the 500 that year. He was in the lead ten laps from the finish, but a sudden drop in oil pressure forced him to switch the engine off (at that time the engine cost $26,000). Graham Hill was the second driver after George Sauders (1927) to win the 500 in his first attempt.

In 1968, in the midst of the full Ford offensive, the turbocharged Offenhauser suc-ceeded in gaining a significant victory thanks to Bobby Unser and his Rislone Leader Cards Inc. More significantly, the construction of the car was the responsibility of Dan Gurney, who also made another contribution to the success of his small factory by coming in second at the wheel of another car built by him, the Olsonite Eagle. The Eagle was entered by All American Racers Inc. and was powered by an 8-cylinder Ford Weslake engine. That year there were also three gas turbine cars.

The gas turbine powered 56 was intended exclusively for the Indianapolis 500. Four were produced, three of which, driven by the Americans Joe Leonard and Art Pollard and the Englishman Graham Hill, took part in the 1968 race, coming in twelfth, thirteenth, and nineteenth, respectively.

Striking in appearance and highly regarded because of its overall achievements, the 56 undoubtedly suffered from the lack of power of its Pratt & Whitney engine. Probably for commercial reasons, the car's sponsors, the Granatelli brothers, were prepared to spend any amount on the car even though they realized that it would be difficult for a gas turbine powered car to win the race.

During trials the 56 achieved a power output of 500 bhp when fueled by gas rather than kerosene, but the previous year it had achieved 550 bhp. In 1968 USAC (the United States Auto Club) ordered that the surface area of the air intake be reduced by 35 percent; this meant that the 56's turbine developed

Car: **Lotus 56**
Maker: **Lotus**
Year: **1968**
Class: **Indianapolis**
Engine: **Pratt & Whitney gas turbine**
Bore × Stroke: —
Capacity: —
Power: **500 bhp (430 bhp)**

only 430 bhp in the version for the race. As a result, it was surprising that after the qualifying trials Leonard and Hill started in the front row and Pollard in the fourth.

The 56 was designed by Colin Chapman and Maurice Phillippe on the basis of their past Indianapolis experience. Their main concern was to avoid a repetition of the lift effects that occur at the high speeds attainable in the straights at Indianapolis. After repeated trials in the wind tunnel, they concluded that the problem could be resolved by adopting a knife-edged front. This completely eliminated pitching during both acceleration and braking and also gave the car much greater stability in the straights.

The 1971 Indy 500 created a great stir more because of the truly exceptional times recorded in practice by Mark Donohue than because of what occurred in the race itself. Donohue recorded an official average of 291.255 km per hour (181.016 mph) at the wheel of a McLaren M 16. This had a wedge-shaped body with radiators positioned halfway along the sides of the car. Other distinguishing features were the rear aileron and the front spoilers. The Ford-Coyotes of Foyt and Donnie Allison also had ailerons.

Al Unser's Colt-Ford, though completely new, followed closely in the tracks of the one Joe Leonard drove in 1970, coming in twenty-fourth. Furthermore, the Colt-Fords started from the Lolas prepared by one of the wizards of Indianapolis, George Bignotti.

In regard to the engines, it was significant that the first three cars on the starting grid were all powered by the turbocharged Offenhauser. The Offenhausers of Peter Revson and Donohue differed in having a stroke of 80 mm rather

Car: **Colt-Ford**
Maker: **Parnelli Jones**
Year: **1971**
Class: **Indianapolis**
Engine: **V-8 Ford**
Bore × Stroke: **95.5 × 72.9 mm**
Capacity: —
Power: —

than 70 mm, which all but one of the marque's other engines had. In Bobby Unser's Olsonite Eagle the stroke had been reduced to 67 mm, making the engine oversquare.

Al Unser's task was made easier by the accidents that were a feature of the race. Miraculously, he avoided all of them. After Revson set a new lap record during official practice, he was considered the favorite. But the cunning Al Unser was able to keep him at a respectful distance and narrowly beat him over the finishing line.

1975 - Eagle Offy

The turbocharged engine is relatively new to European racing technology, introduced by Porsche and Renault in particular. However, at Indianapolis it was first used in 1966 and gained its first victory in 1968. The engine in question was an Offenhauser with a capacity reduced to a little over 2,600 cc and which developed more than 600 bhp. From then on it has won frequently, not surprising considering the extent to which it is used. The regulations limit its capacity to 2,650 cc (it must also have an overhead camshaft) compared to the 4,500 cc for normally aspirated engines.

The Jorgensen Eagle of Bobby Unser, the 1975 winner, was built by Dan Gurney's All American Racers. Bobby Unser had two worthy adversaries in the 1975 race, Johnny Rutherford and A. J. Foyt. The outcome was uncertain for several laps, and was finally decided by a violent thunderstorm that raged over the area for 20 minutes, forcing the organizers to stop the race at the end of the 174th lap. The

Car: **Eagle Offy**
Maker: **All American Racers**
Year: **1975**
Class: **Indianapolis**
Engine: **Turbocharged 4-cylinder in-line Offenhauser**
Bore × Stroke: **111.125 × 67.310 mm**
Capacity: **2,611.27 cc**
Power: **625 bhp at 8,500 rpm**

drivers were ranked according to the positions they had occupied at that moment, Rutherford coming in second and Foyt third. Of the 33 cars that started, all but 6 were powered by the turbocharged Offy. Three of the six used an 8-cylinder engine prepared by Foyt, one a Chevrolet 8-cylinder, and two SGD 4-cylinders.

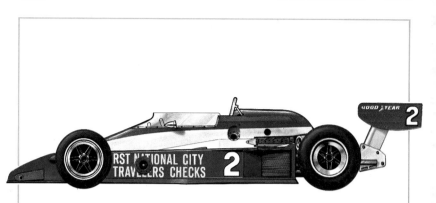

The 8-cylinder Cosworth-Ford's Indianapolis debut took place in 1976 (Al Unser in a Parnelli), achieving an excellent seventh place. In 1977 five cars had these engines, two of them—Tom Sneva's and Al Unser's—starting in the front row and finishing the race second and third overall. In 1978 there were eleven Cosworth 8-cylinders. The winner was Al Unser with a Lola prepared by Jim Hall and powered by this engine. Sneva's Penske (second), Bobby Unser's Eagle (fifth) and Dallenbach's McLaren (sixth) all had similar engines.

Record Cars - From 1898 to the Present

The car was no sooner born than man felt the urge to engage in a competitive struggle, often with fatal consequences. Reckless men, crude vehicles that gradually became immensely powerful, inadequate and dangerous courses: the history of speed is the product more of courage than of reason or science.

Racing is a field in which giant technical strides have been made. It was relatively easy to pass the 100 km per hour (62.15 mph) mark, considering that Jenatzy managed to do so as early as 1902, when the car had been in existence only some four or five years. Seven years later 200 km per hour (124.3 mph) was passed. In 1927, the 300 km per hour (186.45 mph) mark was exceeded; and shortly afterward, in 1932, the 400 km per hour (248.6 mph) barrier was broken. In 1937 Eystone reached 501 km per hour (311.4 mph). Many believed that it was impossible to go beyond this speed. However, despite the break during the war, in 1947 John Cobb went well over the 600 km per hour (373 mph) mark.

With the use of jet and later rocket engines, the history of speed records underwent a sharp change of course, marking the end for piston engines. It would have been foolish to ignore progress. The move to the internal combustion engine from electric traction or steam propulsion was just as revolutionary, but nobody considered trying to prevent it. The difference lies in the fact that neither jet nor, to an even lesser extent, rocket propulsion has ever been associated with the car, with the exception of the Opel Rak I and Rak II of 1928.

Until 1965 the regulations stipulated that a vehicle attempting to break a speed record must have at least two driven wheels. The new propulsion systems have led to the creation of a new category of vehicles for record attempts.

As far as conventional vehicles go, the story closes with the American Summers brothers (Bill and Bob). In 1965, with their Goldenrod powered by two Chrysler engines of about 7,000 cc each, they came close to 700 km per hour (435 mph).

In 1970 Craig Breedlove was the first to exceed 1,000 km per hour (621.5 mph). Ten years later Stan Barrett, another American, demonstrated that what was thought to be an unreachable limit, the sound barrier, could be broken on land.

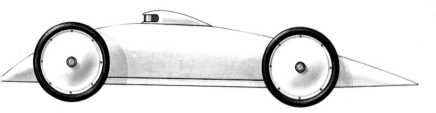

Baker Electric Torpedo 1902: 12 bhp

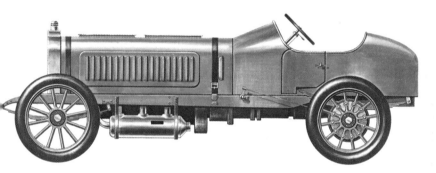

Darracq 1904: 4 cylinders, 11,259 cc, 100 bhp at 1,200 rpm

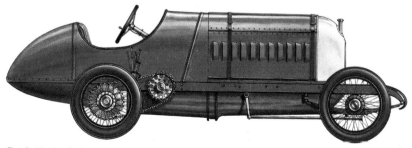

Fiat S. 76: 4 cylinders, 28,353 cc, 290 bhp at 1,900 rpm

The fascinating history of speed begins on December 18, 1898 with a record attempt by the Count de Chasseloup-Laubat. The site of the attempt was a 2 km (1.24 miles) straight in the park of Achères near St. Germain, to the North of Paris. The 2 km was divided, for timing purposes, into two parts. Two time-keepers were placed at the start, two at the end of the first kilometer (0.6215 mile), and two at the end of the second. It was therefore possible to time both a standing and a flying kilometer. The chapter on speed opens with the name of Chasseloup-Laubat, who covered the kilometer in 57 seconds at an average of 63.157 km per hour (39.252 mph). He was driving an electric car weighing 1,400 kg (3,086 lb). The idea of promoting a speed race had come to one of the founders of the Automobile Club de France, Paul Meyan. He had sponsored a hill climb at Chanteloup, 32 km (20 miles), on November 27, 1898 over a course of less than 2 km with a gradient of 12 percent (1 in 8). It was won by the Belgian driver

Car: **Jeantaud**
Designer: —
Year: **1898**
Class: **Record**
Engine: **Fulmen battery electric**

Camille Jenatzy at an average of about 29 km per hour (18 mph). The success of the venture (54 entrants, 47 starters) prompted Meyan to arrange an outright speed race, which took place on December 18 of the same year. It was here that Chasseloup-Laubat set the first world speed record. Jenatzy, who had been unable to take part, challenged Chasseloup-Laubat on January 17, 1899, again at Achères, and beat his rival, reaching a speed of 66.645 km per hour (41.420 mph). However, a few minutes later the record returned to Chasseloup-Laubat (70.297 km per hour/ 43.690 mph). Ten days later Jenatzy went back to Achères and set a new record of 80.321 km per hour (49.920 mph). In March Chasseloup-Laubat overtook Jenatzy again and set a record of 93.724 km per hour (58.250 mph).

In the space of a few months Jenatzy and Chasseloup-Laubat had brought the car forward a long way. In addition to the rivalry that existed between the two, promotional interests had also become involved. Chasseloup-Laubat used a Jeantaud, Jeantaud being the firm that ran the electric taxis of Paris. Jenatzy was sponsored by the Compagnie Internationale des Transports Automobiles Electriques. The stakes were high, which explains why the two fought so tenaciously over the speed record. Instead of being disheartened when, in March 1899, Chasseloup-Laubat regained the record, Jenatzy returned to Achères a few weeks later, on April 1, 1899, with a car he called the Jamais Contente (the never content), as a token of his determination. It had various interesting new features: semi-elliptical leaf spring suspension, wood spoke wheels, Michelin solid rubber tires, and a cigar-shaped body. The body was made of a special alloy called Partinium after its inventor, the Frenchman Henri Partin, and was designed by

Car: **La Jamais Contente**
Designer: —
Year: **1899**
Class: **Record**
Engines: **2 Fulmen battery electric**

Léon Auscher of the Parisian coachbuilders Rothschild. The rear-mounted electric motor rotated at 900 rpm and drove the wheels directly. The vehicle, because of the batteries placed inside the fuselage, weighed 1,450 kg (3,197 lb). Jenatzy's first attempt went up in smoke; in the rush to begin, he had not noticed that the time-keepers had not yet finished marking the course, which had been shifted by 200 meters (219 yds) from that of the previous attempts. He returned 28 days later and this time did not fail. He was the first man in the world to exceed 100 km per hour (62.15 mph), reaching 105.904 km per hour (65.820 mph).

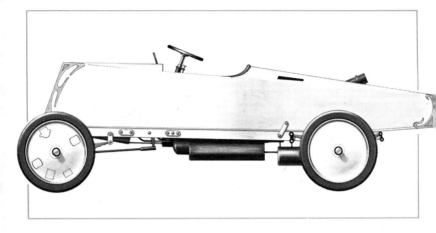

As the century ended, Chasseloup-Laubat and Jenatzy—and with them electric traction—faded completely from the scene. Jenatzy's record, however, remained unbroken until 1902 when it was soundly beaten by Léon Serpollet driving a steam car of his own construction. Steam was in some ways a link between electric and internal combustion engines. The interlude was significant since it established the limits of a system that lacked the potential for great development. He also shifted the setting of the speed record attempt from the straight at Achères to the Promenade des Anglais in Nice during the Semaine de vitesse (speed week) held annually in this city on the Riviera.

As Cyril Posthumus has written in his *Land Speed Record,* there is some doubt about the characteristics of the machine with which Serpollet established the new record on April 13, 1902. Between 1901 and 1903 Serpollet built three steam cars. Two of these were called Oeufs de Pâques (Easter Eggs),

Car: **Serpollet**
Designer: **Léon Serpollet**
Year: **1902**
Class: **Record**
Engine: **Single action 4-cylinder**

because of their shape and because the Semaine de vitesse was held over the Easter period. Serpollet obviously intended his cars to play the role of the "surprise" in the traditional egg. It is known that the Serpollet was powered by a single action 4-cylinder and that it reached a speed of 120.771 km per hour (75.060 mph). Of the thrill experienced he wrote: "I was oblivious of the grandstands and of the public. As I neared the end of the measured stretch, at the moment when I opened the auxiliary pump, I had the dreadful sensation of being shot forward like a bullet fired from a revolver." Serpollet's joy was short lived, lasting from April to November, when the record was beaten by a Mors. This period was also nearly the end for steam.

From the Promenade des Anglais at Nice the speed record was transferred to Dourdan, still in France. It was here that Henri Fournier beat Serpollet, bringing the piston engine to the fore, a development that made his record an historic event. In the meantime world speed record attempts were made by the American William K. Vanderbilt and Henri de Rothschild. Both drove a Mercedes-Simplex 40 S, had vast inheritances, and saw in this type of competition an effective way to make themselves known. Both of them failed, however.

The Belgian Pierre de Caters then had his turn in a Mors. He managed to equal but not surpass Serpollet's time (the attempt took place near Bruges). Vanderbilt tried again, this time with a Mors; but the American multi-millionaire's record was immediately beaten by Henri Fournier, also in a Mors, who reached a speed of 123.249 km per hour (76.560 mph) at Dourdan. Fournier's achievement was also short lived as 15 days later Augières, an amateur driver, estab-

Car: **Mors 60 HP**
Designers: **Brasier and Terrasse**
Year: **1902**
Class: **Record**
Engine: **4-cylinder in-line**
Capacity: **9,200 cc**
Power: **60 bhp**

lished a new record of 124.102 km per hour (77.130 mph) in a car identical to Fournier's.

To sum up, in 1902 the record was beaten three times, the last two occasions being with standard machines, the Paris-Vienna Mors 60 HP 9,200 cc, 4-cylinder with a four-speed transmission. This was the first time in the short history of the world record that the fastest car had not been built specifically for this purpose but for racing in general. The gasoline engine could not have begun in a more convincing fashion.

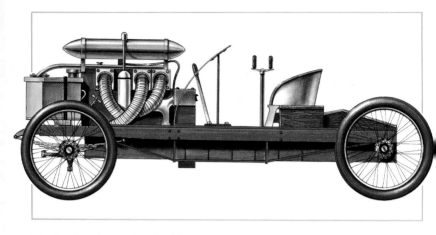

The first American to inscribe his name on the speed record roll of honor, holding it for at least a year was Henry Ford. Like Jenatzy and Chasseloup-Laubat, Ford was prompted by the desire to gain publicity for himself. The attempt took place on the eve of the New York Motor Show of 1903, where Ford launched the new model B. There are two main points to be noted about Ford's record: he had almost no sporting experience as a driver, and for the first time in history a record attempt was made outside French territory, a fact that brought the new record-holder some trouble.

Ford's Arrow was an exact copy of the Ford 999 (from the number of the New York Central Express, the train which in 1893 had reached 180 km per hour/ 111.87 mph near Grimesville). Both cars had shaft drive (the Arrow was also driven by Barney Oldfield, one of the most famous driving aces of the United States); but the 999 record attempt car lacked a gearbox, a differential, and suspension, while the clutch was merely a

Car: **Ford Arrow**
Designer: **Henry Ford**
Year: **1903**
Class: **Record**
Engine: **4-cylinder in-line**
Capacity: **15,700 cc**
Power: **72 bhp**

block of wood that made contact with the flywheel. It also lacked a body and a radiator, the latter being replaced by a container of water mounted above the engine. The Arrow was virtually destroyed in an accident at Milwaukee in 1903 in which the driver was killed. Henry Ford rebuilt it and the record attempt took place on frozen Lake St. Clair, Michigan, not far from Detroit. Ford achieved 147.014 km per hour (91.369 mph). The record established at Ostend in the same year by Duray (136.330 km per hour/ 84.632 mph) in a Gobron-Brillié had been broken. The Automobile Club de France, the only body that could ratify the new record, never officially recognized it.

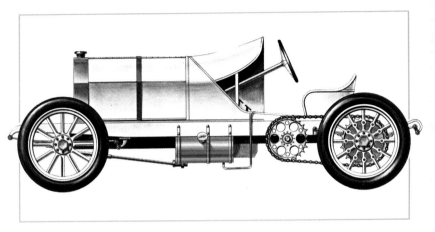

In 1904 the world speed record was broken no less than five times. By then the initiative taken by the French in 1898 had attracted followers in both the United States and Great Britain. In the climb toward ever faster speeds another American, W. K. Vanderbilt, heads the list after Henry Ford. He selected Daytona Beach and a Mercedes 90 and achieved 148.510 km per hour (92.299 mph). However, during the Semaine de vitesse at Nice, Louis Rigolly in a Gobron-Brillié regained the record for France, exceeding 150 km per hour (93.226 mph) for the first time by reaching 152.501 km per hour (95.401 mph). The 100 mph barrier was within reach, a fact that electrified motoring enthusiasts in Britain and America. Rigolly's record was also short lived. Driving a Mercedes 90 Pierre de Caters dethroned him at Ostend, achieving 156.941 km per hour (97.539 mph). Rigolly, however, was not beaten; and with a Gobron-Brillié at Ostend he reached 166.628 km per hour (103.560 mph), well over 100 mph. Before the end

Car: **Mercedes 90**
Designer: **Wilhelm Maybach**
Year: **1904**
Class: **Record**
Engine: **4-cylinder in-line**
Capacity: **11,900 cc**
Power: **90 bhp at 1,150 rpm**

of the year Paul Baras with a Gordon Bennett type Darracq 100 HP overtook his rival, setting a record of 168.188 km per hour (104.530 mph).

Nevertheless, the Mercedes 90 used by Vanderbilt is regarded as the most significant car of the period. Its 4-cylinder, 11,900 cc engine developed 90 bhp (hence its number). It had a four-speed transmission and chain drive, this being regarded at the time as more reliable than shaft drive for high powered engines. It was virtually identical to Caters's car except for an aerodynamic addition at the end of the hood extending almost as far as the steering wheel. The driver was seated lower down than in Caters's car and offered less resistance to forward movement.

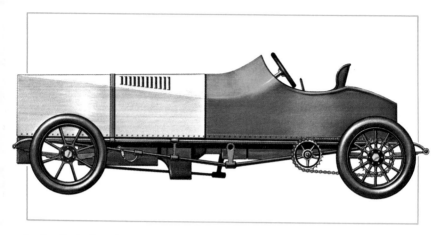

As the illustration clearly shows, Louis Rigolly's Gobron-Brillié, which exceeded first 152 km per hour (94.469 mph) and then 166 km per hour (103.170 mph) complied with certain aerodynamic requirements. The styling indicates that it had been prepared explicitly for the world speed record. It was a virtual twin to the car Duray had used to set his record at Ostend in 1903 (initially 134.325 kmph/83.484 mph and later 136.330 kmph/84.730 mph); however, the 4-cylinder engine had been slightly modified (from 13,500 cc to 13,600 cc) and the power output raised from 110 bhp to 130 bhp. Two features worth noting in this car: the engine had an opposed 4-cylinder layout, and the chassis consisted of welded steel tubes, as in modern racing cars until the advent of the monocoque Lotus 25.

The 1904 Gobron-Brillié gave a demonstration of its versatility when Rigolly, four days after exceeding 100 mph (160.9 km per hour), competed in a race on the Ardennes Circuit, coming in fourth

Car: **Gordon-Brillié**
Designer: —
Year: **1904**
Class: **Record**
Engine: **4-cylinder in-line**
Capacity: **13,600 cc**
Power: **130 bhp**

behind the Panhards of Heath and Teste, and the Clémdnt-Bayard of A. Clemént. This achievement was no slight feat as the circuit of the Ardennes took place over a 600 km course (373 miles). Duray came in sixth in the same race, driving a car identical to Rigolly's. At the end of the first of the five laps, he had been in the lead.

Arthur Duray was born in New York of Belgian parents and was a naturalized Frenchman. For a period he remained faithful to Gobron-Brillié but later raced with Darracq, De Dietrich, Excelsior, and Delage. In 1914 he was second in the Indianapolis 500 with a Peugeot. He made a further attempt on the world speed record with a Fiat but failed because he covered the timed stretch in only one direction.

The first British entry into the arena for an attempt on the world speed record (it was to become a British speciality for many years) was made by Arthur E. Macdonald with a 15,000 cc 6-cylinder Napier. The car developed 90 bhp, had a two-speed transmission, shaft drive, and a front shaped to overcome wind resistance. Macdonald chose the Ormond-Daytona meeting for his attempt and managed to beat seven records, including the world record (168.381 km per hour/104.649 mph), which bettered Baras's mark by a narrow margin. As had happened on other occasions, Macdonald's feat was short lived. Just one hour later, the American Herbert Bowden set a new record at the wheel of a Mercedes powered by two 60 engines, placed one behind the other, and called the Flying Dutchman. The original arrangement of the two engines (developing a total of 120 bhp) in tandem made the car notably longer than the standard racing or record attempt car. In addition the driver's seat was at the rear. The car cost no less than

Car: **Napier 6**
Designer: —
Year: **1905**
Class: **Record**
Engine: **6-cylinder in-line**
Capacity: **15,000 cc**
Power: **90 bhp**

$50,000 at the time. Unfortunately, Bowden had the unpleasant surprise of finding himself disqualified. Although his attempt had been properly timed, his car exceeded the weight limit of 1,000 kg (2,204.6 lb) laid down by the organizers of the Daytona Speed Week. Bowden does not in fact appear in the roll of speed record holders; but his case caused such a stir and the injustice he suffered was so obvious that it forced Great Britain, the United States, and France to finally establish a common set of regulations. It was on this basis alone that the three countries could hold the world speed record or organize record attempts in their own territories.

Bowden's fruitless achievement made it clear that attempts on the world speed record could no longer be made with racing cars transformed for this purpose. It had become necessary to design such cars from start to finish with that particular objective in mind. After Bowden's Mercedes, the Darracq V8 was the first car to be prepared specifically for the speed record. It was designed by the French marque's technical director, Louis Ribeyrolles, who placed two 4-cylinder engines at 90° to each other, thus creating one of the first V-8s in history. It had a total capacity of 22,500 cc and developed 200 bhp at 1,200 rpm. This powerful engine was mounted on a standard chassis and fitted with a two-speed transmission.

The car was entrusted to Victor Hémery, and it amply fulfilled its expectations. It achieved 175.422 km per hour (109.025 mph) over a timed stretch prepared between Arles and Salon in the Camargue, beating Macdonald's record by a full 7 km per hour (4.35 mph). With this successful attempt the record re-

Car: **Darracq V8**
Designer: **Louis Ribeyrolles**
Year: **1905**
Class: **Record**
Engine: **90° V-8**
Capacity: **22,500 cc**
Power: **200 bhp at 1,200 rpm**

turned to France. Every aspect of the attempt—the nationality of the driver, the maker of the vehicle, and the location of the record run—was French.

The very next attempt, that of Marriott, raised the record to the threshold of 200 km per hour (124.301 mph). Marriott, in fact, exceeded that barrier but was not recognized. Over a short time the world speed record had climbed to sensational heights; from 1898 to 1905, drawing the line at Hémery, the record rose from little more than 63 km per hour (39 mph) to more than 175 km per hour (109 mph), often with makeshift or inadequate means. This brief stretch of time was extremely valuable to the engineers, who began to learn about and apply the rudiments of streamlining.

By this time the record belonged to the internal combustion engine. But in 1906 steam had a final success with the Stanley Rocket. The Stanley brothers, who specialized in the construction of steam cars, decided in 1905 to prepare a car capable of matching Serpollet's achievements. They used a standard double-action, twin-cylinder engine; one of its strong features was that it had only 15 moving parts. It was also very light, weighing less than 90 kg (198 lb). Installed at the rear of the chassis, the engine had two crank mechanisms that engaged the rear wheels directly by means of straight cut gearwheels and the differential. The driver (Fred Marriott) had the engine behind him as in a modern Grand Prix single-seater, but the car was steered by using two levers rather than a wheel. The body was built by J. R. Robertson Co. Inc. of Auburndale, Boston, boat specialists, and was of cedar covered with cloth. Another valuable new feature of the Stanley Rocket was the inboard rear brakes, which reduced the

Car: **Stanley Rocket**
Designers: **Francis E. and Freeland O. Stanley**
Year: **1906**
Class: **Record**
Engine: **Horizontal twin-cylinder stream**
Power: **120 bhp at 800 rpm**

unsprung weight. While the overall weight of little over 700 kg (1,543 lb) was low, the power output, 120 bhp, was good, making the car very nimble.

In the 1906 Daytona Speed Week Fred Marriott set five new records while locked in a duel with Louis Chevrolet at the wheel of a Darracq V8. Chevrolet succeeded in bettering Hémery but was immediately overtaken by Marriott, who achieved 205.308 km per hour over the mile (127.600 mph). However, this record was not recognized by the French, who credited Marriott only with the record over the kilometer at a speed of 195.606 km per hour (121.570 mph). The relative ease with which Marriott bested Hémery's mark gave rise to fears that steam was making a comeback. Instead the Stanley Rocket turned out to be its swan song.

The Blitzen is evidence of the importance the Germans had begun to attach to the world speed record for propaganda and publicity purposes. Benz had already made a name for itself in racing, but in 1909 it decided that it would be profitable to become known in the record field. It therefore built a monster of a car with 21,500 cc 4-cylinder engine, having a bore of 185 mm and a stroke of 200 mm. The overhead valves were controlled by pushrods and rockers, and they were larger than the pistons of many modern cars. Ignition was by two Bosch magnetos. Each cylinder had two valves. The engine developed 200 bhp at 1,600 rpm.

The Blitzen (Lightning) had a highly unusual career. Initially it was driven by Hémery, who established a new record at Brooklands in 1909. The car was then purchased by the celebrated American driver Barney Oldfield for, it is said, $10,000. He established a new record at Daytona; but his achievement—once again—was not recognized by the AIACR (Association Internationale des

Car: **Blitzen Benz**
Designer: **Louis de Groulart**
Year: **1910**
Class: **Record**
Engine: **4-cylinder in-line**
Capacity: **21,500 cc**
Power: **200 bhp at 1,600 rpm**

Automobile Clubs Reconnus, based in Paris). In 1911 this institution laid down a new and fair rule for record attempts. It stipulated that the attempts must be made in two directions to rule out any favorable assist from the wind. The Americans, however, did not observe this rule. The task was taken on by the American Bob Burman. Burman had bought the Blitzen from Oldfield and established a new record, still at Daytona, achieving an incredible speed that was probably due to a timing error or an incorrect measurement of the distance.

The record set by the Englishman L. G. Hornsted on June 24, 1914 at the Brooklands track is particularly significant in that it fully complied with the new regulations laid down by the AIACR. Not surprisingly, Hornsted's record was lower than the ones set by Héméry, Oldfield, and Burman. Hornsted, who achieved a speed 13 km per hour (8.1 mph) higher in one direction than in the other, fully justified the AIACR's stipulation that attempts must be made in both directions. He was credited with an average speed of 199.676 km per hour (124.099 mph).

Hornsted's car was similar to the Blitzen except in its appearance, having lost the Teutonic pointed front and the conspicuous lateral exhaust pipes. It looked like a standard racing car but still had the enormous 21,500 cc, 4-cylinder engine that developed 200 bhp. The Blitzen and its sister of 1914 marked the end of a chapter in the history of the speed record. The 1914 Benz was the last German car to feature in the honor roll of pure speed. By then it had become clear that power

Car: **Benz**
Designer: **Louis de Groulart**
Year: **1914**
Class: **Record**
Engine: **4-cylinder in-line**
Capacity: **21,500 cc**
Power: **200 bhp at 1,600 rpm**

outputs such as the Blitzen's were no longer sufficient to make substantial increases in the record. At this point the question arose whether setting a record justified the enormous cost of building a suitable car. The English and the Americans, as we shall see, considered it worth the effort; and a real race developed to find an engine that would produce the required power. Also, new sites for the record attempts had to be found, as the circuits and ordinary roads were no longer suitable.

After the war had ended, the validity of speed records continued to be a highly uncertain matter. The AIACR had stipulated that record attempts must be made in both directions, but the Americans continued to ignore this rule. For this reason the achievements of De Palma and Milton, the former in a Packard and the latter in a Duesenberg, do not, strictly speaking, feature in the roll of records. However, it remains true that both achieved remarkable feats, even if only from the technical point of view. On February 12, 1919, at Daytona, Ralph de Palma reached a speed of about 150 mph (149.875 mph), corresponding to 241.148 km per hour. As he was well aware of the AIACR regulation, it is odd that De Palma did not repeat his attempt in the opposite direction and gain the sanction of the highest international motoring body for his record. Instead he contented himself with recognition in the United States.

The Packard 905 was built in 1916 with a 5,000 cc engine, but for the 1919 rec-

Car: **Packard 905**
Designer: —
Year: **1919**
Class: **Record**
Engine: **V-12**
Capacity: **9,900 cc**
Power: **240 bhp at 2,400 rpm**

ord attempt a 10,000 cc engine replaced it. In type an aircraft engine, it was a 12-cylinder and developed 240 bhp at 2,400 rpm. It used the modified chassis of a standard production car, the Twin Six, and weighed 1,536 kg (3,386 lb). It had a three-speed transmission and disc wheels. The 905 was probably one of the first racing cars to be fitted with a headrest for the driver. In the case of this American car, it formed an integral part of the shape of the body, and this was obviously the reason for its presence. Not until many years later did the headrest become a safety feature.

On April 27, 1920 an identical situation to De Palma's arose. This time the protagonist was another famous American driver of the time, Tommy Milton. It appears that the idea of making an attempt on the speed record came to him in 1919 while he was convalescing from serious burns suffered in an accident that year. He proposed to the Duesenberg brothers that they build a car for a record attempt using two 5,000 cc engines. These engines could no longer power the standard racing cars they built since in 1920 the capacity of the American formula had been reduced to 3,000 cc. The Duesenbergs accepted. The two engines were arranged side by side and had separate transmission shafts. The new car had a single-seater body with a highly angled front, an elongated tail, and a headrest for the driver.

With the Double Duesey, as it was called, Milton achieved 156.030 mph (251.052 km per hour). It seems certain that he intended to make a run in the opposite direction over the timed stretch,

Car: **Duesenberg**
Designers: **Fred and August Duesenberg**
Year: **1920**
Class: **Record**
Engines: **Two 8-cylinder in-line, each 5,000 cc**
Capacity: **10,000 cc**
Power: **184 bhp at 3,800 rpm**

but his car caught fire. Milton obviously wanted his record to be recognized on both sides of the Atlantic; but because of his bad luck he, too, had to be content with holding only a U.S. speed record. However, it remains a fact that, the skill and courage of the driver aside, the Duesenberg brothers produced an excellent car in all respects, including appearance. The Double Duesey, like the Packard 905, was not some monster of a car built for a record attempt. With it the Duesenberg brothers' ability to design and build racing cars received, in a certain sense, official recognition.

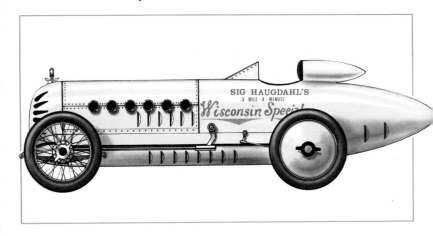

Did this car and its driver (Sigmund "Sig" Haugdahl) succeed in breaking the world speed record? Haugdahl had no support for his claim because this time not even the American Automobile Association would recognize it, and it has never been entered in any record book. The car, however, certainly existed. It had a 6-cylinder aircraft engine whose power output was increased to 250 bhp. Haugdahl, who was also the builder, used a suitably reinforced touring car chassis and a highly streamlined single-seater body fitted with a windshield and a headrest. It had double disc (inner and outer) wheels, but whether Haugdahl actually used them is unclear.

He left an account of his attempt, emphasizing at several points the danger involved, particularly at over 150 mph, if the wheels were not properly balanced. Of the record itself there is no trace since there were no timekeepers. A photograph distributed by Haugdahl featured the phrase "Sig Haugdahl's 3 Mile-a-Minute Wisconsin Special." The driver

Car: **Wisconsin Special**
Designer: **Sigmund Haugdahl**
Year: **1922**
Class: **Record**
Engine: **6-cylinder in-line Wisconsin**
Capacity: **12,500 cc**
Power: **250 bhp**

had, according to his own statement, reached 180 mph (289 km per hour). The press, on the other hand, credited him with a maximum speed of 170.700 mph (274.656 km per hour) and 162 mph (260.658 km per hour) over the flying kilometer. None of these speeds has ever been confirmed.

The course of the world record is littered with Walter Mitty–like characters. Sig Haugdahl was probably one of these, but it must be granted that at least he built a car that was potentially capable of making him the fastest man in the world.

On May 17, 1922 the English driver Kenelm Lee Guinness broke the world record. Guinness was also well known in the industrial field as the founder of a spark plug manufacturer bearing his initials (KLG), which still exists today. The record is particularly dear to English hearts; it was the last one to be set on the Brooklands circuit, which, by then, was no longer suitable for such attempts. Sunbeam gave Guinness the means to challenge destiny. Not much care had been taken over the shape of the car; but it had a 12-cylinder aircraft engine, the Manitou, that developed 350 bhp at 2,100 rpm. It had one camshaft per bank of cylinders and three valves (one inlet, two exhaust) per cylinder. It is thought that the two engines, which were angled at 60° to each other, were not exactly the same size. If this is true it could indicate that the attempt was made with whatever equipment was available. The 12-cylinder had a capacity of 18,300 cc and there was a four-speed transmission. The overall weight was quite low (1,625

Car: **Sunbeam 350 HP**
Designer: **Louis H. Coatalen**
Year: **1922**
Class: **Record**
Engine: **60° V-12**
Capacity: **18,300 cc**
Power: **350 bhp at 2,100 rpm**

kg/3,582.5 lb). Guinness experienced some difficulty in the acceleration phase as the Brooklands circuit did not permit an effective run up. Despite this, he achieved 130.350 mph (209.733 km per hour) over the flying kilometer in one direction and 137.150 mph (221.640 km per hour) in the other. He was recognized as setting a record of 133.750 mph (215.250 km per hour).

Oddly, Guinness's record stood for two years. Then, once again, record fever began to spread, affecting the English in particular. In 1924 René Thomas and Eldridge brought to the fore two marques new to this field (Delage and Fiat). Both were making use of an new area of racing, and for both it was to be a venture into the field of pure speed that was not repeated.

At this point in the history of the world record, events moved swiftly if erratically. The title of the "fastest man in the world," or rather who was to be regarded as the fastest, came to be decided more by officialdom than by the skill of the technicians or the courage of the drivers.

In 1923 Malcolm Campbell, a name that was to become familiar in this field, prepared a Sunbeam Special, contributing personally to its development. This car was in fact very similar to the one with which Guinness had set a new record. Campbell chose the International Speed Trial Meeting at Fanöe in Denmark. He achieved his aim, reaching 136.310 mph (219.322 km per hour) over the flying kilometer and 137.720 mph (221.591 km per hour) over the flying mile. However, his attempt was not recognized since the timing apparatus was not approved by the AIACR. While he was considering another attempt, a rival came forward—Renè Thomas. Delage had placed at his disposal a car powered by a 10,600 cc, overhead valve, 12-cylinder

Car: **Delage**
Designers: **Plancton and Lory**
Year: **1924**
Class: **Record**
Engine: **60° V-12**
Capacity: **10,600 cc**
Power: **280 bhp at 3,200 rpm**

engine (two 6-cylinders angled at 60° to each other) that developed 280 bhp at 3,200 rpm. Thomas and Delage selected the unsuitable and dangerous Arpajon straight, and he reached a speed of 230.634 km per hour (143.340 mph) there. The Englishman Ernest Eldridge with the Fiat Special—the modernized version of the old 1908 Mefistofele—was also at Arpajon. Despite having to make great efforts to keep his powerful car on the road, he managed to improve over Thomas. However, Thomas, rather unsportingly, immediately filed an official objection against Eldridge on the grounds that his car, contrary to the regulations, did not have a reverse gear. His objection was accepted.

Malcolm Campbell did not give up his quest for the title, but his early efforts bore little fruit. After the initial mishap at Fanöe, he suffered another accident when he lost a wheel that struck and killed a young spectator. Fanöe was thus ruled out once and for all as a site for record attempts. Campbell then found another site at Pendine Sands in South Wales that was about 11.5 km (7.15 miles) long. It was suitably equipped, and in September 1924 Campbell made a new attempt to break the record. The uneven surface of the sand caused problems; firm, compact stretches alternated with crumbly, soft patches that slowed the car and forced the driver to take great care. He did, however, succeed this time, reaching a speed of 235.217 km per hour (146.221 mph), bettering Eldridge's speed by less than 1 km per hour (0.6215 mph). His Sunbeam had been modified, the camshaft and the wheels having been replaced. Campbell, who had tremendous will power and ambition, intended to improve his record further with

Car: **Sunbeam**
Designer: **Louis H. Coatalen**
Year: **1924**
Class: **Record**
Engine: **V-12**
Capacity: **18,300 cc**
Power: **350 bhp**

a different car. However, a new ruling by the AIACR forced him to make yet another attempt with the car that had already enabled him to become, for the moment, the fastest man in the world. His Sunbeam was dusted off and taken to Pendine again. The sand was in perfect condition, and Campbell had no difficulty in exceeding, for the first time in the history of the speed record, 150 mph, reaching 242.800 km per hour (150.901 mph). The speeds recorded in this attempt were more reliable than had previously been the case; a new ruling stipulated, among other things, that the timing must be automatic and accurate to one hundredth of a second.

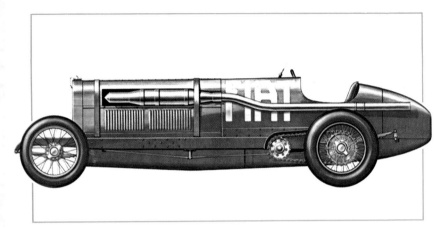

This car had a lengthy history behind it. It originated in 1908 as the S.B.-4 and was powered by a 18,146 cc twin block 4-cylinder. It was used in the duel at Brooklands between Nazzaro and Newton, the latter replacing Selwyn Edge. The S.B.-4 remained in England, racing again at Brooklands with its new owner, the Englishman George Abercromby. When Abercromby moved abroad he sold it, and the car came into the hands of another English amateur, Noel Macklin. He in his turn sold it to Engley. The car was not seen again on any circuit until the end of World War I. It ended up in the hands of John Duff, who bought it for £100 from a garage in Fulham. In 1921 Duff modified the original engine, replacing the pistons and increasing the compression ratio. The car was used in a long-distance race on Whitsunday 1922 but was unable to stand the strain, and it suffered irreparable damage. It seemed that its days were over; however, the following year it reappeared at Brooklands almost totally rebuilt, including the body.

Car: **Fiat Mefistofele**
Maker: **Fiat**
Year: **1924**
Class: **Record**
Engine: **6-cylinder in-line aircraft engine (A.12 bis)**
Bore × Stroke: **160 × 180 mm**
Capacity: **21,714 cc**
Power: **320 bhp at 1,800 rpm**

It was driven by its new owner, Sir Ernest A. D. Eldridge. The original engine, which by then had been destroyed, was replaced by a Fiat aircraft engine (A.12 bis). This made various other modifications, such as the installation of a special radiator, essential. This Fiat engine was a 21,714 cc vertical straight-6 that developed 320 bhp at 1,800 rpm. Eldridge set a world speed record of 234.890 km per hour (145.985 mph) with the Mefistofele at Arpajon in 1924. After again rebuilding it, its final owner sold the car in a fitting gesture to Fiat. Today it is on display in the firm's historical museum.

The next assault on the speed record was made by yet another Sunbeam, though very different from the ones Guinness and Malcolm Campbell had driven. Sunbeam had great racing experience; however, its car was very light, powered by a 12-cylinder engine of just 4,000 cc produced by pairing two 2,000 cc Grand Prix 6-cylinders at 75° to each other. It was fitted with a Rocts supercharger and a single Solex carburetor and developed 306 bhp at 5,300 rpm. This engine was mounted on the chassis of a Grand Prix car, and although the power output was not much less than the 18,300 cc V-12's, the new V-12 weighed a full 650 kg (1,433 lb) less. The car resembled a normal racing car in all respects.

Henry Segrave, one of the most prominent drivers of the period and the winner—with a Sunbeam—of the 1923 French Grand Prix, was chosen to drive it. On March 16 he succeeded at Southport, a new site, in surpassing the record of his fellow countryman, Malcolm

Car: **Sunbeam**
Designer: **Louis H. Coatalen**
Year: **1926**
Class: **Record**
Engine: **75° V-12**
Capacity: **4,000 cc**
Power: **306 bhp at 5,300 rpm**

Campbell, though by less than 3 km per hour (1.865 mph). He was extremely fortunate as, on coming up out of a hollow caused by the run-off of water over the beach, the Sunbeam flew through the air and the engine cut out. However, Segrave had already covered a sufficient distance at a high enough speed to give him the record.

The most interesting feature of this successful attempt was that the engine of Segrave's car had less than a quarter of the capacity of Campbell's. As such it restored a certain amount of sanity to this field of competition. The trend proved short lived, however, as from then on the engines of cars making record attempts became out and out monsters.

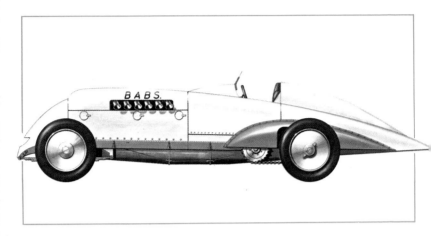

The Babs is one of the speed record cars that has remained dearest to the hearts of the English, whether motoring enthusiasts or not, both for its achievements and for the legendary figure of its driver and maker. John Godfrey Parry Thomas, a Welshman, made his name by tuning the Leyland Eight, a luxury touring car, and using a prototype derived from it to establish a record at Brooklands in 1925.

For his attempt to beat the world speed record, he purchased for a mere £125 the Higham Special, which had belonged to the late Zborowsky. He removed its 26,900 cc, V-12 Liberty engine, which developed 400 bhp, and mounted it on a chassis reinforced by longitudinal members and built by Rubery Owen. The four-speed transmission came from an old Benz. It had chain drive. The body was designed by Thomas himself and was somewhat similar to the Leyland.

Thomas made his first attempt at Pendine on April 27, 1927, but the condition of the sand prevented him from exploiting

Car: **Babs**
Designer: **John Godfrey Parry Thomas**
Year: **1927**
Class: **Record**
Engine: **45° Liberty V-12**
Capacity: **26,900 cc**
Power: **400 bhp**

the potential of his car to the fullest. Nevertheless, he achieved 272.403 km per hour (169.300 mph) over the flying kilometer (0.6215 miles). The record was already his, but he was not satisfied. He adjusted the carburation, which had left a little to be desired on the first attempt, and tried again. This time he achieved 275.229 km per hour (171.056 mph) over the flying mile. Segrave's record had been shattered, but the Babs and Parry Thomas had further surprises up their sleeves. They were both active, for the last time, the following year.

In order to regain the record, Malcolm Campbell embarked on a major undertaking, ordering the construction of a car to be used exclusively for the land speed record. He mobilized an army of technicians and firms, each specializing in some aspect of the construction process. The chassis was designed by Amherts Villiers and built by Vickers Ltd. (the Robin Hood Engineering Works carried out the assembly). The overall design of the car was entrusted to the Italian technician Joseph Maina, a friend of Campbell's trusted mechanic, Leo Villa. Dunlop was given the job of preparing the tires after Campbell and his advisers had expressed the opinion that the best thing to do, to avoid running too great a risk, was to use solid rubber tires. There remained the principal problem, the engine. Campbell, with his standing and the iron will that distinguished him, succeeded in getting permission from the British Air Ministry to use the 12-cylinder Napier Lion, widely used to power a variety of civilian and RAF planes. It seemed im-

Car: **Napier-Campbell Bluebird**
Designers: **A. Villiers - J. Maina**
Year: **1927**
Class: **Record**
Engine: **12-cylinder Napier Lion, in three groups of four**
Capacity: **22,300 cc**
Power: **450 bhp**

possible that such an engine, whose specifications to a certain extent were military secrets, could be used for other purposes; but Campbell succeeded in overcoming all reluctance. It is said that the Napier-Campbell cost its maker £9,500, as opposed to the less than £1,000 Parry Thomas paid for the Babs.

Impatient and permanently on edge, Campbell made his first attempt at Pendine on January 2, 1927; but the condition of the sand prevented him from regaining the record. He made another attempt on the following day, again without success. He returned in March and this time succeeded (setting a record of 281.447 km per hour/174.920 mph), though he risked his life in the attempt.

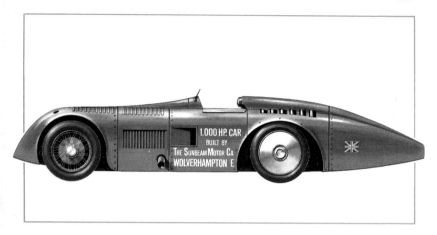

On March 29, 1927, Henry Segrave became the first man in the world to exceed 200 mph (321.8 km per hour). The speed record was becoming a question of increasing interest, and Sunbeam believed it would be profitable to regain the world record. Louis Coatalen was once again responsible for the new car; but unlike in his 1926 car, which had a capacity of just 4,000 cc, in this one he used two V-12s built during the war by Sunbeam and arranged them one behind the other with the driver's seat in between. These engines—the Metabele—each had a capacity of 22,500 cc, 48 valves, and developed 435 bhp at 2,000 rpm. The total power output was therefore 870 bhp, but the car was called the 1000 HP car. Complete with body, which wrapped around the wheels, it weighed four tons. It had two three-speed transmissions with a single control.

The task of attacking the record was given to Henry Segrave. He believed that it would not be possible to break the record on any course in Britain. Even though

Car: **Sunbeam 1000 HP**
Designer: **Louis H. Coatalen**
Year: **1927**
Class: **Record**
Engine: **V-24 Sunbeam**
Capacity: **45,000 cc**
Power: **870 bhp**

it was against the wishes of the firms sponsoring the attempt, he obtained permission to go to Daytona. In order to get AIACR approval of the record, he had to persuade the Americans to comply with the rules laid down by that organization.

Segrave achieved his aim completely and succeeded in raising the record to 327.981 km per hour (203.842 mph). The previous record (281.477 km per hour/174.939 mph) set by Campbell's Napier was shattered by more than 46 km per hour (28.6 mph).

Nobody thought for a moment that Campbell would give up. The following year, he returned to the fray with virtually the same car as in 1927.

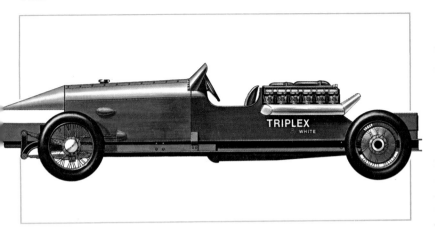

Unlike the Black Hawk of Frank Lockhart, Ray Keech's White Triplex was a wild beast of monstrous proportions both inside and out. It took its name from J. M. White, a Philadelphia cable manufacturer, who sponsored Ray Keech. It was powered by three 12-cylinder Liberty aircraft engines of 27,000 cc each, giving a total capacity of 81,000 cc. An original arrangement was used for the engines: one was mounted at the front and the other two at the rear, side by side. It had neither a gearbox nor a clutch but only an accelerator pedal and a brake pedal that acted on the rear wheels. It also lacked a normal reverse gear. Keech, knowing full well that any record would not be recognized without such a mechanism, arranged an ingenious system that kept him within the rules. Two auxiliary wheels in back of the rear axle were kept raised; by means of a lever they could be lowered to the ground and, driven by a worm gear, would propel the car backward at a speed of one mph.

After failing in an attempt during the

Car: **White Triplex**
Designer: **J. M. White**
Year: **1908**
Class: **Record**
Engine: **V-36 Triplex Liberty**
Capacity: **81,000 cc**
Power: **1,200 bhp**

Speed Meet, Keech returned to Daytona in April. This time he managed to push his impressive car (all of four tons and about 1,200 bhp) up to 334.022 km per hour (207.596 mph), slightly above Campbell's speed of 333.062 km per hour (206.999 mph).

After 22 years the record had returned to the United States, much to the satisfaction of the spectators. However, only three days later, many of them were to witness the death of Frank Lockhart.

Malcolm Campbell's 1928 record immediately came under attack from two American contenders, Frank Lockhart with the Stutz Black Hawk and Ray Keech with the White Triplex. Neither of them succeeded in dethroning the English driver during the Speed Meet. The first to make another attempt several weeks later was Frank Lockhart. As he was running along one of the stretches, he lost control of the car, and it ended up in the sea, upside down. He was rescued by the crowd; considering the spectacular nature of the accident, he pulled the car out relatively unscathed. It was then Ray Keech's turn. He achieved his goal on April 22, 1928. Three days later Frank Lockhart tried again. On the return stretch, a tire blew out and this courageous driver lost his life.

Frank Lockhart was not only one of the most highly thought-of drivers of the time (among other achievements, he won the 1926 Indianapolis 500), he was also a well-respected technician. The Stutz Black Hawk was the fruit of his inventive-

Car: **Stutz Black Hawk**
Designer: **Frank Lockhart**
Year: **1928**
Class: **Record**
Engine: **V-16 Duesenberg**
Capacity: **3,000 cc**
Power: **385 bhp at 7,500 rpm**

ness. Lockhart designed it while working in the experimental department of Stutz at Indianapolis. Lockhart linked together two 91 (1,500 cc) double overhead camshaft engines, producing a 3,000 cc, 16-cylinder. Despite its more than modest capacity for a car intended for the speed record, it developed 385 bhp at 7,500 rpm with two centrifugal superchargers and two Zenith down-draft carburetors. A feature of this car was its four hydraulic brakes, the first record class car to be so equipped. The body of the Black Hawk was a minor masterpiece, beautifully built and expertly streamlined.

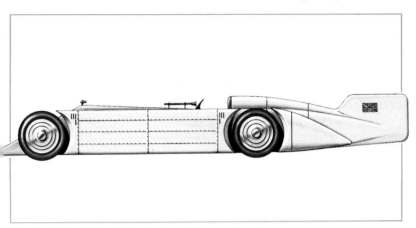

In 1929 Henry Segrave set a record of more than 334 km per hour (207.6 mph) with the Golden Arrow Irving Napier. The engine chosen was the Napier used for the Schneider Cup. It developed more than 900 bhp at 3,300 rpm. To make the body as streamlined as possible and minimize wind resistance, it was built as three bodies, two enclosing the wheels and the central one the engine and the driver's seat. The two lateral bodies may be compared to those of the 1954 Lancia D50 designed by Vittorio Jano. The car was built at the Robin Hood works of KLG at Putney Vale. It had a servo-assisted, multi-plate clutch; a three-speed transmission; and a double propeller shaft (without differential) to keep the driver's seat as low as possible, placing it between the two counter-rotating shafts.

In March 1929 the great Henry Segrave made his first attempt, but threatening weather conditions persauded him to call it off. Fifteen days passed. The gigantic proportions of the car and the fact that Segrave hoped to take the record from an American (Keech) attracted a crowd estimated at more than 100,000 to Daytona. After the regulation two runs Segrave was the fastest man in the world, having greatly exceeded his predecessor's record.

Car: **Golden Arrow Irving Napier**
Designer: **J. B. Irving**
Year: **1929**
Class: **Record**
Engine: **12-cylinder, in three rows of four**
Capacity: **26,900 cc**
Power: **925 bhp at 3,300 rpm**

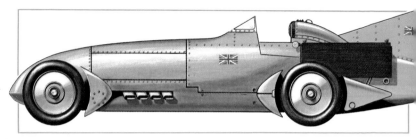

The large margin by which Henry Segrave had beaten Campbell's mark goaded Campbell on to regain the record. This time he approached the matter economically, placing all his trust in his 1927 car, which was modified only in some details.

Campbell also believed that Daytona was the only place where record attempts could be made. The fact that Segrave had succeeded there and that his records had been ratified by the AIACR drew to the famous American locality the attention of not only the public but also of all those who were in some way connected with this kind of competition. For its part the Daytona Chamber of Commerce had the happy idea of organizing a Speed Meet to celebrate the 25th anniversary of the day on which the track had first become a site for world record attempts.

Car: **Napier-Campbell Bluebird**
Designer: —
Year: **1928**
Class: **Record**
Engine: **12-cylinder Napier Lion**
Capacity: **22,300 cc**
Power: **450 bhp**

Several drivers took part in the Speed Meet. However, the first to go into action was yet again Malcolm Campbell, impatient as ever, who hurled himself into a tremendous run, regaining the world record by a whisker (333.062 km per hour/206.999 mph). Excited and on edge, the English driver made the return run without changing the tires as had been arranged with the Dunlop technicians. Fortunately the tires held out, and he succeeded in covering the second run without any particular difficulty. However, he met a strong head wind, which lowered his overall average.

Ray Keech remained in possession of the record for less than a year; it was broken on March 11, 1929 by Henry Segrave with the Golden Arrow. Campbell then improved the record five times in a row. Only his will power and ambition enabled him to overcome the tremendous difficulties that confronted him. Even before Segrave had beaten Keech's record, Campbell was searching for a new site. He thought he had found one at Verneuk Pan in South Africa, but it proved unsuitable. This venture, which was a total failure in spite of the help offered to him by the South African government, cost Campbell a great deal of time and an estimated £7,000. Far from being beaten, he returned home and commissioned a completely new car. The design was entrusted to a highly talented young man, Reid R. Railton, who worked for Thomson & Taylor of Brooklands. Railton, who was searching for a more powerful engine, asked for and obtained a 1929 supercharged Napier Lion. Campbell was, reluctantly, forced to return to Daytona, where in February 1931 he regained the record, just failing to break 400 km per hour (248.602 mph), with

395.469 km per hour (245.786 mph). Slightly over a year later he returned to Daytona and raised his record to 408.621 km per hour (253.960 mph), the Bluebird having undergone only minor modifications. In 1933 the record leaped forward when Campbell pushed it to 438.123 km per hour (272.295 mph). He was using the same Bluebird as in previous years, but it had been re-engined with a supercharged Rolls-Royce V-12 which had won the 1931 Schneider Cup (36,500 cc capacity, 2,300 bhp). It was fitted with a new clutch, and the body was altered, particularly at the front, to improve the engine cooling.

Campbell used this car to set two other world records, on March 7, and September 3, 1935. For these record runs the front of the body had been further modified and the rear wheels paired.

Car: **Napier-Railton Bluebird**
Designer: **Reid R. Railton**
Year: **1933**
Class: **Record**
Engine: **Supercharged Rolls-Royce V-12**
Capacity: **36,500 cc**
Power: **2,300 bhp**

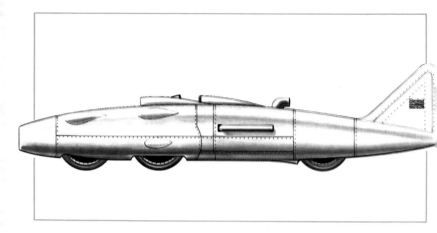

In 1935 Campbell improved his record with a Bluebird that had been substantially modified, particularly in its body. On the technical side, it was the first car used in a record attempt to have paired wheels. The use of air brakes was a further important innovation. Another new feature was the driver's use of an aircraft-type safety belt. Campbell hoped to exceed 300 mph. In this he failed, but he did break his old record. In the same year he made good his promise to bid farewell to the land speed record once he had broken the 300 mph (484.818 km per hour) barrier, doing so at another site, Bonneville.

His successor was a fellow countryman, Captain George Eyston, whose vehicle was the Thunderbolt. The French aerodynamics expert Jean Andreau and the Bean works of Tipton were involved in its construction. It was powered by two Rolls-Royce aircraft engines (Schneider Cup) with a total capacity of 73,000 cc and power output of 4,700 bhp. It had a three-speed transmission. Its most in-

Car: **Thunderbolt**
Designers: **George Eyston and Jean Andreau**
Year: **1937**
Class: **Record**
Engines: **2 supercharged Rolls-Royce V-12s**
Capacity: **73,000 cc**
Power: **4,700 bhp**

teresting new feature was the arrangement of the wheels: the four front wheels were in two pairs and were all steerable while the rear four were twinned. The forward pair of the four front wheels had a narrower track than the other pair so that the front could be tapered. Other notable points included the independent suspensions, inboard front disc brakes, and the rear disc brake. The position of the driver, behind the two pairs of front wheels but in front of the engines, was another original feature. Eyston also chose Bonneville for his attempt and set a record of 501.374 km per hour (311.606 mph).

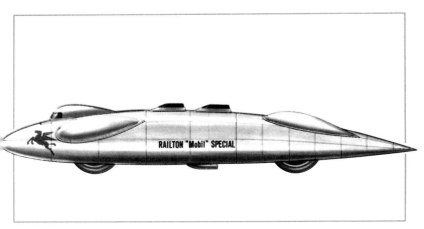

Speed record attempts were resumed in 1947; but before the war had interrupted them, Eyston's record of more than 500 km per hour (310.752 mph) was improved on three times: by Eyston himself in 1938 (536.471 km per hour/333.419 mph), by Eyston again in the same year (555.909 km per hour/345.500 mph), and by a new record holder, John Cobb, in 1939 (595.560 km per hour/370.143 mph).

The task of designing the car with which John Cobb would attempt to dethrone Captain George Eyston was given to the brilliant Reid R. Railton. Railton was already highly experienced in this field, having designed Campbell's Bluebird. He again resorted to the by then rather old Napier Lion, using two of them. Since at Bonneville at least 11 percent of their power would be lost because of the altitude, he concentrated on reducing the weight to a minimum, keeping it below three tons, as opposed to the Thunderbolt's seven. He dispensed with the flywheel and the clutch. There was no

Car: **Railton Mobil Special**
Designer: **Reid R. Railton**
Year: **1938**
Class: **Record**
Engines: **2 supercharged Napier Lion 12-cylinders**
Capacity: **26,900 cc**
Power: **1,250 bhp**

radiator, the cooling being by blocks of ice. The brakes acted only on the transmission shaft and were cooled by water falling from the blocks of ice, which was then expelled. It had independent front suspension and coil spring rear suspension. The rear track was narrower than the front one. The tires were specially made by Dunlop, their tread a mere fiftieth of an inch thick. The single-piece body was made of aluminium and weighed just over 200 kg (440.9 lb). Perhaps the most interesting feature of the Railton Mobil Special was the arrangement of the two offset engines. Each had its own three-speed transmission, and one drove the front wheels while the other drove the rear ones.

241

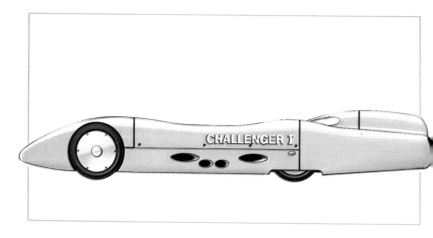

This was one of the last conventional machines to attempt to break the speed record. Likewise, its builder and designer, the American Mike Thompson, was one of the last to make the attempt with a relatively low cost vehicle. Challenger 1 was powered by four 6,700 cc Pontiac engines, all bought from scrap yards, mounted in pairs on a tubular chassis also made from salvaged material. Each engine was fitted with Hilborn-Travers injection and had a clutch and a three-speed transmission. The two engines in the front drove the front wheels while the rear engines drove the rear wheels. The magnesium alloy wheels were supplied by Halibrand, and the tubeless tires were supplied by Goodyear. The rear track was 17.5 cm (6.89 in) narrower than the front one. The car weighed about two tons.

Challenger 1 initially underwent trials at Edwards Air Force Base, but Thompson was only able to reach about 320 km per hour (199 mph) and suffered an accident. At Bonneville he exceeded

Car: **Challenger 1**
Designer: **Mike Thompson**
Year: **1960**
Class: **Record**
Engines: **4 V-8 Pontiacs, each 6,700 cc**
Capacity: **26,800 cc**
Power: **2,800 bhp**

545 km per hour (338.720 mph). His car, meanwhile, had been fitted with two brake parachutes instead of one (it was the first car involved in a record attempt to use this method of deceleration). The first proper attempt on the record was made in September 1959, and he reached just under 600 km per hour (372.902 mph). In 1960 Challenger 1 was fitted with Roots superchargers, used by General Motors in diesel engines, which increased the power of the four Pontiac engines by more than 30 percent from 2,000 bhp to 2,800 bhp. In a final attempt that year, he succeeded in breaking the 400 mph barrier, being timed at 653.254 km per hour (406 mph). This achievement was enough for Thompson.

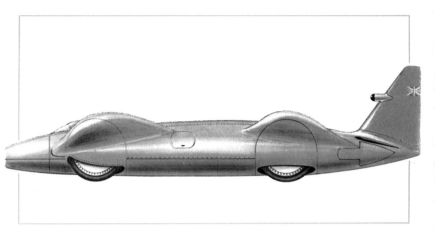

The deeds of Sir Malcolm Campbell, who was created a Baronet in honor of his legendary exploits, were continued by his son Donald. He too had records in his blood, having already broken the water speed record several times. His great ambition was to surpass 400 km per hour (248.602 mph) on water. He had already exceeded 320 km per hour (198.881 mph) and 400 mph (more than 643 km per hour) on land. With this intention he commissioned a land vehicle from Norris Brothers of Burgess Hill, Sussex, the company that had previously supplied him with a highly successful boat for the water speed record. For the power unit the Norrises selected a Bristol-Siddeley Proteus turbine, used in the Bristol Britannia aircraft. It had a power output of 4,100 bhp at 11,000 rpm. The wheels were driven via two David Brown single-speed gearboxes without clutch or differential. The vehicle did not have a chassis. The independent suspensions had oleopneumatic dampers. It had compressed air disc brakes and air

Car: **Bluebird Proteus**
Designer: **Norris Brothers**
Year: **1964**
Class: **Record**
Engine: **Bristol-Siddeley Proteus turbine**
Power: **4,100 bhp at 11,000 rpm**

brakes at the tail. The Dunlop tires were designed to stand a maximum speed of 475 mph (more than 764 kmph). In running trim Bluebird weighed 4,320 kg (9,523.8 lb) and consumed, on average, at full speed four and a half liters of kerosene every 2.4 kilometers (1.14 mpg). It also had an excellent aerodynamic design. Its only drawback was its cost (more than one and a half thousand million Italian lire of the time). Campbell virtually destroyed it during an unsuccessful record attempt, but the Owen Organization came to his assistance and another one was built. This time Donald Campbell selected Lake Eyre in Australia for the site; and on October 5, 1964 he set a record of 648.728 km per hour (403.187 mph).

Spirit of America–1964
Spirit of American Sonic 1

In 1963 the speed record was, in line with the times, radically altered, both in spirit and in letter, by the appearance of the first jet-propelled vehicle.

The first records set by Breedlove's Spirit of America were not recognized. Besides having three rather than four wheels—as decreed by the FIA (Fédération Internationale de l'Automobile), which had replaced the AIACR—the new car failed to comply with the regulations laid down by this the highest international motoring body by failing to have at least two driven wheels. None of this, however, bothered its driver and builder, the American Craig Breedlove, who had built the Spirit of America for his own amusement in his home garage. He had first bought a General Electric J47 jet engine cheaply and, with the help of two experts in aerodynamics, produced a highly promising preliminary study. Struck by his enthusiasm and ingenuity, Shell and Goodyear came to his assistance.

Breedlove began by placing a model in a wind tunnel to develop his design. The Spirit of America was ready in 1962. In trials Breedlove easily reached 365 mph (587 km per hour). After having made a few modifications to the vehicle, including moving the front wheel further back, he resumed his program. On August 5, 1963 he achieved a top speed of 704 km per hour (437.539 mph) on one run. Officially he was credited with an average speed of 655.696 km per hour (407.518 mph). On October 13, 1964 Breedlove returned to Bonneville. He had made further modifications to his Spirit of America, fitting it with a new J47 engine capable of producing more thrust and improving its streamlining. He easily set a new record of 754.296 km per hour (468.798 mph). In 1965 Breedlove resumed his attempts and raised the record to 893.921 km per hour (555.576 mph) on November 2 and 966.528 km per hour (600.701 mph) on November 15. He was still driving his Spirit of America, but a number of important modifications had been made to it. It was now powered by a General Electric J79 turbojet and was known as

1965 - Spirit of America Sonic I   USA

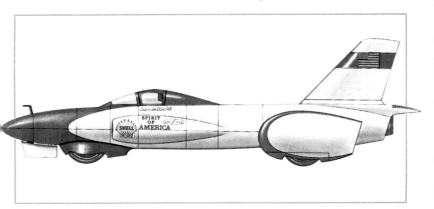

▲
Car: **Spirit of America**
Designer: **Craig Breedlove**
Year: **1964**
Class: **Record**
Engine: **General Electric J47**
Power: **5,200 lb of thrust**

Spirit of America Sonic I. It no longer had
three wheels but four and was virtually
triangular in shape. The engine was
mounted in the tail and potentially could
reach a speed of about 1,300 km per
hour (807.955 mph).

Car: **Spirit of America Sonic I**
Designer: **Craig Breedlove**
Year: **1965**
Class: **Record**
Engine: **General Electric J79**
Power: **15,000 lb of thrust**
▼

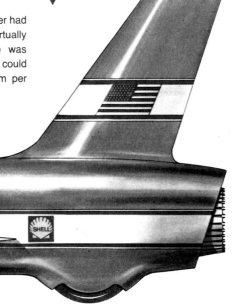

Wingfoot Express–1964
Wingfoot Express II–1965

Speed fever gripped the brothers Walt and Art Arfons of Akron, Ohio. The fact that they had both set themselves the same target, the world speed record, prevented them from collaborating; and they went their separate ways virtually ignoring each other. Walt Arfons, with the help of the technician Tom Green and the sponsorship of Goodyear (hence the name of the vehicle), built the Wingfoot Express. It was powered by a Westing-

house J46 "triple-jet" which developed 10,000 lb of thrust. It had four wheels, oleopneumatic front and rear suspension, and a very pointed body.

The Wingfoot Express was ready in the spring of 1963 and underwent trials without showing any great promise. In 1964 the job of driving it was assumed by Tom Green, as Walt Arfons had suffered a heart attack and was no longer fit enough *(Continued on page 248)*

▲

Car: **Wingfoot Express**
Designers: **Walt Arfons and Tom Green**
Year: **1964**
Class: **Record**
Engine: **Westinghouse J46 "triple-jet"**
Power: **10,000 lb of thrust**

Car: **Wingfoot Express II**
Designers: **Walt Arfons, Tom Green
and John Wolf**
Year: **1965**
Class: **Record**
Engine: **25 Aerojet rockets**
Power: **25,000 lb of thrust**

▼

USA

Wingfoot Express II - 1965

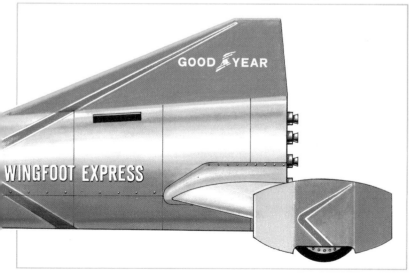

(Continued from page 248)

for such a challenge. Green made several runs but failed to come near the existing record. As a result, with the agreement of Walt Arfons, he replaced the J46 with a new unit of the same type. This engine functioned to perfection; and despite the fact that he had little experience as a driver, Green reached 420.070 mph (664.950 km per hour). However, Green's record with the Wingfoot Express lasted a mere three days. It was successfully attacked by Art Arfons. Art Arfons, 38, was nine years younger than his brother Walt; but he worked with no less passion and acumen.

Walt Arfons's decision to abandon jet-propelled vehicles, such as the Wingfoot Express, in favor of rocket propulsion marks a major innovation in the history of record attempts. The idea was not totally new; in May 1928 Fritz von Opel had achieved 195 km per hour (121.193 mph) on the Avus track in Berlin with a car based on the same principle. Walt Arfons and Tom Green, together with another technician, John Wolf, reckoned that the Aerojet JATO (jet-assisted-take-off) rockets would suit their needs. These were solid fuel rockets used to assist the take-off of heavily loaded aircraft. The Wingfoot Express II was built along these lines and was propelled by a battery of 1,000-lb-thrust JATOs. The Achilles heel of the rockets was that their thrust lasted only about 14 seconds. Arfons and his collaborators tried to get around this problem by increasing the number of rockets from 15 to 25.

The Wingfoot Express II was on the verge of setting a new overall world speed record when, on October 22, driven by Bobby Tatroe, it reached 580 mph (more than 933 mph). Once again, the rockets burned out before the vehicle had managed to cover the regulation distance (it had covered just over half the flying mile). Without this drawback, which proved to be insurmountable, the Wingfoot Express might have achieved a staggering speed.

Green Monster–1965

With the disappearance of Walt Arfons and the Wingfoot Express from the scene, the number of contenders for the world speed record was reduced to two: Art Arfons and Craig Breedlove. The decisive year was 1965. The overall speed record was broken three times, all within the space of a few days. In addition the Summers brothers challenged the record for cars powered by conventional engines. On November 2, Craig Breedlove appeared on the scene and took the record away from Art Arfons, raising it to 893.921 km per hour (555.576 mph). His joy was short lived as on November 7, just a few days later, Art Arfons with the Green Monster dethroned him and raised the record to 927.829 km per hour (576.649 mph). At this point the record was advancing in leaps and bounds. One statistic will suffice to explain why Arfons's vehicle was nicknamed the monster: it consumed over 250 liters (55 gal) of kerosene per minute. On November 15, only eight days later, Craig Breedlove regained the record, in the process passing one of the milestones in the history of the land speed record. He became the first man in the world to break the 600 mph barrier, reaching 600.601 mph (966.528 km per hour).

Car: **Green Monster**
Designer: **Art Arfons**
Year: **1965**
Class: **Record**
Engine: **General Electric J79 jet**
Power: **17,500 lb of thrust**

USA   **Green Monster - 1965**

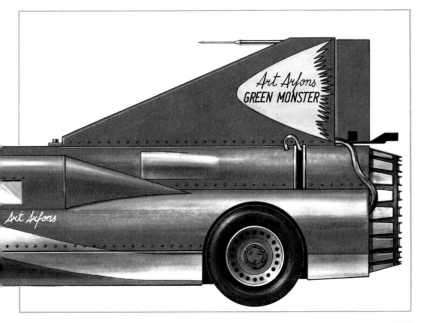

1965 - Goldenrod

USA

In October 1964 the FIA finally restored some order to the question of records. It recognized as valid the attempts made by cars powered by jet engines and created two classes of records: one for cars with at least two driven wheels and one for cars powered by jet engines or exploiting ground effect. Given this sub-division two Californians, Bob and Bill Summers, decided to attack Donald Campbell's record. Following Mike Thompson's example, they bought four production engines (Chryslers with hemispherical heads). They fitted them with fuel injection; each developed 608 bhp. Unlike Thompson, who had mounted the engines in pairs, the Summers brothers placed them one behind the other. All four wheels were driven via two four-speed transmissions. The vehi-

1970 - The Blue Flame

USA

After the electrifying duel between Craig Breedlove and Art Arfons in November 1965 the track at Bonneville disappeared from the headlines for five years. For how long would Craig Breedlove remain the fastest man in the world? Did jet propulsion have any strings left to its bow?

Walt Arfons's idea of using rockets for the propulsive force was taken up by two American technicians Ray Dausman and Dick Keller. The latter had worked in the American Institute of Gas Technology. The crucial problem of Walt Arfons's Wingfoot Express II was the rapid expenditure of thrust. The problem could be bypassed by using liquid fuel, as in the internal combustion engine, rather than solid. In 1964 Keller and Dausman completed their prototype. It was fueled by hydrogen peroxide, a liquid known for its antiseptic properties. The initial applications were carried out with a dragster,

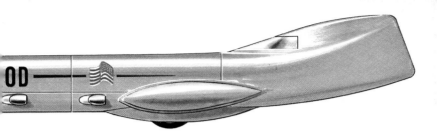

cle was very low, rather long (about 10 m/32 ft 9.7 in) and had a very reduced front section. The driver (28-year-old Bob Summers) sat right at the rear of the vehicle, behind the last of the four engines. The car was called the Goldenrod because of the golden color of the body. On November 11, 1965 it set a record of 658.636 km per hour (409.344 mph).

Car: **Goldenrod**
Designers: **Bob and Bill Summers**
Year: **1965**
Class: **Record**
Engines: **4 V-8 Chryslers, each 6,900 cc**
Capacity: **29,400 cc**
Power: **2,432 bhp**

and the two technicians were joined by an expert on the subject, Peter Farnsworth of Reaction Dynamics. The decision was made to fuel the vehicle with a mixture of natural gas and hydrogen peroxide, and the Gas Technology Institute proved to be a generous sponsor. The car was christened The Blue Flame. The driver was Gary Gabelich, a young man who had made a name for himself as a driver of hot-rods and

Car: **The Blue Flame**
Designers: **Dick Keller and Ray Dausman**
Year: **1970**
Class: **Record**
Engine: **Reaction Dynamics liquid fuel rocket**
Power: **13,000 lb of thrust**

dragsters and as a test pilot of space capsules. On October 23, 1970 he broke the 1,000 km per hour (621.5 mph) barrier with a remarkable 1,014.496 km per hour (630.513 mph).

Index